JEWISH IDENTITY IN MODERN TIMES

Leo Baeck and German Protestantism

EUROPEAN JUDAISM

General Editor: Jonathan Magonet
We are pleased to announce a multidisciplinary series of monographs and essay collections, to be published in conjunction with Leo Baeck College, exploring contemporary issues in Jewish life and thought. As with the complementary journal *European Judaism*, it reflects the wide range of academic, social, historical and theological areas that are studied at Leo Baeck College with its multinational staff and student body and its unique position as the only progressive Jewish seminary operating in Europe.

Vol. 1: **Jewish Explorations of Sexuality**
Edited by Jonathan Magonet

Vol. 2: **Jewish Identity in Modern Times**
Leo Baeck and German Protestantism
Walter Homolka

Jewish Identity in Modern Times
Leo Baeck and German Protestantism

Walter Homolka

With a foreword by Albert H. Friedlander
and an epilogue by Esther Seidel

Berghahn Books
Providence • Oxford

First published in 1995 by
Berghahn Books

Editorial offices:
165 Taber Avenue, Providence, RI 02906, USA
Bush House, Merewood Avenue, Oxford, OX3 8EF, UK

Library of Congress Cataloging-in-Publication Data
Homolka, Walter.
    Jewish identity in modern times : Leo Baeck and German
Protestantism / Walter Homolka ; with an introduction by
Albert H. Friedlander and an epilogue by Esther Seidel.
      p.   cm. -- (European Judaism ; v. 2)
    Includes bibliographical references and index.
    ISBN 1-57181-059-5 (alk. paper)
    1. Baeck, Leo, 1873-1956. 2. Judaism--Relations--Christianity.
3. Christianity and other religions--Judaism. 4. Protestant
churches--Germany--History--20th century. I. Title. II. Series:
European Judaism (Providence, R.I.) ; v. 2.
BM755.B32H66   1995
296.3'872--dc20   95-17238
                                      CIP

British Library Cataloguing in Publication Data
A catalogue record for this book is available from the British Library.

Printed in the United States on acid-free paper.

CONTENTS

Acknowledgements

No matter what accomplishments you make, somebody helps you.

Althea Gibson

A study of this nature draws upon the scholarship of all who have preceded the writer. The debt owed to the scholars who were quoted and whose advice was utilised is freely and gratefully acknowledged. Special mention must be made of Professor Dr Reinhard Schwarz, Professor Dr Wolfgang Harms, Rabbi Dr Walter Jacob, Rabbi Dr Albert H.Friedlander, Rabbi Dr Jonathan Magonet, Rabbi Julia Neuberger, Professor Dr Dr Kurt Nowak, Pastor Dr Michael Führer and Pastor Dorothee Schlenke.

Acknowledgements are also made to the British Library, London, the Bavarian State Library, Munich, and the German Library, Leipzig. At the Staatsbibliothek Preußischer Kulturbesitz, Berlin, the archives with their original sources on Adolf von Harnack were put at the disposal of the author.

I am also grateful to Monika Preuß, Heidelberg, Allison Brown, Berlin, and William Templer for their essential assistance.

My special and grateful appreciation, though, belongs to Professor Dr Christoph Schwöbel at King's College, London, and Kiel University. His scholarly advice and personal counsel have made the endeavour of this study a remarkable experience of creative partnership. Without his continuing interest and concern this work could not have been finished.

Munich, spring 1995, Walter Homolka

Leo Baeck, portrait by Ludwig Meidner, 1937.

LEO BAECK IN THERESIENSTADT
by Albert H. Friedlander

There is no doubt about Baeck's contribution to Jewish theology in the twentieth century: it has been significant. Without ever departing completely from the ancient wellsprings of orthodoxy, he was a studious observer of the intellectual currents of his time and surroundings; under the influence of liberal Jewish theology, he drew on and reworked those currents, weaving them into his own theological thought. A special aspect of Baeck's work is that he remained in critical confrontation with Christianity throughout his life, acting as a kind of builder of bridges between the two faiths. The decisive rupture in his life and work was the existential threat posed to Jews and Judaism by National Socialism and his traumatic experiences as a concentration camp inmate in Theresienstadt – an experience suffered by so many German Jews who had, in their harrowed history, passed from the initial euphoria of emancipation to sobering disillusionment during the Second Reich, and then on into the horrors inflicted upon them by the Third.

Theresienstadt was a transit point on the Nazi route to annihilation – from here victims were sent on to the ovens of Treblinka and Auschwitz. One of Theresienstadt's inmates was Rabbi Leo Baeck, whose life and work are a living testimony to the resistance of soul and intellect, a spark that was not extinguished even in the Nazi death camps. This specific aspect of Leo Baeck's biography and personality must constitute the point of departure for any attempt to deal with his theological work. Only when viewed against this historical backdrop does the analysis explored in the present volume take on adequate depth. Although it is important to recognise Baeck's significance for Christian-Jewish dialogue in Germany and

Europe, we must always be mindful of the dire concrete circumstances under which Baeck pursued his theological interests, and the heavy burdens placed on his existence as a scholar.

I intend to focus on intellectual resistance, illustrating this stance by the life and work of one of Theresienstadt's camp inmates, Rabbi Leo Baeck. This does not mean to suggest that Baeck was in any way unique or an exception. Each and every person who was sent to suffer here deserves our respect. Whether accompanied by physical resistance or not, resistance of the intellect and human spirit was very much alive in Theresienstadt.

I was visited a few years back by Kerry Woodward, then on the staff of the BBC music department. Woodward had with him a copy of the opera *Der Kaiser von Atlantis* (a work which was later given the awful English title *Death takes a Holiday*). While reading the libretto, I discovered that the text had been written down on the back of questionnaire forms of the kind that inmates in the concentration camps had been forced to fill out. So I started to pore over these reverse pages, searching for some name possibly familiar to me. Whatever has come to us from Theresienstadt – be it music, poetry, pictorial material or theological lectures – it is necessary to see the anonymous totality that lies behind such expressive manifestations. And one must always be mindful of the individuals and their names – human beings brought here by force, sent here to die. This also holds true in the case of Leo Baeck. Baeck had been deported to Theresienstadt in his capacity as the leader of German Jewry – and thus its representative – and he became a symbol, a myth. We humans have always needed myth in order to transcend reality, to distance it from the world we live in – and to glorify or demonise the past. Those who wish to view German Jews as assimilated, weak and incapable of resisting the Nazis, can, via the distorted representation of a single individual, give rise to the formation of a distorted image of an entire group, namely German Jewry as a whole. But Leo Baeck cannot be misused for such purposes. His integrity and greatness are beyond dispute. Yet neither should he be made into some kind of saint. That would place too much distance between him and us, between him and generations to come – normal people who are most certainly anything but saints. His humanity, his fears and insecurities, his doubts and torments – yes, even his mistaken judgments – are a necessary part of any historical study that would attempt to describe the specific Jewish reactions to the greatest evil of our time.

What was Leo Baeck's importance in and for Theresienstadt? The president of the 'Reich Association of German Jews' was deported to Theresienstadt on 27 January 1943 together with Dr Paul Epstein and Philipp Kozower.

It was not even 6 a.m. when there was a ring at the front door. (Baeck later commented: 'The only ones it could have been at that time was the Gestapo.') They told Baeck he had to leave immediately. He refused, asking for another hour so he could arrange his affairs. The Gestapo men contacted their superiors, and he was granted the additional time he had requested. Baeck wrote a farewell letter to his family and filled out some postal cheque forms to pay his gas and electricity. That act can be seen as an expression of German pedantry or a Jewish sense of duty. Or it might be reminiscent of that famous scene in Plato's *Apology* where Socrates, putting the cup of hemlock to his lips, instructs his friends to pay his outstanding debts. In Baeck's case, everything we know about him suggests that the latter interpretation is more correct.

There were approximately 47,000 Jews in the camp when Baeck arrived in Theresienstadt. Half of them were under the age of sixty, the rest were older; many were very debilitated. The prisoner Leo Baeck became a number: inmate 187984. He was immediately detailed to a work squad, and assigned to the task of hauling a cart through the camp, collecting refuse. A short time thereafter, following his seventieth birthday, Baeck was relieved of these strenuous duties. Later on, he was given responsibilty for social services in the camp. In recognition of his position, Baeck was made an honorary member of the council of elders *(Ältestenrat)*, a body that had been created before his arrival. But Baeck himself no longer wanted to exercise any official duties – he had had enough of such power in the past, and there were others in the camp to take on these functions. Rather, he wished to continue his work as a spiritual counsellor, to visit the sick, attempting to console them to the best of his ability, even under these horrifying conditions. Baeck's sisters had also been deported to Theresienstadt and had died there. The scholar met former associates in Theresienstadt with whom he had worked in years gone by.

Baeck's lectures in Theresienstadt were a source of consolation and inspiration for many inmates who understood that what mattered now was no longer the academic study of Greek and Roman history and philosophy; rather, it was a question of the survival of the human will faced with structures designed to destroy their spirit, transmogrifying them into creatures that were no longer human. When we hear friends who speak about those terrible times as living witnesses and survivors, we realise that Theresienstadt (or Terezin) was a living hell, albeit disguised, camouflaged. The inmates were humiliated mentally and physically, mistreated, their personalities systematically destroyed. Their only emotion was boundless despair.

Baeck knew that the great danger was not hunger, not the crowded conditions, the filth and vermin. In his preface to H. G.

Adler's book on Theresienstadt, Baeck saw the camp as a gruesome
Nazi experiment:

> The Theresienstadt concentration camp, designed exclusively for Jews,
> was in a very particular way just such an experiment in the will to evil. ...
> Theresienstadt: a maximum chance to fall ill – linked with a minimum
> possibility for staying healthy. Space for existence was replaced by space
> to die in. That was one aspect. Mounting multitudes crammed into an
> ever more cramped and narrow area, so that people repeatedly were
> bumping into and scrapping up against each other: all forms of egoism
> and their associated greed were meant to proliferate, all decency to
> wither. That was the second element. Finally, the third factor was that
> Jews from many parts of Europe had been crowded together there,
> human beings who for many generations had had different homelands,
> different cultures and languages. In this atmosphere, all type and manner
> of petty jealousy – or so it seemed – had to erupt, and any sentiment for
> one's shared fate to wilt and perish[1]

The reality described here suggests the closeness of the writer to
the theology of suffering – an element of Jewish thought in which
dialogue and the attempt to draw nearer to one's fellow expand the
space for living, delineating a hard and clear difference between the
hunted and their hunters. The theology of suffering is unable to
describe those organisational structures that crystallise in every
community of prisoners, creating privileges for some individuals or
groups, while denying them to others. Nor should that theology
essay such a description. The unavoidable accusations along these
lines raised against Baeck had their ultimate origin in partisan differences: the Orthodox rabbis were deeply disturbed by the circumstance that Baeck, a Reform rabbi, was being accorded so much
respect. And the fact that Baeck had also concerned himself with
the fate of Christians rendered him suspect in their eyes. Yet even
Recha Freier, and Hannah Arendt later on as well, always stressed
Baeck's integrity, despite their questions about the position he took.
Indeed, Hannah Arendt even expressly took back the doubts and
reservations she had earlier articulated. There were simply too
many people who had known Leo Baeck directly in Theresienstadt,
and whose respect he had earned as a beam of light in the darkness,
a solid rock of unassailable probity. The question remains: should
Baeck have openly voiced his worst fears (which later hardened
into virtual certainty) that the ultimate destination of the transports
being organised from Theresienstadt was death, and not resettle-
ment? He was unable to force himself to make that decision. Baeck
had an abiding conviction: 'To destroy all hope would lead to
despair and death in Theresienstadt.'

1. Leo Baeck, Geleitwort, in H. G. Adler, *Theresienstadt 1941–1945. Das Antlitz einer
Zwangsgemeinschaft* (Tübingen, 1955), VII.

Remaining faithful to this perspective, Baeck stayed a scholar even under the harrowing conditions of the camp, pursuing his work with unwavering resolve. In so doing, he became a living paragon of the resistance of the spirit and intellect – a stance that had a concrete impact on his fellow inmates in that dark place. He gave lectures in the camp, in an untiring effort to strengthen the many hundreds who listened, crowded in the oppressive cramped confinement of the barracks, to that quiet voice: a beacon that lit up new vistas for them as it spoke about the history and philosophy of past eras. This philosophy was remembered here in the camp, while in the barbarism raging outside it seemed to have been forgotten, finally and irrevocably.

1945 brought freedom for the survivors. Yet even after liberation, many stayed on in the camps to be at the side of the sick and dying – including Leo Baeck. A typhoid epidemic had broken out among the weakened, exhausted inmates, and Baeck refused to 'leave his flock' – just as, back in 1939, he had refused to leave Germany. He was still the spiritual counsellor, the man of consolation, whose task was to ease the suffering of the living and bury the dead.[2]

Nor should one think that this final service rendered to the dead is unimportant. On the contrary: the rituals accompanying death lie at the very heart of Jewish belief, and Baeck occupied a position of inestimable value in Theresienstadt, since he was able to provide a modicum of dignity for sufferers in an ambience where, in the words of Paul Celan, 'Death is a master from Deutschland' – an abyss where no effort was spared to rob both the living and the dead of their human dignity.

Many of those assisting at the burials were unable to bear the sight of the corpses. In contrast, Baeck saw in them 'only the external mortal shells, cast off by their souls, which now were free'.

Finally, Baeck too left Theresienstadt: 'On July 1, 1945, I left the concentration camp Terezin; an American bomber brought me to Paris. I had to wait there for some documents, and then was flown July 5th by military plane to London, where I was reunited once again – after a separation of six years – with my daughter, son-in-law and granddaughter.'

Leaving the camp was one more existential caesura for Baeck, a further rupture with all that happened before. Yet it is impossible truly to understand Baeck's later thought and teaching if we know nothing about Theresienstadt, where he taught and served in the most hellish of times.

---

2. Leonard Baker, *Days of Sorrow and Pain. Leo Baeck and the Berlin Jews* (New York/ London, 1978. Baker's book is a comprehensive and detailed biography of Baeck and was awarded the Pulitzer Prize in 1979.

The most important section of Baeck's work *This People* was written in Theresienstadt. It was in the form of a kind of *Midrash:* an ancient rabbinical method for the exposition of the underlying significance of a text that took on ever greater importance in Baeck's work. Crucial here is the fact that his work remains silent about the darkness enveloping its genesis. Or, as Ernst Ludwig Ehrlich formulated it:

> A 'no' becomes visible which – like everything in Baeck's thinking – is primal in its Jewishness: his silence about Christianity in the book *Dieses Volk.* In rabbinical Judaism, silence is the most effective polemic. Baeck was of the opinion – a view shared by many other Jews as well – that the great majority of Christians, and their institutions, had failed to pass the test imposed upon them in the years 1933-1945. That knowledge ... of course did not exclude the deep sense of gratitude he felt toward those few who had remained faithful to the Jews, especially Gertrud Luckner ... or that unknown man on the street who had secretly passed on an apple to someone branded by the yellow star.[3]

Nonetheless, this teaching, this Midrash from Theresienstadt, asks about the ultimate meaning of human existence. In a time of greatest persecution for the people of Israel, Baeck attempts to see Israel as a model for all humankind, as the veritable revelation of the significance of human existence. Ehrlich is correct in his view that the resounding silence in *Dieses Volk* amounts to a judgment on the failure of the Christians. Yet when Baeck wrote in Theresienstadt about the 'covenant', he was referring not only to Israel – he meant all humankind. In his later teachings, Baeck came to view the common basis of Jews and Christians, the asymmetrical relation between the world's peoples, seemingly fixed and frozen, as part of the never dissolved covenant between God and Israel.

Leo Baeck's stature as a human being, and the unwavering resoluteness with which he travelled down his path, render the study of his work obligatory. His struggle for Jewish identity is rooted in a profound sense of piety, coupled with a living and vital confrontation with the intellectual currents of his time. He measures Christianity with a sharp and critical eye – though never persisting in a perspective that there are irreconcilable differences between the two faiths. Thus, Baeck remains an important link for the building of understanding between Jews and Christians, grounded in respect, against the backdrop of the unspeakable suffering this century has visited upon the Jewish people.

3. Ernst Ludwig Ehrlich, in *Freiburger Rundbriefe* 25 (1973), pp. 75–8.

INTRODUCTION

The present study aims at analysing one specific Jewish approach
to define its essence and identity as it has been presented by Leo
Baeck (1873–1956) – generally considered to have been the last great
exponent of German liberal Judaism. We focus on the attempt to
evaluate the connection of liberal Jewish theology and liberal Christian theology at the turn of the twentieth century. This will serve as
background in order to explain Baeck's contribution to the Jewish-
Christian dialogue.

The Socio-Economic Background of Post-Enlightenment Judaism

In order to understand the specific situation of German Jewish life
and thinking before the Second World War we have to keep in mind
that German Jewry underwent a twofold revolution: the encounter
with both the culture and society of its Christian environment during
the emancipation period (1780–1871).

Speaking in political terms, the emancipation of Jews in Germany
resulted in the abolition of civil autonomy for Jewish communities on
the one hand and the end of the feudal status of German Jewry on the
other. With the creation of the modern German state Jews became
integrated into the legal, economic and social system of a Christian
society. Although one must assert that the fruits of Jewish emancipation
remained quite incomplete and the social integration of Jews was somewhat partial the nineteenth century can nevertheless be seen as a
period of intense cultural productiveness on the part of German Jewry.

Many of the religious movements of modern times, Reform, Conservative, and Neo-Orthodox, were brought into being by German Jewish thought. One of the outstanding results of Jewish intellectual endeavour in the nineteenth century was the establishment of the science of Judaism *(Wissenschaft des Judentums)*, a school of thought that developed the idea of an evolutionary process of religious thought within Judaism against the static idea of a Jewish faith that is totally based on an unquestionable act of revelation.

Thus, the religious crisis in nineteenth-century German Judaism was a result of both political as well as social changes and the lack of accessibility of an ancient Jewish faith. It was the great achievement of the science of Judaism to offer an approach for re-defining Jewish identity in a way that contributes to the growth of a new identity.

It was no longer the walls of the ghettos that made the Jew a Jew. Individual reason searched for an enlightened approach to the values of Judaism, the Jewish cultural and religious heritage, and a specific Jewish history.

These scholarly developments did not find a home within the normal university system of that time.[1] Jews had to establish their own institutions of higher education dealing with religious thought. So in 1854, the first Jewish Theological Seminary was established in Breslau, and in 1872, the *Lehranstalt für die Wissenschaft des Judentums* was founded in Berlin. Both of them became central for the science of Judaism.

So one might conclude that liberal Jewish theology, which was highly dependent on the rational findings of the science of Judaism in the areas of philosophy, religion and biblical exegesis, was one of Judaism's most influential responses to the uncertain intellectual and religious situation of Jews in nineteenth century Germany.

What is Liberal Theology?

Trutz Rendtorff has offered quite a fine definition, which serves both Jews and Christians well, when he said that 'liberal theology' in a general sense is every theology that tries to identify modern developments and by doing so also tries to shape and influence them in a constructive way.[2]

Let us focus for a while on the phenomenon of 'liberal theology' at the end of the nineteenth century.

1. See Trutz Rendtorff, 'Das Verhältnis von liberaler Theologie und Judentum um die Jahrhundertwende', in *Das deutsche Judentum und der Liberalismus: German Jewry and Liberalism,* edited by Friedrich-Naumann-Stiftung (Sankt Augustin, 1986), pp. 96–112, here pp. 104–6.
2. Ibid., p. 96.

The following picture emerges: during the first decades of the Second Empire (1870–1914) we realise a specific relationship between political Liberalism that was highly influenced by liberal Protestantism on the one side[3] and a liberal Jewish society on the other. Liberal Jews and liberal Protestants seemed to share a common ground in their set of values as well as their political goals. Liberal Jewish Theology – with its spokesmen Joseph Eschelbacher, Moritz Lazarus, Moritz Güdemann, Ludwig Geiger and Leo Baeck, to name but a few – and liberal Protestant theology – to name among its exponents Ernst Troeltsch, Albert Ritschl, Martin Rade and Adolf von Harnack – were both concerned with finding solutions to questions each of them raised in the same way. And by searching for solutions they found themselves on common ground.

Both groups stressed the neo-Kantian ideal of a human being enabled by ethics to devote all life to an a priori system of principles. It can be said that liberal Protestantism and liberal Judaism tried in the same way to reinterpret religious traditions on the basis of modern rationality. And both attempted to purge their faiths of irrational components.[4]

There was one decisive divergence, though, that separated liberal Jewish theology and liberal Protestant theology: the assertion of Christian theology that Christianity is superior to Judaism and the hypothesis that Judaism must have been quite a decadent faith even prior to Jesus.

The lectures of Adolf von Harnack on the 'Essence of Christianity' *(Wesen des Christentums)*, which were published in 1900, may be seen in this light; Judaism seems to be characterised as an initial and antiquated stage of religion preceding Christianity. It is hardly surprising that Harnack's lectures resulted in heavy criticism among Jewish scholars, orthodox and liberal alike, immediately after they had been so successfully published. One of the first Jewish reactions, however, came from Leo Baeck.

Baeck published a review of Harnack's book in the *Monatsschrift für Geschichte und Wissenschaft des Judentums*[5] in 1901. This may well be seen as the starting point of Baeck's interest in Christianity. The present study attempts to verify that the topic remained his continuing concern. Using overt polemics Baeck tries to draw a sketch of the 'essence of Judaism' by criticising Christianity as it is presented by Harnack.

3. For the development of liberalism and the influences of liberal Protestant theology see Uriel Tal, 'Liberal Protestantism and the Jews in the Second Reich 1870–1914', in *Jewish Social Studies* 26 (1964), pp. 23–41.
4. Cf. ibid., pp. 35–6.
5. *Monatsschrift für Geschichte und Wissenschaft des Judentums* 45 (1901), pp. 97–120

What are the main points of Baeck's criticism concerning Harnack's *Essence of Christianity?* Firstly the lack of appreciation of Jewish scholarship and literature. This, he argues, leads to a misinterpretion of Judaism as it was in the time of Jesus. Secondly, Baeck demonstrates the apologetic intention of Harnack's book.

It was not until four years later that Baeck published his book on the 'Essence of Judaism' *(Wesen des Judentums),*[6] which offers a much more elaborate answer to Harnack's theories. In 1922 a second and enlarged edition followed. Against Harnack's description of Judaism Baeck presents the image of a Jewish faith defined by ethics, 'intellectually orientated' *(geistig),* and genuinely universal; the corresponding piety emphasises good deeds and trust. The 'essence' of Judaism, according to Baeck, lies in the ethical monotheism of the prophets. Although neither Harnack nor Christianity are mentioned explicitly throughout the whole book Baeck's intention is obvious: *Essence of Judaism* is the apologetic answer to Harnack's *Essence of Christianity.*

From then on Baeck's interest in Christianity as the counterpart to Jewish theology is present throughout his work. The bibliography of Baeck's writings contains more than thirty titles on Judaism and Christianity, approximately half of them written during the Weimar Republic, five of them even during the Third Reich.

Baeck's methodology in criticising Christianity is characterised by polarity – a model where 'classical' and 'romantic' religion oppose each other and correspond to the elements of 'mystery' *(Geheimnis)* and 'commandment' *(Gebot),* that is 'mysticism' and 'ethics'. When Judaism and Christianity are analysed in depth each of the two religions may be judged by the criteria offered by this polarity.

Speaking of Christianity, Baeck identifies and distinguishes two main streams of tradition: Paul, Augustine and Martin Luther represent the element of 'mystery'; Jesus, Pelagius and Calvin are identified with the element of 'commandment'. 'Classical religion' (i.e. Judaism) is readily described as a perfect balance between 'mystery' and 'commandment', Christianity is predominantly shaped by Paul and Luther and therefore described as 'Romantic Religion' per se.

Are there any sources of contemporary thought that may shed light on the origin of Baeck's model? The terms 'mystery' and 'commandment' should really be seen in the context of the renaissance of mysticism in the 1920s and the ongoing scholarly interest in mysticism. Furthermore, we can assert an influence by the debate on natural law *(Naturrechtsdebatte)* and its impact on the development of social ethics in post-Enlightenment times. This debate was of special

6. Leo Baeck, *Das Wesen des Judentums,* 1st edn (Berlin, 1905).

interest for Protestant scholars and will undoubtedly have had some resonance in a Judaism heavily influenced by Hegelian and neo-Kantian thought.

Baeck develops his typology by concentrating on the theology of Martin Luther and its Pauline sources. It can be easily detected that Baeck is mainly interested in two topics of Luther's theology: the question of *liberum* or *servum arbitrium* (whether or not our will is free) and the doctrine of two kingdoms. Baeck shows the reader an image of Lutheranism that is deeply influenced by the Prussian Protestant state church *(Staatskirche)*, and the Jewish perception of this alliance of Protestant church and state. So the description of Luther's theology often seems to be rather critical, one-sided and based on a contemporary Jewish prejudice.

This study does not intend to correct Baeck's – often polemic and problematical – view of Christianity and above all of Luther's theology. Rather, we shall attempt to show in which particular way both Christian and Jewish scholars at the turn of the twentieth century tried to formulate what they understood to be the very 'essence' – of their religions.

There have been various attempts to define an 'essence'; it should be mentioned that Alfred Loisy tried the same for Catholicism with *L'Évangile et l'Église* in 1902. However, one may conclude that these attempts to determine the superiority of a certain faith over the others failed miserably. We may conclude that the search for 'essence' did not foster the coexistence of Judaism and Christianity but had the aim of bringing them into a position of apologetic polarity: two camps from each of which the potential opponent on the other side can be carefully detected from a safe distance.

A solution emerged when the historical outlook changed perspective. Liberal theology, Christian and Jewish theologians alike, had to take into account at a later stage that it is impossible to cling on to the idea of exclusive definition of an 'essence' that should then dominate culture, politics and state. Rather, theology has to concentrate on finding and describing the phenomeon of 'identity'.

This new perspective seems crucial for the development of a pluralistic society. 'Identity' requires an inclusive approach to an individual's or a group's faith rather than trying to exclude all influences that seem to distract from the 'essence' of a particular religion. The achievement of some form of identity enables one to accept what differs and what one has in common with people of another faith. It will be interesting to note that Baeck himself exchanges the rather static concept of 'essence' later for the flexible concept of 'existence', thereby acknowledging the changes in the underlying basis of the identity problem.

Baeck described the cornerstones of a true Jewish-Christian dialogue in his lecture on *Judaism, Christianity, and Islam*[7] the knowledge and the acceptance of the differences and similarities of religions; in order to understand those, one has to be aware of one's own religious identity.

What is Attempted?

This study will concentrate on the Jewish aspect of liberal theology. Therefore, Christianity will serve mainly as a backdrop to Jewish theological development at the turn of the twentieth century and is not a main subject in its own right.

Some more details of Leo Baeck's biography will provide the basis for further investigation (chapter 1).

Afterwards, I shall sketch the historical background of the rapid changes which German Judaism had to experience in the nineteenth century (chapter 2).

We will then discuss into depth the essence debate (chapters 3 to 5) in its Christian and Jewish aspects. After an examination of modern Jewish theology (chapter 6), I shall try to outline the theological system of Baeck's thinking (chapter 7).

Then I shall look closely at Baeck's perception of central themes in Luther's thought. I will evaluate this understanding, assess it with regard to the intellectual environment we had discussed in the earlier chapters and try to come to a conclusion on the validity of Baeck's interpretation of Luther: the aim and function of Baeck's particular way of presenting his opponent and an assertion on the underlying problem that Baeck has in mind when challenging Luther (chapter 8).

In conclusion I will discuss the trend towards a genuinely Jewish systematic theology (chapter 8).

It is hoped that a picture emerges that illuminates the situation of Jewish thought between the emancipation of the post-Enlightenment age and the dawn of a pluralistic society, a problem for Judaism and Christianity alike.

---

7. Leo Baeck, *Judentum, Christentum und Islam: Rede gehalten von Ehren-Großpräsident Dr. Leo Baeck anlässlich der Studientagung der Districts-Loge Kontinental-Europa XIX in Bruxelles,* (22 April 1956); here p. 4.

Chapter 1

LEO BAECK – JEWISH LEADER IN A CHRISTIAN NATION

A True Leader of German Judaism

Leo Baeck lived from 1873 to 1956. He is considered one of the most significant representatives of German Judaism and, at the same time, as the *spiritus rector*, the spiritual leader of progressive Judaism. Albert H. Friedlander, in his comprehensive biography *Leo Baeck: Teacher of Theresienstadt*, refers to Baeck in terms of his outstanding importance, his versatile talents and his scholarly knowledge, as follows:

> he was the leader of German Jewry, the last duly elected and appointed leader of a community which had come to an end after more than a thousand years of historic existence. He was one of the great scholars of his generation; what he had to say about Christianity and concerning mysticism or ancient philosophy was received with as much attention as his great writings on the essence of Judaism. Grand Master of the German B'nai Brith fraternal organization of Jews, the leading rabbi of the Jewish community of Berlin, professor of the last Jewish seminary in Germany still secretly ordaining young men as rabbis to a dying community, Leo Baeck had refused to leave Germany, despite the insistence of Jews all over the world, of the German leaders themselves.[1]

On the other hand, Leo Baeck was and still is considered controversial, even among Jews.

There are some people who are qualified to be 'representatives' of their community because they reflect all of the characteristics of that community, so that this overall picture is not disturbed by idiosyn-

---

1. Albert H. Friedlander, *Leo Baeck: Teacher of Theresienstadt* (New York, 1958).

crasies or individual traits showing through. Others represent their community by embodying a single distinctive characteristic that is expressed so strongly and distinctly that it leaves a lasting impression. Then again there are some people who have the strength to stick to their own, individual convictions, yet still retain the ability, in spite of their individuality – even in the face of numerous obstacles – to embody the entirety of their community, diverse though it may be. Leo Baeck was such a man. As a result, he was both unconditionally German – a pioneer of the organisation of Jewish German citizens, the *Centralverein deutscher Staatsbürger jüdischen Glaubens*, as well as one of the few rabbis who refused, in 1897, to participate in a protest against the 1st Zionist Congress.

Baeck was twenty-four years old at the time and had just received his first rabbinical appointment. He boldly risked his future career and, just as boldly, he later offered his services to the Zionist Fund and the 'Jewish Agency for Palestine', despite the common suspicion that such groups were attempting to undermine the civic roots of assimilation so important to Jewish middle-class society. And, finally, he happily welcomed the state of Israel, without letting that support stop him from loudly and openly opposing the terrorism based on nationalism which preceded the founding of the state.

Youth in Lissa

Leo Baeck, the seventh of eleven children, was born in Lissa in the Province of Poznan, on 23 May 1873. His ancestors came from Moravia and Hungary. There were rabbis on both sides of his family, including his father, Dr Samuel Bäck, who enjoyed a high reputation as a scholar and author as a result of his book on the history of the Jewish people and their literature from Babylonian times to the present.

Leo Baeck was raised in a religious family, which did not withdraw from the future-orientated spirit of an emerging epoch. The environment in which he grew up was filled with a sense of joyful humanity, but at the same time contributed to the contemplative young boy's rejection of the feelings of optimism toward the future that were, albeit much later, revealed to be rather superficial. At the time, many Jews embraced this optimism because they wanted to overcome the narrowness of their living space, similar to conditions in the Middle Ages, from which they had emerged only fifty to a hundred years earlier.

As a Jew in Lissa, he could observe the members of three Christian denominations: Lutheran, Calvinist and Catholic. Baeck's respect for the Calvinist minister in Lissa played a role in his affinity for the Calvinists, which later developed theological roots. The house in which the Baeck family lived belonged to the minister, who charged them a very low rent and who refused to accept the increase that the Baecks offered.

The relationship between the Germans and the Poles in Lissa was strained. The Jews were hardly affected by anti-Polish sentiment, but they considered themselves German, based on their language, culture and political affinity. At the time, Germans in the area did not object to the Jewish identification of themselves as Germans. During the Second World War, Baeck found the following words to express the position of the Jews among various peoples and nationalities:

> The struggle in which the soul of this people – its union with God – once opposed the peoples of Canaan and the surrounding peoples, was, above all, a struggle for purity ...
> This was especially the case in times when eras or cultures submerged and new forms of life revealed themselves.
> The danger of unhealthy assimilation was ever-present – an assimilation by which more evil and cruelty than that which is noble and life-giving was adopted from the surroundings The inner core of this people was thereby attacked. A real, healing assimilation does exist ...
> The essence of this people has hardly been limited by this; in fact, its spirit was generally enriched. But when they allowed themselves to be embraced by the arms of Canaan, then the core of life, the union with God, lost its strength.[2]

Studies in Breslau and Berlin

Baeck was first taught by his father and he then graduated from the *Gymnasium*, the German grammar school. In 1891, he left the city of his birth to attend the conservative 'Jewish Theological Seminary' in Breslau. He continued his studies in 1894 at the liberal 'Institute for the Science of Judaism' and at the University of Berlin, where Dilthey was one of his teachers. Both at the University of Breslau and the University of Berlin, Baeck studied oriental and ancient languages in addition to philosophy, theology and history. He was barely twenty-two years old when he completed his doctorate in Berlin and published his dissertation on Spinoza's early influence in Germany.

At the time when Baeck first started writing, his way of thinking was considered to support Reform or liberal Judaism. Although his deep insight into the imperfection of religion led him to approach

2. Hans G. Adler, 'Rechenschaft in dunkler Zeit: Leo Baeck und sein Werk' in *Leo Baeck: Lehrer under Helfer in schwerer Zeit*, Arnoldshainer Texte 20, Werner Licharz (ed.) (Frankfurt am Main), p. 64.

these tendencies, in later years he repeatedly emphasised that he did not consider himself to belong to any reform movement and that piousness, as he understood it and which could only rightly refer to old Jewish piousness, had nothing in common with the vague term 'liberal'.

Instead of reform, he hoped for substantial progress that would not be superficial, but what he referred to as *progressus*, a history that Baeck depicted theologically as 'a history of encounters with God'.[3]

He compared religious liberalism, however – not to be confused with mere tolerance – with liberal conservatism, preservation and remembrance that is open to the new, and reflects on the prophetic words of God: 'For my thoughts are not your thoughts and your ways are not mine.'[4] It was an expression of this type of progress and conservatism when Baeck declared, in the conclusion to his work *Dieses Volk (This People)*:

> It is an illusion of people and peoples when they think they can deter-mine history, the course of generations, in a way they would like. This will not make things easy for them; responsibility in which freedom reveals itself as freedom is much more difficult … Tradition cannot be created, let alone coerced; only freedom which is capable of developing can really take its place.[5]

The Rabbinate in the Weimar Republic

In 1897, as a young rabbi, Baeck was sent to Oppeln in Upper Silesia. There, he married a graceful and dignified woman, Natalie Ham-burger, and his only child, Ruth, was born. In 1907, Baeck went to Düsseldorf where he served as a rabbi, and in 1912 he moved to Berlin where he was both a rabbi and a lecturer at the Institute for the Science of Judaism.

Thirty years later, in the summer of 1942, when this institute was closed, he was the last remaining teacher, having only three students. Baeck held seminars and lectures on ancient exegetical writings *(Midrash)*, homiletics, Jewish mysticism, the historical background of the Revelation of John, the history of religion and comparative sci-ence of religion. His lectures were analytic, systematic and appeared to be unbiased. Whoever heard him speak never forgot the im-pression he made – his melodious voice, in spite of a slightly scratchy intonation, which was always deeply affected by the topic he was speaking on. One of Baeck's students described him as follows:

3. Ibid., p. 67.
4. Isa. 55:8.
5. Adler, 'Rechenschaft', in *Leo Baeck*, Licharz (ed.), p. 67.

When Leo Baeck preached, he wasn't condescending to his listeners. He carefully chose each word, considered weighting and sound, forming each sentence accordingly.

He spoke in a monotone with an unusual vibrating, high-pitched voice, emphasising sentences here and there with a movement of his sensitive hands; more often, though, he showed the importance of a thought through the increased severity of his glance. He seemed to expect the response to his speech from somewhere far beyond the congregation.

Baeck's sermons ... always had some kind of personal character. A pious scholar asked questions of the Bible, a highly educated man conversed with history and literature. He spoke *with* them, not *about* them. And although his sermons were complete, they usually lacked a final conclusion; they showed a person in search of the truth.

He told his students: 'Do not forget that the preacher has a special position: the listeners cannot ask questions, cannot contradict; the preacher always has the last word.'[6]

Many of Baeck's students speak of the joy and the seriousness that he brought to his work as a rabbi. Bruno Italiener specifically remarked that, of his many tasks, Baeck was particularly devoted to the sermon. Regarding Baeck's opening lecture at the institute, Italiener said:

The lecture, which gave essential new insights into the historical development of the sermon, closed with Baeck's own thoughts on the task of the modern sermon.

In the demands that he placed on the sermon, Baeck reflected his deep moral earnestness. The preacher must always remember that 'the dignity of the religion is his responsibility'. Accordingly, it is his duty 'to teach and to elevate'. He should not, however, be misguided by the wish to be liked. He also shouldn't 'step down' to his listeners just because it is easier. Much more, he should 'remain true to his own, the best of Judaism'. Only in this way will he feel the joy of being able to respect himself.

In this sense, not only did Baeck educate a generation of rabbis who could sit at his feet as students, but he himself lived according to these beliefs.[7]

During the First World War, Baeck was a Jewish chaplain on both the western and the eastern fronts. After the war he was President of the liberal rabbinical association *(Allgemeiner Rabbinerverband)* and was considered a spokesperson for Judaism. Soon he became the (officially) recognised spokesperson for Jewry in Germany, respected by the majority of followers of different religious and political sympathies. Baeck was an active member of the executive board of the *Centralverein deutscher Staatsbürger jüdischen Glaubens*, which represented the old programme of national incorporation into German society while unconditionally holding on to the religion of ancestry. Unlike many other rabbis, he never condescended to participating in

---

6. Fritz Bamberger, 'Leo Baeck: Der Mensch und die Idee', in *Worte des Gedenkens für Leo Baeck*, Eva G.Reichmann (ed.) (Heidelberg, 1959), p. 76.

7. Bruno Italiener, 'Der Rabbiner', in *Worte des Gedenkens*, Reichmann (ed.), p. 165.

a protest against national Zionism. He considered it an obligation to be involved in general Jewish organizations in which non-Zionists and Zionists worked together toward the construction of a home in Palestine for any Jews who wished to settle there, whether out of conviction or out of need.

His advice was considered definitive by the state authorities. Baeck was the expert consultant for the Prussian Ministry of Education and the Arts for Jewish Affairs[8] and, starting in 1924, he was both the Grand Master of the German district of B'nai Brith lodges and the President of the central welfare bureau for German Jews *(Zentralwohlfahrtsstelle der deutschen Juden)*. In addition, he was not only a religious and secular leader, but a leading representative of the science of Judaism as well.

Leo Baeck and the Third Reich

1933 did not catch Leo Baeck unawares. Of course he could not have foreseen the immensity of the developing horror; almost no one possessed the ability to imagine the crimes which were to come.

Baeck sought to perpetuate the hope that Germany's Jews had, that at least a trace of civilised behaviour would be preserved. When the goal of the Nazi persecution, the annihilation of the Jews, could no longer be denied, Baeck tried to save as many potential victims as possible.

The creation of a central office for the protection of basic rights and needs had been neglected for far too long and it was not until 1933 that the Association of German Jews was founded, headed by Leo Baeck. The office dealt daily with the authorities, mostly the secret police (Gestapo), in order to support emigration, to intercede for those in danger, to avoid or at least alleviate extreme hardship, as well as to lend emotional and other support by constructing welfare facilities and schools.

In those years, Baeck was arrested five times. He was quickly released each time and was never intimidated or defeated. After the notorious 'Nuremberg Laws' of 1935 were made known, Baeck wrote the following prayer, which he had asked to be read in all synagogues on Yom Kippur:

> In this hour, all of Israel stands before God who judges and forgives. With the same strength with which we admit our sins, both our individual and our common sins, we declare with disgust and outrage that we see the lie that is being used against us, the slander that attacks our religion and those who bear witness.

8. This position he shared with Ernst Troeltsch, who also acted as government adviser.

We profess our faith and our trust in our future.

We counter all this abuse with the sovereignty of our religion, and all the offences committed against us with our efforts to follow the path of Judaism, fulfilling His commandments. Do not despair and do not become embittered. Trust in Him to Whom all times belong.[9]

It is remarkable that even in those stormy times, Baeck continued his studies, wrote books and even had them published. With his work from 1905 on the essence of Judaism, Baeck had responded to the lectures on the essence of Christianity written by Harnack, the respected Protestant theologian. It is significant that during the period of Nazi rule, Baeck felt compelled to delve more deeply into Christianity than ever before, and to contribute, as a Jew, to its understanding. Baeck's contribution is referred to as a contribution to 'Jewish-Christian dialogue', a phrase unfortunately so overused as to resemble a faded slogan.

From 1933 to 1939, in an effort to distil the oldest parts of the New Testament from later Greek elements, Baeck, three times, translated the parts he considered the earliest layers of tradition from the original Greek into Hebrew. In 1938, Baeck's work on the 'Gospel as a Document of the History of the Jewish Faith' *(Das Evangelium als Urkunde der jüdischen Glaubensgeschichte)*[10] was published, in which Baeck examined the records, the events and the proverbs and parables of the four gospels. In the preface he explained his intention:

> The question how the Gospels in the New Testament could have developed out of the ancient message of Jesus the messiah has been much disputed. But like the question of the original meaning of these tidings, it can really be approached in one way only: by way of the sphere in which all those events took shape. Only in terms of its own space and time will everything become clear to us. We must understand the nature of oral tradition as it was then alive in Palestinian Judaism. We must penetrate its very soul and grasp the essentially poetic manner in which tradition in those days was handed down and apprehended. Only then will harmony and discrepancy in our Gospels be grasped, too. For the Gospels must be understood, not in terms of textual sources out of which they might have been composed, but in terms of the tradition out of which they originated …
>
> A life of Jesus can be written, if at all, only after one has determined what the first generation after Jesus related and handed down …
>
> Our conclusion was not summoned; it appeared: the Gospel emerges as a piece, not inconsiderable, of Jewish history – a testimony of Jewish faith.[11]

9. Fritz Bamberger, ' Leo Baeck: Der Mensch und die Idee', in Reichmann (ed.), *Worte des Gedenkens*, p. 80.
10. German: Berlin, 1938; English in *Judaism and Christianity* (translated and edited by Walter Kaufmann) (New York, 1958).
11. Leo Baeck, 'The Gospel as a Document of the History of the Jewish Faith', in *Judaism and Christianity* (New York, 1958), p. 41f.

After the pogroms in November 1938, the Association of German
Jews (Reichsvertretung der deutschen Juden) was transformed with a
new name into an organisation with compulsory membership and representation of the German Jewish community under the supervision of
the Gestapo. Under the watchful eyes of Heydrich and Eichmann,
independent, autonomous activities became increasingly difficult and
dangerous, but Baeck remained in his position as director and refused
all appointments he received outside Germany. He never considered
his own personal safety.

In the summer of 1939 Baeck travelled to London, where his
daughter and her family lived, to negotiate possibilities for emigration for German Jews, but he did not let himself be dissuaded from
returning to Germany after hearing information about the impend-
ing war. 'As long as one single Jew still remains in Germany, that is
where I belong and I will not leave the country.'[12]

The most difficult time began; for Baeck it was a time of personal
challenge during which his countless tasks continued to multiply.
Later in life Baeck disclosed surprising information regarding his
activities during the war:

> I was in constant contact with the men in the Resistance. My intermedi-
> ary was a director of the Bosch factory in Stuttgart ... This man had con-
> tact with Goerdeler as well as with the military ... .
> An appeal to the German people was to be written and I was one of
> those asked to help draft such an appeal. My intermediary told me that
> my version was chosen for the 'Day After'.
> We all knew that the independent newspapers that would appear fol-
> lowing the defeat of the regime would need material for three months, and
> newspaper articles and political literature were, therefore, being prepared.
> There was also to be a book on the development of the status of Jews
> in Europe and I worked on this book from 1938 to 1941.[13]

When he was deported to Theresienstadt on 28 January 1943, Leo
Baeck took this book with him, as well as the opening chapter of the
first volume of *This People (Dieses Volk)*, which he completed while in
the concentration camp. He was almost seventy years old at the
time. He quickly became the head of the council of elders, but more
significant was that he was a sincere person, a true friend and helper
to the other prisoners.

H.G. Adler gave an impressive description of what Baeck was
able to do and what he did in Theresienstadt:

> Shortly after Leo Baeck arrived on 28 January 1943, word had already
> gone round, not only among the German Jews, most of whom had

12. Adler, 'Rechenschaft', in *Leo Baeck*, Licharz (ed.), p. 70.
13. Ibid., p. 70f.

already heard of him, but also among the other prisoners, that a very special man had come, someone who was not satisfied with the dubious honour of receiving a leadership position in the fettered 'self-government', but rather a man who took on his job in a way very different from most of his co-workers, but without ever actively supporting a resistance, as we know from the venerable example of the Warsaw ghetto and other camps in eastern Europe.

Certainly he would not have refused to devote himself to such a political resistance movement, but that was in any case not a possibility considering the social mix of prisoners in Theresienstadt.

Leo Baeck, as he put it himself, was the centre of a moral resistance. He practised and taught this resistance, that is, he behaved as he felt a person should behave – always, everywhere, no matter how adverse the conditions – kind, honest and benevolent.[14]

After the end of the war and the liberation of the concentration camp, Leo Baeck went to London. Soon after, he was elected to several highly important offices. He was President of the 'Council of Jews from Germany' and Chairperson of the 'World Union for Progressive Judaism'. His later activities included extensive teaching and travelling, and finally he became a professor of the history of the Jewish religion at Hebrew Union College in Cincinnati, Ohio.

Baeck died on 2 November 1956. The Hebrew inscription on his tombstone reads: *'Aus rabbinischem Stamm'*, of rabbinical roots.

In the winter semester of 1940, Dr Baeck taught classes in Berlin on the fundamental thought of Judaism.

He spoke of power that exists only in order to perish. Every thought, on the other hand, remains forever, it is everlasting. No idea has ever been destroyed by any catastrophe. Biblical heritage is seeing the small in the great and the great in the small. 'God laughs in Heaven.'

Baeck's Interest in Christianity

Baeck had a special relationship to the Jewish-Christian dialogue throughout his life. In a certain sense, he was its spiritual precursor. To Baeck, Jewish-Christian co-operation meant mutual respect for differences and not an empty, meaningless balancing out of the centuries of sacred traditions. However, this mild-mannered man, so often willing to compromise, had no patience with attempts at defamation or misrepresention of his faith.

On the other hand, his portrayal of Christianity was not always free of theoretical construction and displayed no lack of polemics.

---

14. Hans G. Adler, 'Leo Baeck in Theresienstadt', in *Worte des Gedenkens*, Reichmann (ed.), p. 63.

Perhaps the century-long persecution of the Jews by Christians brought out this way of thinking, making it almost excusable, but today we must admit that Baeck was not always fair in his description of Christianity. He did, however, view the church as the successor of ancient Graeco-Roman civilisation, which was characterised by the ideal of beauty and harmony. All its elements were designed to be perfect, complete and in tune with one another. Whether in Greek art or in philosophy, the perfection and the balance of things right up to the harmony of the kingdoms is its strongest characteristic.

This civilisation lacked a dynamic element, however, restlessness and dissatisfaction with the world as it is. A driving messianic momentum, the prophetic protest against the imperfection and unjust order of the world, was absent. For this reason, a hideous contempt for humanity, along with brutality, terror and slavery, could exist in Greece and Rome, side by side with the admirable achievements of art, the mind, technology and culture. This was not viewed as contradictory and posed no serious problem. Prophetic criticism was absent, as well as a sense of ethical absoluteness, of the sanctity of each human life and, beyond that, of nature in general. An Amos, an Isaiah or a Jeremiah could not have existed there.

As the successor to Rome, the church adopted the structure of Graeco-Roman civilisation. In his essay on 'Romantic Religion', Baeck analysed Christian and Jewish religion. The church emphasises harmony and perfection, as did ancient Greek culture. Salvation is part of this reality; it is not achieved on the basis of any human effort or the help of God. In his sense, the church also lacked the dynamism and forward-looking impatience that is embodied in Judaism. The church was characterised by passivity and an immobile self-centred sense of salvation.

Baeck is most critical of Lutheranism. The 'Doctrine of the Two Kingdoms', which divided the sphere of human beings into that which belonged to the state and that which belonged to God, is here taken to an extreme.

In Baeck's view, the Lutheran Church relinquished all responsibility for the worldly condition of the people and left it to state authorities. Morality became so removed from religion that individuals seemed to be guaranteed a clear conscience concerning worldly affairs. What did matters of the world have to do with the individual anyway? These tendencies led in Baeck's view to an authoritarian state and the silent acceptance of National Socialism by many. A police state allowing no room for individual decisions was, according to Baeck, a direct development of Lutheranism. The Nazi state was the logical consequence of such a misguided theological evolution.

On the other hand, Baeck was one of the Jewish intellectuals who enthusiastically supported the 'reclaiming of Jesus' into Judaism. In 1938, at the height of National Socialism, he published his book on the 'Gospel as a document of the history of the Jewish faith', *Das Evangelium als Urkunde der jüdischen Glaubensgeschichte.* He showed that Jesus led his entire life as an exemplary Jew ;who would never have considered founding a new religion, not to speak of being worshipped as God. Baeck described Jesus as follows:

we behold a man who is Jewish in every feature and trait of his character, manifesting in every particular what is pure and good in Judaism. This man could have developed as he came to be only on the soil of Judaism; and only on this soil, too, could he find his disciples and followers as they were. Here alone, in this Jewish sphere, in this Jewish atmosphere of trust and longing, could this man live his life and meet his death – a Jew among Jews.[15]

The bibliography of Baeck's writings contains more than thirty titles on the relationship between Judaism and Christianity. Seventeen of them were published in the Weimar Republic, five of the most important works even during the Third Reich.[16] One may say that the work of Leo Baeck is characterised by a permanent discussion with Christianity, even in most difficult times like the Third Reich.

It is remarkable that it is through the argument with the liberal Protestant Adolf von Harnack that Leo Baeck became known to a large public. Harnack's book on the *Wesen des Christentums* (Essence of Christianity) inspired Baeck to write his apologetic *Wesen des Judentums* (Essence of Judaism), which was published in 1905, four years after Harnack's book. We may see this as the starting point of Baeck's interest in Christianity.

The following chapter is dedicated to the historical background and the social climate of the emergence of a science of Judaism and its confrontation with liberal Protestantism in the *Wesensdebatte* (essence debate). It will be the aim to present and discuss the main arguments of both the Christian and Jewish thinkers taking part in this debate. Special emphasis will be given to Adolf von Harnack and the Jewish response to his ideas from Leo Baeck and others including Joseph Eschelbacher, Felix Perles and Martin Schreiner.

15. Baeck, *Judaism and Christianity*, p. 101.
16. Theodore Wiener, *The Writings of Leo Baeck, Studies in Bibliography and Booklore*, vol. 1, no. 3 (Cincinnati, Ohio, 1954); see also Robert R. Geis et al., *Versuche des Verstehens* (Munich, 1966), p. 50.

Chapter 2

THE JEWISH FIGHT FOR EQUALITY

Emancipation and Antisemitism during the Second German Empire

The twofold nature of the 'Jewish question' in the nineteenth century is marked by emancipation and antisemitism.[1] The emancipatory period started at the end of the eighteenth century and continued up to a judicial act of emancipation, the law of the North German Confederation of 1869. The background leading up to this is supplied by the Enlightenment: in its secularisation process and, most importantly, in the transformation of society from feudalism to modern bourgeois capitalism.

In the liberal consciousness of the Enlightenment, emancipation was seen as a kind of collective educational process of Judaism, based on the dissolution of Jewish group identity and, with that, of the confessional status of the Jewish religion (De-judaisation). The Jewish acceptance of this emancipation took place in a dynamic process of adaptation to the developing structures of modern society. This was characterised by the increasing number of mixed marriages and conversion to Christianity, as well as by a growing indifference

1. Reinhard Rürup, 'Emanzipation und Krise: Zur Geschichte der "Judenfrage" in Deutschland vor 1890', in *Juden in Wilhelminischen Deutschland 1890–1914: Ein Sammelband*, Werner E. Mosse and Arnold Paucker (eds), Schriftenreihe wissenschaftlicher Abhandlungen des Leo Baeck Instituts 33 (Tübingen, 1976) pp. 1–56; and Reinhard Rürup, 'Die "Judenfrage" der bürgerlichen Gesellschaft und die Entstehung des modernen Antisemitismus', in *Emanzipation und Antisemitismus: Studien zur 'Judenfrage' der bürgerlichen Gesellschaft*, Kritische Studien zur Geschichtswissenschaft 15 (Göttingen, 1975), pp. 74–94; for a general overview, cf. further: Jacob Katz, *Zur Assimilation und Emanzipation der Juden* (Darmstadt, 1982).

of Jews to their own religion.[2] In the hope of accelerating the emancipation process, Jews demonstrated primarily liberally orientated politics.[3] The connection between the emancipatory 'Jewish question' and the emergence of a bourgeois capitalist society was, at the same time, the necessary condition for the antisemitic turn of events that took place during the stabilisation crisis of the German Empire. The Catholic stereotyping of the cultural struggle as a 'war of Judaism against Christianity', the defeat of the Liberals in the election of 1878/79 and Bismarck's antiliberal turnaround intensified this process.[4] In this sense, modern, racist antisemitism was a post-emancipatory phenomenon that represented the ideological bond of the 'antagonistic nationalism'[5] of the Empire, therefore acquiring the quality of a world view.[6]

The situation at the turn of the century was greatly influenced by the 'Berlin Antisemitism Debate', which was triggered by Heinrich von Treitschke in 1879, based on the speeches leading up to the debate by Adolf Stoecker, one of the court chaplains at the time.[7]

2. Cf. G. Mai, 'Sozialgeschichtliche Bedingungen von Judentum und Antisemitismus im Kaiserreich', in *Judentum und Antisemitismus von der Antike bis zur Gegenwart*, T. Klein, V. Losemann and G. Mai (eds), prepared for the Department of History of the Philipps-Universität Marburg (Düsseldorf, 1984), pp. 113–36; and Monika Richarz, (ed.), *Jüdisches Leben in Deutschland*, Publication of the Leo Baeck Institut 3 vols (Stuttgart, 1976/78/82), here vol. 2: *Selbstzeugnisse zur Sozialgeschichte im Kaiserreich* (Stuttgart, 1978), p. 16.

3. Cf. Jacob Toury, *Die politischen Orientierungen der Juden in Deutschland: Von Jena bis Weimar*, Schriftenreihe wissenschaftlicher Abhandlungen des Leo Baeck Instituts 15 (Tübingen, 1966).

4. However, Bismarck was not seen from a Jewish perspective as being antisemitic out of conviction; antisemitism was merely a political tool of incitement for him; cf. 'Bismarck posthumus', *Allgemeine Zeitung des Judenthums: Ein unparteiisches Organ für alles jüdische Interesse*, (founded by Rabbi Dr L. Phillipson; ed: Dr G.Karpeles; from 1909, L. Geiger) (Leipzig, Berlin, 1870 onwards) 63 (1899), nr 15 of 14 Apr., pp. 169–71.

5. Hans-Ulrich Wehler, *Das deutsche Kaiserreich 1871–1918*, Deutsche Geschichte 9, 4th edn (revised and with expanded bibliography) (Göttingen, 1980 [1973]), p. 108.

6. Cf. Rürup, *Die Judenfrage' der bürgerlichen Gesellschaft*, p.91; on the history of the term 'antisemitism', cf. P. Nipperday and Reinhard Rürup, 'Antisemitismus', in *Geschichtliche Grundbegriffe: Historisches Lexikon zur politisch-sozialen Sprache*, Otto Brunner, Werner Conze and Reinhart Koselleck (eds), vol. 1 (Stuttgart, 1972), pp. 129–53; quoted in the reprint, Rürup, *Die Judenfrage' der bürgerlichen Gesellschaft*, pp. 95–114; ibid., p. 74, clearly differentiates between modern antisemitism and pre-bourgeois, religiously motivated enmity toward Jews; for another view, cf. Uriel Tal, *Christians and Jews in Germany: Religion, Politics and Ideology in the Second Reich, 1870–1914* (translated from Hebrew by N.J. Jacobs) (Ithaca/London, 1975) (Jerusalem, 1969), p. 305.

7. Cf. the important bibliography: Walter Boehlich, (ed.), *Der Berliner Antisemitismusstreit (Quellensammlung)* (Frankfurt am Main, 1965). On Treitschke, cf. Liebeschütz, Hans, *Das Judentum im deutschen Geschichtsbild: Von Hegel bis Max Weber,*

Theodor Mommsen, supporter of the liberal resistance to Treitschke recognised very early that this debate made antisemitism socially acceptable. The reins of shame[8] were loosened, no longer holding the movement in check; the debate became an issue of academia.[9] As early as 1890, prominent liberals such as Mommsen, H. Rickert and others, founded the *'Verein zur Abwehr des Antisemitismus'*, an organisation dedicated to fighting antisemitism. The most prominent member representing a theological perspective was Otto Baumgarten.

Soon after, in 1893, German Jews formed their own association, the 'Central Association of German Citizens of Jewish Faith' *('Centralverein deutscher Staatsbürger jüdischen Glaubens')*.[10] Around the turn of the century, antisemitism was by no means an explicit social movement, but an albeit hidden antisemitic tendency definitely existed in society.[11] The Jewish attitude at this time was ambivalent. The old dream of total assimilation was retained by some,[12] while others, most notably the Zionists, had already abandoned the concept of assimilation.[13] It became more and more obvious that, for the sheer sake of preserving Judaism, 'assimilation' was desirable only if a distinctive Jewish group identity could be maintained. That is, Jewish tradition needed to be reformulated in such a way as to be compatible with the conditions of modern society and culture.

The historical significance of 'liberal' and also of 'conservative' Judaism, from the very beginning and especially at the turn of the century, is determined by their involvement in this task.

Harnack's *Wesen des Christentum (The Essence of Christianity)* came in the midst of this atmosphere of intensified Jewish sensibility

---

Schriftenreihe wissenschaftlicher Abhandlungen des Leo Baeck Instituts 17 (Tübingen, 1967), pp. 157–91.

8. Theodor Mommsen, *Auch ein Wort über unsere Juden* (Berlin, 1880), p. 11.

9. Cf. Norbert Kampe, 'Akademisierung der Juden und Beginn eines studentischen Antisemitismus', in *Jüdisches Leben*, Berliner Topografien 4, Museumspädagogischer Dienst Berlin – Ästhetik und Kommunikation, Wolfgang Dreßen (ed.) (Berlin, 1985), pp. 10–23.

10. Cf. Arnold Paucker, 'Zur Problematik einer jüdischen Abwehrstrategie in der deutschen Gesellschaft', in *Juden in Wilhelminischen Deutschland*, Mosse and Paucker (eds), pp. 479–548.

11. For the Jewish perception of antisemitism around the turn of the century, cf. M. Phillipson, 'Jahresüberblicke', in *JJGL (Jahrbuch für jüdische Geschichte und Literatur in Deutschland)* edited by Verband der Vereine für jüdische Geschichte und Literatur in Deutschland (Berlin, 1989 onwards) and Gustav Karpeles, in *AZdJ* (1898 onwards).

12. See Richarz, *Jüdisches Leben*, 2, for an eloquent example.

13. On the relationship of the 'Centralverein' to the Zionist Movement, cf. Jehuda Reinharz, *Fatherland or Promised Land: The dilemma of the German Jew 1893–1914* (Ann Arbor, 1975), esp. the summary (pp. 225–34) and the extensive bibliography (pp. 290–312).

regarding the conditions for forming a Jewish identity. The Jewish response to Harnack and its intensity must, therefore, be understood within this framework.

Liberal Judaism and the 'Science of Judaism'

The historical period of upheaval in Judaism around the turn of the century, as described above, is also reflected in the corresponding intellectual and scholarly development within the Jewish community, one of the necessary prerequisites for the debate on the question of the essence of Judaism. Leopold Zunz's book, *Die gottesdienstlichen Vorträge der Juden historisch entwickelt*,[14] was published in 1832, marking what is considered the birth of the 'science of Judaism' and scholarly reform of Judaism. By giving evidence for an evolutionary process in the history of Judaism, Zunz gave scientific grounds for Reform ideology.[15]

Zunz inspired the first generation of liberal rabbis, of whom Abraham Geiger (1810–74) was the leading representative. In their conceptions of this evolution, Jewish tradition, which had been considered as a unified whole up to that point, was divided into a persevering 'core' and its changing temporal manifestations; i.e. the fundamental elements of the 'essence' were defined.[16]

This process of historicisation was accelerated through emancipation and assimilation. The validity claims regarding apparently obsolete aspects of Jewish tradition were disposed of by Jews through consistent historicisation. A science of Judaism that was emancipated and dissociated from theology was to aid the integration into modern society as it developed.[17]

14. Cf. Caesar Seligmann, *Geschichte der jüdischen Reformbewegung von Mendelssohn bis zur Gegenwart* (Frankfurt am Main, 1922), p. 88; on the entire development, cf: Friedrich W. Niewöhner, 'Judentum. Wesen des Judentums', in *Historisches Wörterbuch der Philosophie*, vol. 4, Joachim Ritter and Karlfried Gründer (eds) (Darmstadt, 1976); and Heinz M. Graupe, *Die Entstehung des modernen Judentums: Geistesgeschichte der deutschen Juden 1650–1942*, Hamburger Beiträge zur Geschichte der Juden 1 (Hamburg, 1969).
15. Cf. Gösta Lindeskog, *Die Jesusfrage im neuzeitlichen Judentum. Ein Beitrag zur Geschichte der Leben-Jesu-Forschung*, with an epilogue to the reprint (Darmstadt, 1973 [Uppsala, 1938]), p. 41.
16. Cf. Bernhard Isaac, 'Der Religionsliberalismus im deutschen Judentum' (unpubl. doctoral dissertation, Univeristy of Leipzig, 1933), pp. 48f.
17. Cf. Kurt Wilhelm, (ed.) *Wissenschaft des Judentums im deutschen Sprachbereich: Ein Querschnitt*, Schriftenreihe wissenschaftlicher Abhandlungen des Leo Baeck Instituts 16, 2 vols (Tübingen, 1967), here: vol. 1, pp. 3f.; and Lindeskog, *Die Jesusfrage*, pp.40f.; cf. also the negative comments of Leo Baeck on the resulting develop-

As early as 1836, Geiger called for the founding of a Jewish theological faculty representing this new approach; in 1854, the first Jewish Theological Seminary was established in Breslau, and in 1872, the *Lehranstalt für die Wissenschaft des Judentums*, an educational institution for the science of Judaism, was founded in Berlin.

The growing controversy, in which assimilation was regarded as an insertion into a Christian-dominated culture, resulted in a return to specific aspects of Jewish tradition. This had a twofold effect on modern Jewish theology: first, the revival of the old apologetics under new conditions, and second, the first historical-critical research into the emergence of Christianity with the intention of qualifying it as a historical phenomenon.

Since the figure of Jesus was also placed within the context of the history of the Israelite-Jewish religion, the demand for a specifically Jewish authority for the recording of its history grew. It was only with the consolidation of liberal Judaism that a positive picture of Jesus was attained, which at the same time brought a novel intensity to the Jewish-Christian discussion.[18]

Even though, following emancipation (1869), the majority of German Jews showed relatively little interest in a scientific reappraisal of their tradition, this gradually changed with rising antisemitism. Harnack's *Wesen des Christentums* confronted the science of Judaism in this very period of transition and performed a catalytic function, so to speak, on the further development of the science and its Jewish acceptance and support.

We have seen how emancipation had helped the German Jews to come to terms with their own tradition. The scholarly approach of the science of Judaism not only helped to foster this reappraisal but also became the necessary tool for an intellectual defence against antisemitism in church and society.

---

ment: 'Das Judentum wurde ein historisches ...', in Leo Baeck, *Aus drei Jahrtausenden: Wissenschaftliche Untersuchungen und Abhandlungen zur Geschichte des jüdischen Glaubens*, with an introduction by H. Liebeschütz (Tübingen, 1958), p. 33; cf. also his positive appraisal of Troeltsch in this context: ibid., pp. 30–2; on the emergence of the 'science of Judaism' from historicism, cf. Liebeschütz, *Das Judentum*, pp.113–56.

18. Cf. Lindeskog, *Die Jesusfrage*, pp. 63–77; see also the 'Bibliographie der jüdischen Leben-Jesu-Forschung, p. 33, of which most entries are from 1890 (!); cf. also Gösta Lindeskog, 'Jesus als religionsgeschichtliches und religiöses Problem in der modernen jüdischen Theologie', in *Judaica* 6 (1950), pp. 190–229, 241–68; and Schalom Ben-Chorin, 'Das Jesusbild im modernen Judentum', in *Zeitschrift für Religions- und Geistesgeschichte* 5 (1953), pp. 231–57.

In the following chapter we shall look at one exponent of Christian misunderstanding of Judaism: Adolf von Harnack. His *What is Christianity?* (*Essence of Christianity*, to translate the German original literally) is reconstructed and his ambivalent evaluation of the Jewish religion is traced back to early historical criticism, specifically to Julius Wellhausen.

Chapter 3

CHRISTIAN ABSOLUTISM IN THE CROSSFIRE OF THE JEWISH ESSENCE DEBATE

Adolf von Harnack's Essence of Christianity

Harnack's lectures were not originally intended for print; this was made possible through student notes.[1] Because of their generalised form, Harnack abstained from using any scholarly apparatus whatsoever; the text itself remained unchanged throughout all editions, although several notes were added in 1908.[2]

The following reconstruction of the text emphasises – more explicitly than in Harnack's own words – the connections between 'historical' methods and the determination of the essence, in order, supported by elaborate quotations, to depict the targets of Jewish criticism more clearly.

The Essence of Christianity – A Reconstruction

'What is Christianity?'[3] – Harnack attempts to answer this question in a purely historical manner in his lectures. 'Historical', according to

1. The following refers to the *second* printing (1985) of the Gütersloh edition of Harnack's *Das Wesen des Christentums* (1977) or the English translation of 1986.
2. Cf. Adolf von Harnack himself, Introduction to 56th – 60th Thousand: *Das Wesen des Christentums,* reprinted for the 50th anniversary of the first edition, with a preface by R. Bultmann, Stuttgart 1950 (Leipzig 1900), p. xx.
3. Adolf von Harnack, *What is Christianity?* (Philadelphia, 1986).

Harnack, means a specific linking of the 'methods of historical science, and the experience of life gained by studying the actual course of history'.[4] The historical method is, therefore, also the mode of the modern consciousness in understanding itself, since 'what we are and what we possess, in any high sense, we possess from the past and by the past – only so much of it, of course, as has had results and makes its influence felt up to the present day'.[5] With this determination of the character of historical understanding on the basis of historical influence, the tension – inherent in the essence – between the permanent core of something and its respective contemporary manifestation is given by means of its influence.

For historians, this results in the highest duty being the 'determination of what is of permanent value ... what is essential'.[6] This includes the idea that

[i]n history absolute judgments are impossible. ... History can only show how things have been; and even where we can throw light upon the past, and understand and criticize it, we must not presume to think that by any process of abstraction absolute judgments as to the value to be assigned to past events can be obtained from the results of a purely historical survey. Such judgments are the creation only of feeling and of will; they are a subjective act. The false notion that the understanding can produce them is a heritage of that protracted epoch in which knowing and knowledge were expected to accomplish everything; in which it was believed that they could be stretched so as to be capable of covering and satisfying all the needs of the mind and heart. That they cannot do.[7]

The historical method determined in this way is based on Christianity itself, for its 'material' is 'Jesus Christ and his Gospel', whereby the essence of a historical personality can only be determined when one looks at its historical influence.[8] The Gospel 'contains something which, under differing historical forms, is of permanent validity, i.e. "the Gospel within the Gospel".'[9]

---

4. Harnack (1986), p. 6; On Harnack's concept of history and his opinions on the writing of history, cf. esp. Peter Meinhold, 'Adolf von Harnack', in *Geschichte der kirchlichen Historiographie*, Orbis Academicus, III/5, 2 vols (Freiburg/Munich, 1967); here: vol. 2, pp. 263–87; and Klauspeter Blaser, *Geschichte – Kirchengeschichte – Dogmengeschichte in Adolf von Harnacks Denken: Ein Beitrag zur Problematik der historisch-theologischen Disziplinen*, (Mainz, 1964), pp. 22ff., 37ff.

5. Harnack (1986), p. 4.

6. Ibid., p. 13; cf. also Harnack's introduction: Harnack (1950), pp. xvii, xix.

7. Harnack (1986), p. 18.

8. Harnack (1985), p. 17; cf. also Adolf von Harnack, 'Das Christentum und die Geschichte' (1896), p. 19, in *Reden und Aufsätze*, 2nd edn, vol. 2 (Gießen, 1906), pp. 1–21; and Carl-Jürgen Kaltenborn, *Adolf von Harnack als Lehrer Dietrich Bonhoeffers*, Theologische Arbeiten, 31, (Berlin (GDR), 1973) p. 35.

9. Harnack (1986), p. 14.

Harnack's reference back to the creative personality of Jesus tries to determine historically the essence of Christianity and is also an expression of the connection between personality and historical development that is constitutive of his sense of history.[10] It also represents the systematic unfolding of his thesis – based on the development of dogmas – of the emergence of dogma as a product of the Hellenisation of the Gospel.[11] If, for Harnack, the undogmatic Christianity of Jesus' proclamation of the Gospel represents original essential Christianity, then he has to emphasise the *creative* element in the appearance of Jesus, as distinct from its contemporary conditions.

Judaism at the time of Jesus, therefore, is not presented in terms of its own conditions, but rather primarily as a surpassed, obsolete preliminary stage of Christianity, which is threatened with becoming a merely rhetorical antithesis: monotheism had long been established in the piety of the Old Testament; the Psalmists demonstrated what Harnack calls 'a religious individualism of depth and vigour'; the content of Jesus' preaching is also found in the Prophets, the Jewish tradition passed down to his time, and even in the Pharisees. But, according to Wellhausen, as quoted by Harnack:

> the Pharisees ... unfortunately ... were in possession of much else besides ... They reduced everything to one dead level ... The spring of holiness had indeed, long been opened; but it was choked with sand and dirt, and its water was polluted. For rabbis and theologians to come afterwards and distil this water, even if they were successful, makes no difference.[12]

Even though the Pharisees had already preached the centrality of the need 'to love God and thy neighbour', it had no impact because it was weak and, therefore, harmful. It was not until the 'power of the personality of Jesus' appeared that this proclamation acquired historical influence.[13] This is also based on the 'sovereignty of the Gospel' itself, for it makes its appeal to the inner man, which remains unchanged throughout all historical changes.[14]

Through his emphasis on the individual as God's child, Jesus expresses for the first time and in an unsurpassable manner, the idea of the 'infinite value of the human soul'. The essence of Christianity, according to Harnack, consists in this directness of the religious rela-

---

10. This is most clearly expressed in Adolf von Harnack, 'Über die Sicherheit und die Grenzen geschichtlicher Erkenntnis' (1917), pp. 21f., in *Erforschtes und Erlebtes: Reden und Aufsätze*, new volume, vol. 4 (Gießen, 1923), pp. 3–23; cf. also Harnack 1985, pp. 89, 98.

11. Cf. Adolf von Harnack, *Lehrbuch der Dogmengeschichte*, 3 vols, (Tübingen 1909/10) (last edition of the work of 1886–90, which was re-edited and expanded by Harnack himself); here: vol. 1, p. 20.

12. Harnack (1986), p. 47f.

13. Ibid., p. 48f.

14. Ibid., pp. 114f.

tionship of the individual to God as the Father. In this sense, the Gospel is *'religion itself'*.[15] The enabling of a consciousness of individuality, the directness of the religious relationship as the *imitatio Christi* in thought *and* deed – i.e. religion 'a man has himself experienced' – becomes the inherent criterion of Harnack's portrayal of Christianity in the three main sections of his lectures.[16]

The preaching of Jesus as presented in the first section, with its constant reference to the image of the Kingdom of God, differs from Jewish assumptions in the Old Testament in that it cuts off the eudemonistic expectations of a mundane and political character, which had been connected with the notion of the Kingdom of God, thereby emphasising its inward nature.[17] This stresses its ethical content in a new way.

The ethicisation of monotheism, representing an enormous advance in the history of religion, had already been achieved by the prophets of the Old Testament[18] and although there existed 'an ample and profound ethical system' in the Judaism of the time of Jesus, it had been so petrified in ritual observance that it was almost transformed into something that was the direct opposite of it. Jesus countered this by proclaiming a higher righteousness, characterised by a close combination of religion and morality, with faith as its inner criterion, and characterised as well by love and mercy, rather than the 'eye for an eye, tooth for a tooth' type of justice of the Old Testament.[19]

In the second part of the lectures, the examination of the main bearings of the Gospel, the antithesis to the Pharisees played an important role, most importantly in the sections on 'the Gospel and the poor' and 'the Gospel and law'. Jesus

> came into immediate opposition with the official leaders of the people, and in them with ordinary human nature in general. They thought of God as the despot ... They made this religion into an earthly trade, and there was nothing more detestable ... [The Pharisees] had little feeling for the needs of the people ... The priests and the Pharisees held the nation in bondage and murdered its soul.[20]

Regarding the question of Jesus' Messianic selfconsciousness, Harnack emphasises Jesus' description of himself as the Messiah, for this was 'an assumption that was simply necessary if the man who felt the inward call was to gain an absolute recognition within the lines of

15. Ibid., p. 63.
16. Ibid., p. 148.
17. Ibid., p. 52.
18. Ibid., p. 76, 70f.
19. Ibid., pp. 75ff.
20. Ibid., p. 50f., 91, 103.

Jewish religious history',[21] even if Jesus then transcended the Old Testament idea of the Messiah.

In the second main part of the lectures, on 'the Gospel in History', Harnack describes the most decisive development as Christianity's clear break with Judaism and Jewish Christianity. Herein lies the great world-historical significance of the Apostle Paul. Through his interpretation of the Gospel, in particular the Christology, Paul made this break possible, thereby, according to Harnack, transforming Christianity into a universal religion.[22] 'What was kernel here and what was husk, history has itself showed with unmistakable plainness, and by the shortest process. Husk were the whole of the Jewish limitations attaching to Jesus' message ... '[23] This form of Christianity was itself in subsequent history subject to certain limitations and alienation processes, as Harnack shows in his description of the history of the break between Greek and Roman Catholicism. A motivating element of the negative development, according to Harnack, was the danger of the Old Testament as an inferior and obsolete principle of the past forcing its way into Christianity, thus threatening Christian freedom.[24]

A critical reduction by the Reformation brought religion back again to itself, according to Harnack, to the Gospel and its corresponding religious experience,[25] to faith in a merciful God.

We may, therefore, conclude: Harnack feels that modern Protestantism must reconnect particularly with the intentions and the principles of the Reformation. This would be the only way to achieve a conception of Christianity that is compatible with the present intellectual conditions of modern culture, that could prove itself in the new task of attending to social issues. Harnack's lectures culminate in his personal declaration of belief in religion as a formative force in life: 'It is religion, the love of God and neighbour, which gives life a meaning; knowledge cannot do it.'[26]

Harnack's Reference to Julius Wellhausen

Harnack's ambivalent evaluation of the Jewish religion in the Old Testament is based on a particular perspective of Jewish-Israelite religious history, which can be traced back, specifically, to Julius

21. Ibid., p. 141.
22. Ibid., pp. 176ff.
23. Ibid., pp. 179f.
24. Ibid., p. 186.
25. Ibid., p. 268.
26. Cf. ibid., pp. 299f.

Wellhausen. Following the approaches of W.M.L. de Wette, W. Vatke and K.H. Graf, Wellhausen provided a literary critical foundation to support the distinction between 'Hebraism' and 'Judaism', referring to the pre- and post-exilic periods respectively.[27] This distinction was first introduced in the early nineteenth century by de Wette, with reference to Herder's romantic transfiguration of the early days of religion.

In his 1878 published work, *Geschichte Israels*,[28] Wellhausen showed a convergence between the religious development of Israel and a historical gradation of the literary-critical levels of the Old Testament. The post-exilic dating of the priestly code corresponded to legalistic *('gesetzliche')* Judaism as the final stage of the religious development, as it unfolds in the Old Testament. Wellhausen's decisive thesis was based on the early dating of the prophets and its corresponding religious pre-eminence.

In Wellhausen's work on Israelite and Jewish history, *Israelitische und Jüdische Geschichte*, published in 1894, he clearly speaks of a post-exilic religious and national process of decline of Israel to 'Judaism', within which a faith free of prophecy was degraded to 'nomocracy', ending in Pharisaism.[29] According to Wellhausen, Jesus was the first to re-establish the connection to the ethical ideals and the religious individualism of the prophets, thereby completing the religious history of the Old Testament.[30] This was the common view held by historical-critical research at the turn of the century;[31] it also corresponded to one of the main contentions of liberal theology: 'Original undogmatic Christianity took up the pure prophetic-Messianic roots of the religion

27. Cf. here and in the following: Liebeschütz, *Judentum im deutschen Geschichtsbild*, pp. 245–68; Hans-Joachim Kraus, *Geschichte der historisch-kritischen Erforschung des Alten Testaments*, 3rd expanded edn, (Neukirchen-Vluyn, 1982 [1956]), pp. 255–74; Rolf Rendtorff, 'Die hebräische Bibel als Grundlage christlich-theologischer Aussagen über das Judentum', p. 37, in *Jüdische Existenz und die Erneuerung der christlichen Theologie*, Martin Stöhr (ed.) (Munich, 1981), pp. 32–47.
    On the philosophical and scientific historical factors influencing Wellhausen, cf. esp. Lothar Perlitt, *Vatke und Wellhausen: Geschichtsphilosophische Voraussetzungen und historiographische Motive für die Darstellung der Religion und Geschichte Israels durch Wilhelm Vatke und Julius Wellhausen*, Beihefte zur Zeitschrift für alttestamentliche Wissenschaft 94, (Berlin, 1965).
28. *Geschichte Israels* appeared under the better known title *Prolegomena zur Geschichte Israels* starting with the 2nd printing.
29. Cf. Julius Wellhausen, *Israelitische und Jüdische Geschichte*, 3rd edn (Berlin, 1897 [1894]), p. 17: 'Das Gesetz ist das Product der geistigen Entwicklung Israels, nicht der Ausgangspunkt derselben.'
30. Cf. Klaus Koch, *Ratlos vor der Apokalyptik* (Gütersloh, 1970), p. 35.
31. Cf. Hermann Gunkel, 'Das Alte Testament im Licht der modernen Forschung', pp. 40–76 and also the other articles in *Beiträge zur Weiterentwicklung der christlichen Religion*, A. Deissmann (ed.) (Munich, 1905); cf. also Uriel Tal, 'Theologische Debatte um das 'Wesen des Judentums', pp. 612ff., in Mosse (ed.), *Juden im Wilhelminischen Deutschland*, pp. 599–632.

of the Old Testament as they existed before any of the post-exilic reinforcement processes.'[32]

How close is Adolf von Harnack's reception of Wellhausen's ideas? Harnack considers Wellhausen the most significant historian of religion of our time[33] and agrees with him down to the terminology he uses. The best example of this is the use of the debris *('Schutt-Quellen')* metaphor for the relationship of Jesus to the Judaism of his time.[34]

Harnack saw Wellhausen's stance of disregarding post-exilic Jewish history as an important basis for his attempt at determining the essense of Christianity by historical means. This was the main point Jewish critics held against Harnack. And we may now also say that it was to some degree explicitly aimed at Wellhausen[35] and the bias of early historical criticism in the exegetical methods.

In our next step it shall become clear how Jewish academia reacted on such a one-sided perception of the basis of Christian religion.

32. Cf. ibid., pp. 615f.; Bousset, *Wesen*, p. 89 considers Harnack (1985) and Wellhausen (1897) as the representative works of so-called modern theology.
33. Harnack (1985), p. 108.
34. Cf. ibid., p. 38 and Wellhausen (1897), p. 384.
35. In this context it is interesting that H. Cohen, who was a close friend of Wellhausen's during their time together in Marburg (1885–92) was always explicitly obliged to Wellhausen's pre-dating of the Prophets for his own theory of ethical monotheism, without seeing the resulting consequences for the concept of an historical continuity of Judaism; cf. Hans Liebeschütz, *Von Georg Simmel zu Franz Rosenzweig: Studien zum Jüdischen Denken im deutschen Kulturbereich,* with an epilogue by R. Weltsch, Schriftenreihe wissenschaftlicher Abhandlungen des Leo Baeck Instituts 23 (Tübingen, 1970), pp. 36–8.

Chapter 4

THE ESSENCE OF JUDAISM

The History of the Concept of the Essence of Judaism

The concept of an 'the essence of Judaism' is not a genuinely intra-Jewish expression. It was externally motivated, through the historical and intellectual upheaval in the Judaism of the nineteenth century.[1] Apart from a few scattered occurrences from the beginning of the nineteenth century,[2] it was not until the gradual development of Jewish emancipation, often conceived as the insertion of Judaism into a Christian-western culture, that the question of the essence of Judaism took on a sense of urgency.

At this time, the question became the necessary search for the determining characteristics of Judaism which would enable the preservation of a specifically Jewish identity under the conditions of emancipation and assimilation. This was the task of the so-called 'science of Judaism' *(Wissenschaft des Judentums)* (cf. chapter 2, 'Liberal Judaism and the "Science of Judaism"'). Following this early discussion on the essence of Judaism, the most important context of the use of the term that attracted considerable public attention was the debate that was triggered by Harnack's essence of Christianity. The concept 'essence of Judaism' clearly became a religious notion, countered by the more aggressive national interpretation of the developing Zion-

---

1. Cf. for the following: Friedrich W. Niewöhner, 'Judentum, Wesen des Judentums', in *Historisches Wörterbuch*, Joachim Ritter and Karlfried Gründer (eds.) (Darmstadt, 1976), pp. 649–653.
2. The earliest evidence can be found in the German-Jewish magazine *Sulamith* from 1807; cf. Tal, 'Theologische Debatte', p. 607, note 11; for further examples, see Niewöhner, 'Judentum', p. 650.

ism. As early as 1904, Hermann Cohen spoke of the imitated expression 'the essence of Judaism'.[3] The *historically defensive* or *apologetically motivated* emergence of the concept 'essence of Judaism' is reflected up to the present day in the circumstance that no Jewish or Israeli encyclopedia includes an article on the 'essence of Judaism'.[4] Even the *Neues Lexikon des Judentums*[5] of 1992 does not contain this technical term, which may again indicate that 'essence' is really a term with no continuing basis and resonance for Jewish theology.

Motives for Jewish Interest in Harnack

As a result of his exceptional position within protestant theology,[6] as well as his political activity in the field of academic education, Adolf von Harnack was considered *the* representative of German academic culture by the Jewish community. Representing a controversial position in the efforts for academic freedom,[7] he was, as a historian and critic of Christian dogma, of particular interest to modern Jewish theology up until the early decades of this century.

The anti-Judaic polemic in Harnack's 'essense of Christianity' was intensified for the Jewish reception through the general character of his lectures (*für Hörer aller Fakultäten* – for an audience from all faculties of the university).

This was especially the case in Berlin, both the city where academic antisemitism began and, at the same time, the city with the largest Jewish community and, second only to Frankfurt, the centre of liberal Judaism and the science of Judaism.

Based on the specific historical situation of Judaism at the turn of the century (cf. chapter 2, 'Emancipation and Antisemitism'), Harnack's theses, with their strong anti-Judaic polemic, could only be interpreted as immensely threatening by the Jewish community. The science of

3. Cf. Hermann Cohen, 'Die Errichtung von Lehrstühlen für Ethik und Religionsphilosophie an den jüdischen theologischen Lehranstalten (1904)', p. 115, in *Zur jüdischen Zeitgeschichte*, Jüdische Schriften 2, with an introduction by F. Rosenzweig. B. Strauß (ed.), Veröffentlichungen der Akademie für die Wissenschaft des Judentums/V. Philosophische Sektion (Berlin, 1924), pp. 108–25.
4. Cf. Niewöhner, *Judentum*, p. 652.
5. Julius H. Schoeps, (ed.), *Neues Lexikon des Judentums* (Gütersloh/Munich, 1992).
6. Cf. for the following also Friedrich W. Marquardt, 'Unabgegoltenes in der Kritik Baecks an Adolf von Harnack', pp. 172f., in *Leo Baeck: Lehrer und Helfer in schwerer Zeit*, Werner Licharz (ed.), Arnoldshainer Texte 20, (Frankfurt am Main, 1983), pp. 169–87.
7. Cf. Felix Perles, *Was lehrt uns Harnack?* (Frankfurt am Main, 1902) (first published as 'What Jews may learn from Harnack' in *The Jewish Quarterly Review* 14 [1902] pp. 517–43; reprinted in F. Perles *Jüdische Skizzen*, [Leipzig, 1912], pp. 208–31), p. 8.

Judaism, which was in the process of being established, was relatively unprepared for a response. The initial intellectual defence mechanism to antisemitism was channelled into the founding of numerous popular Jewish literary associations (cf. chapter 2, 'Liberal Judaism').[8]

The rabbinical seminaries 'degenerated' into specialised theological institutions for the education of clergy only, which to some seemed isolated from general scholarly activity.[9] In the state universities, a Jewish academic was usually limited to the position of a *Privatdozent*,[10] i.e. a university lecturer without tenured status and adequate income.

There was also considerable unawareness and religious indifference on the part of the educated Jews; the findings of critico-historical Protestant Bible studies and, to a large degree, Harnack's lectures themselves, encouraged the conversion of many Jews to Christianity. The Jewish press clearly spoke of the 'subversive influence ... that tendentious writings like Harnack's *Wesen des Christentums* exert on the Jewish intelligentsia, who were defenceless in many regards'.[11] Harnack's lectures had a catalytic effect on the intellectual and scientific structure of Judaism in this situation.[12]

As early as 1902, the Society for the Promotion of the Science of Judaism *(Gesellschaft zur Förderung der Wissenschaft des Judentums)* was founded in Berlin. Its greatest task was the publishing of an outline of the science of Judaism.[13] Leo Baeck's and Joseph Eschenbacher's contributions to the essence debate were the first titles published by this organisation. Also in 1902, the *'Liberale Verein für die Angelegenheiten der Jüdischen Gemeinde zu Berlin'*, a liberal organisation, founded in 1895, of the Jewish community in Berlin, issued a call for papers in the *Berliner Tageblatt (Berlin Daily)* offering a prize for the best work on the 'essence of Judaism'.[14]

---

8. The unsatisfactory situation of Jewish science is strongly criticised throughout the *AZdJ* (1870 onwards), and in the *JJGJ* (1898 onwards) especially from 1900 onwards; cf. esp. Gustav Karpeles, 'Literarische Jahresrevue', in: *JJGL* 4 (1901), pp. 18f., and *JJGL* 5 (1902), p. 30; cf. also 'Ein Wort über die jüdische Wissenschaft', in: *AZdJ* 65 (1901), no. 50, (13 Dec.), pp. 589f.

9. Cf. *AZdJ*, ibid., and Note 65, p. 589.

10. Cf. Fritz K. Ringer, *Die Gelehrten: Der Niedergang der deutschen Mandarine 1890–1933*, translated from U.S. English by K. Laermann (Stuttgart, 1983) (Cambridge, 1969).

11. *AZdJ* 67 (1903), no. 20 (15 May), p. 235.

12. Cf. *AZdJ* 73 (1909), No. 9 (26 Feb.), p. 98: Gustav Karpeles, looking back on this development: 'The best and only defense of Judaism will always be knowledge of Judaism.'

13. On the report of the inaugural meeting and the intentions of the 'Gesellschaft' cf. *JJGL* 6 (1903), pp. 55–63; further: *Monatsschrift für Geschichte und Wissenschaft des Judentums (MGWJ)*, 48 (1904), pp. 52–64.

14. Cf. Karpeles, 'Literarische Jahresrevue', p. 20. Regarding the text of the announcement, cf. the reprint in *Chronik der Christlichen Welt* 12 (1902), no. 7 (13 Feb.), p. 77.

Jewish scholars like Leo Baeck were thus quite prepared to take up the dispute on 'essence', which really became an issue of superiority over one another for both Judaism and Christianity. The following section sums up the Jewish critique that Harnack had to face.

The Points of Jewish Criticism of Harnack

The Jewish debate on Harnack's *Essence of Christianity* was of an explicitly public nature.[15] Writings on the subject of essence consisted primarily of the publication of lectures given for a wide variety of audiences: congregations, scholarly societies, etc. The discussion took place not only in theological journals such as the *Monatsschrift für Geschichte und Wissenschaft des Judentums*, but also in newspapers, such as the main organ of liberal Judaism, the *Allgemeine Zeitung des Judentums*. In this way it was related to the contemporary (self-)perception of Judaism.

In addition to Leo Baeck's contributions, the most important writings were: Felix Perles (1874–1933), Rabbi of Königsberg: *Was lehrt uns Harnack?* (1902); Martin Schreiner (1863–1926), Arabic scholar and Professor of Jewish history and literature at the Berlin Lehranstalt: *Die jüngsten Urteile über das Judentum* (1902); and two works of the Breslau Rabbi Joseph Eschelbacher (1848–1916): *Das Judentum und das Wesen des Christentums* (1904) and *Das Judentum im Urteil der modernen protestantischen Theologie* (1907).

The main target of Jewish criticism was Harnack's thesis of a religious degeneration process in post-exilic Judaism, taken from Julius Wellhausen. As a result the fact of Christianity's origin in Judaism was played down.[16] This meant a twofold negation of Judaism, that is, of historical as well as of modern Judaism, since modern Judaism is only to be understood as part of the continuum of the history of Judaism.[17]

---

15. Cf. Tal , 'Theologische Debatte', p. 602.
16. Harnack's relationship to Wellhausen on this was seen very clearly; cf. Joseph Eschelbacher, 'Das Judentum und das Wesen des Christentums: Vergleichende Studien', in *Schriften*, edited by Gesellschaft zur Förderung der Wissenschaft des Judentums (Berlin, 1908 [1904]), pp. 21–3; Martin Schreiner, *Die jüngsten Urteile über das Judentum: Kritisch untersucht* (Berlin, 1902), pp. 14f.; any kind of historical-critical research was perceived very sensitively from a Jewish point of view; cf. Joseph Eschelbacher, *Das Judentum*, pp. 2–8 and Joseph Eschelbacher, 'Das Judentum im Urteil der modernen protestantischen Theologie', in *Schriften*, edited by Gesellschaft zur Förderung der Wissenschaft des Judentums (Leipzig, 1907), pp. 1–22; cf. also the Felix Perles-Wilhelm Bousset conflict in the discussion by Heinrich Holtzmann, 'Besprechung der Kontroverse zwischen F. Perles und W. Bousset', in *Theologische Literaturzeitung* 29 (1904), pp. 43–6.
17. According to Perles, *Was lehrt uns Harnack?*, pp. 29f.

From a Jewish perspective, the reasons[18] for this judgment were as follows:

1. The disregard of the research results of the science of Judaism, above all regarding the relation between Jesus or early Christianity and the Judaism of the time. (Jüdische Leben-Jesu-Forschung).[19]
2. The lack of awareness of rabbinical literature. In this context, Harnack's equating of Halacha and Haggadah was criticised, which is perhaps one factor in the rise of the so-called *Flächentheorie*, i.e. the theory of the nondifferentiation between ritual and ethic provisions in the Talmud.[20]

According to M. Schreiner, 'subjective' or theological bias also exists, as he clearly specified:

1. The 'Christological view of history': the prejudiced Christian view of Old Testament Jewish faith with regard to the concept of the Messiah made the subordination of Judaism under Christianity possible in the first place.[21]
2. The 'Pauline psychology of religion', i.e. Paul's pejorative understanding of the religion of the law.
3. The 'unconscious striving to glorify the Indo-Germanic race'.[22]

From a Jewish point of view, these factors were seen as expressions of the supposedly legitimate academic 'special treatment' of Judaism.[23]

The main feature of the Jewish constructive critique of Harnack was the assertion of a continuity between pre- and post-exilic Judaism and, following from that, of the constitutive relationship between Jesus and the Judaism of his time. The emphasis on this continuity, above all in view of the theological content, was clearly intended to show that Judaism cannot be considered as an obsolete preliminary stage of Christianity, but rather represents an essential foundation.

The evidence of Jesus' rabbinical-Jewish education and knowledge also served as an argument for modern Judaism's right to exist in the present-day Christian-dominated culture. The Jewish demand for recognition was expressed as follows: '... that our religion in any civilised state receive the same rights as Christian denominations,

---

18. Cf. for the following: Schreiner, *Die jüngsten Urteile*, 'Vorwort', pp. v–vii.
19. Gösta Lindeskog, 'Bibliographie der Leben-Jesu-Forschung', in *Die Jesusfrage im neuzeitlichen Judentum: Ein Beitrag zur Geschichte der Leben-Jesu-Forschung*, reprint (Darmstadt, 1973).
20. Cf. ibid., pp. 15–18; Perles, *Was lehrt uns Harnack?*, pp. 23f.; Eschelbacher, *Das Judentum*, p. 25; on the 'Flächentheorie', cf. also Michael Guttman, *Das Judentum und seine Umwelt* (Berlin, 1927), pp. 338ff.
21. Cf. Schreiner, *Die jüngsten Urteile*, 'Vorwort', pp. v–vii and Note 75, Eschelbacher, *Das Judentum*, p. 48.
22. Schreiner, *Die jüngsten Urteile*, 'Vorwort', p. vi.
23. According to Aron Ackermann, *Judentum und Christentum* (Leipzig, 1903), p. 12; cf. also Leo Baeck, 'Harnack's Vorlesungen über das Wesen des Christenthums', in *MGWJ* 45 (1901), p. 118.

entitled to space for the spiritual life of civilised peoples and that it be recognised that this represents an enrichment of the national spirit'.[24]

The focal point of the debate was the question of Jesus' Messianism, and here the Jewish argument went further. The relevant phrase of Harnack was often quoted, that Jesus' Gospel proclamation was nothing new.

It was a central argument of Jewish theologians and scholars that the elements that separated[25] Judaism and Christianity were first introduced into Christianity through Paul. From a Jewish perspective, this meant (1) the appropriation of Jesus through the dogmatic interpretation of his teachings according to the ideology of the Logos-Christology, (2) the limiting of the concept of monotheism through the doctrine of the Trinity, and (3) the stripping away of the ethical content of Jesus' preaching through dogmatisation.

The emergence of dogma was understood as a result of the supersession of Judaism or Jewish Christianity by the universal Christianity of Paul's making, and the development initiated by that process.[26] This not only illustrates a definite connection between the Jewish position and Harnack's findings concerning the development of dogma; it is also most important to note that it signifies the general affinity of the Jewish critique of Pauline Christianity with liberal Protestant theology when both oppose the established authoritative interpretation of Christianity in Catholicism and conservative Protestantism.[27]

Harnack's referring back to the pre-Gentile and pre-pagan, purely monotheistic elements of Jesus' preaching in defining the essence of Christianity was welcomed, therefore, from the Jewish perspective, as a return to Judaism. Perles, for example, understood Harnack's *Essence of Christianity* as 'the most splendid justification for Judaism that we could have wished for'.[28] In the same way, Harnack's explanation of the Reformation was interpreted as a return to elements of genuine Jewish faith. In his reply to Heinrich von Treitschke in 1880 regarding the Reformation, Hermann Cohen stated 'that we Jews converge with

---

24. Schreiner, *Die jüngsten Urteile*, 'Vorwort', p. vi.
25. Cf. here and in the following, Perles, *Was lehrt uns Harnack?*, pp. 11f., 26f.; Eschelbacher, *Das Judentum*, pp. 15f., 61ff., 142; Schreiner, *Die jüngsten Urteile*, pp. 38f., 44; cf. also Tal, 'Theologische Debatte', pp. 617ff.
26. Cf. Eschelbacher, *Das Judentum*, pp. 154f.
27. Cf. Tal, 'Theologische Debatte', p. 617.
28. Perles, *Was lehrt uns Harnack?*, p. 9; cf. also Eschelbacher, *Das Judentum*, p. 19; Eduard von Hartmann, 'Das Wesen des Christentums in neuester Beleuchtung', in *Die Gegenwart* 59 (1901), pp. 4–8, 210–12, 230–32, here p. 6; as early as 1901, Hartmann accused Harnack of 'Rejudaisierung': 'Die Person Jesu wird zu einem sanften, liebenswürdigen, volkstümlichen Rabbi, den jeder Reformjude von ganzem Herzen als Vertreter seiner Tendenzen reclamiren kann.'

the historical tendency of Protestantism'.[29]For this reason, a major part of Jewish writings on essence focuses on explaining the Jewish-rabbinical origin of the essential elements of Jesus' Gospel proclamation.[30]

The continuity of ethical content was particularly emphasised, i.e. (1) the Jewish origins of belief in God the Father, (2) the concept of the inwardness of the Kingdom of God, and (3) the rabbinical parallels to the Sermon on the Mount and the Lord's Prayer.

The infinite value of the human soul is depicted through the Old Testament concept of human beings created in God's image in the story of the Creation, and through the Jewish fundamental belief in individual moral autonomy.

The centrality of 'loving God and thy neighbour' also represents the epitome of Judaism. This is already extended in the Old Testament to include strangers and enemies in need, even if not generally understood as love of one's enemies, which, according to Jewish belief, is regarded as unattainable anyway and bordering on self-denial.[31]In addition, the commandments in the Old Testament regarding social welfare and the poor, as well as their interpretation and execution by the Pharisees and the scribes, are stressed to show the importance of ethical conduct.

The Jewish argument successfully highlighted the fact that Harnack's undogmatic reference back to Jesus' teaching in the Gospels was *not* tied to an enhancement of Judaism at the time of Jesus, but rather (as shown in chapter 3, 'The Essence of Christianity'), from the point of view of his historical methodology, was indeed consistent in its intended devaluation. It can be asserted that it is exactly this curious mixture of closeness and total opposition to Judaism that is the *theological* reason for the great intensity of the Jewish debate on Harnack's *Wesen des Christentums*.

Harnack's interpretation of Judaism was necessarily adopted by liberal Protestant theology. It was clear that it could succeed in separating Judaism from its own undogmatic Christianity only by introducing an artificial antithesis to Judaism.[32] As a result of pressure for emancipation and assimilation, the first generation of liberal Judaism (Zunz, Geiger, etc.; cf. chapter 2, 'Liberal Judaism') eliminated the

29. Cohen, *Zur Jüdischen Zeitgeschichte*, p. 93; cf. also Eschelbacher, *Das Judentum*, p. 65; Perles, *Was lehrt uns Harnack?*, p. 33.

30. The most explicit example of this is in Eschelbacher, *Das Judentum*, pp. 32–94, in the main section of the work, where he directly parallels Harnack's work .

31. Cf. here Eschelbacher, *Das Judentum*, pp. 57, 74f. and Walter Homolka and Albert Friedlander, *The Gate to Perfection* (Oxford, 1994), p. xiii.

32. Cf. Perles, *Was lehrt uns Harnack?*, pp. 14–17; this is most clearly expressed in: Abraham Wolf, 'Professor Harnack's "What is Christianity?"', pp. 672f., in *The Jewish Quarterly Review* 16 (1904), pp. 668–89, here pp. 672f.

traditions of Judaism that presented problems for Christian understanding (e.g. the normative authority of the Halacha and the Talmud, the so-called ceremonial law, the national particularistic
aspects of Judaism, etc.) through consistent historicisation of their
claims to validity.[33]

The intensive essence debate, as carried on in Jewish circles, led
to a need for a fundamental renewal of the specific 'essence' of one's
own religion. The external criticism of Jewish tradition was inter-
nalised, as it were, constructively, through positive recollection and
reintegration of those elements in the religion that seemed problematic, by interpreting them in terms of the possibility of their universality. In this way, the selection of Israel was understood as the moral
task of Israel or of Judaism; the historical, preserving function of the
Pharisees and the ceremonial law for the preservation of the univer-
salist elements of the Jewish religion was explicitly emphasised; the
Pharisaic goal of completely ritualising everyday life was understood
as a 'democratic' intention.[34]

The most original of all dismissals of the accusations of particularism is demonstrated by Isaak Goldschmidt's definition of the
essence of Judaism as an order, characterised by the parallel existence of universalism with regard to the content of its belief and, at
the same time, formal particularism with regard to its membership.[35]

The Jewish essence debate in opposition to Harnack was intensified by his *Rektoratsrede*, his inaugural address in 1901 as Principal of
the University of Berlin. The address, entitled 'The task of the theological faculties and general history of religion',[36] confirmed, from a
Jewish point of view, Harnack's evaluation of Judaism as the mere
pre-history of Christianity.

On this presupposition, Harnack's principle for the study of religions developed in this address did not seem at all applicable to
Judaism:[37] 'True understanding can only be gained from religion
which is alive and the perception of devotion'.[38]

33. An isolated example of such a radical reform perspective is Israel Jelski, *Das Wesen
    des Judentums* (Berlin, 1902); cf. also Tal, 'Theologische Debatte', pp. 621–23.
34. According to Ackermann, *Judentum und Christentum*, p. 15.
35. Cf. Israel Goldschmidt, *Das Wesen des Judentums nach Bibel, Talmud, Tradition und
    religiöser Praxis* (Frankfurt, 1907), pp. 210, 217ff.; cf. also the harsh criticism of M.
    Cahn, an orthodox rabbi, pp. 332–70.
36. Adolf von Harnack, 'Die Aufgabe der theologischen Fakultäten und die allgemeine
    Religionsgeschichte, nebst einem Nachwort' (1901), in *Reden und Aufsätze*, vol. 2,
    (Gießen, 1906), pp. 159–87.
37. According to Perles, *Was lehrt uns Harnack?*, pp. 30f.; Ackermann, *Judentum und
    Christentum*, pp. 7f.
38. Harnack (1906), p. 171; regarding Old Testament religious history as 'prehistory',
    a preliminary to Christianity, cf. p. 169 and 172.

The so-called *Babel-Bible Debate*,[39] which was provoked by the orientalist and specialist in Assyrian culture Friedrich Delitzsch in 1902, also had a catalysing effect. Delitzsch contested the religious-historical authenticity of the Old Testament on the basis of parallel Babylonian-Assyrian evidence. He was fiercely contradicted, not only by Jewish,[40] but also by Protestant theologians, above all by Hermann Gunkel and Harnack himself. In spite of the gap between Judaism and liberal Protestant theology, which appeared to be widening, especially in the course of the essence debate, the Jewish position always stressed the possibility of future agreement.

The cultural and historical significance of Judaism and its lasting religious greatness was seen in the establishment of a prophetic and ethical monotheism; the significance of Christianity for the history of the world was seen as spreading this message in a gentile and pagan world, which was made possible through the concept of incarnation.[41] An explicit *ethical* understanding of religion was operative here. The conclusion of Harnack's lectures was expressly cited: Harnack's reference to religion as 'loving God and thy neighbour' was understood as genuine Jewish thought.

Based on this concept of religion, peaceful agreement between Judaism and Christianity could also be expected from a Jewish perspective, where this agreement was also seen as having to prove itself in actual neighbourly love regarding social tasks in the present and the future.[42]

Therefore, two central tasks of the Jewish contribution to the essence debate can be distinguished: Judaism's claim for equality and its acceptance as a living faith both in Jesus' as well as in modern times. Agreement on these two topics could have been the basis of harmonious coexistence and co-operation between Christians and Jews. However, most Jewish essence writings remained too strongly restricted to direct confrontation with Harnack. Leo Baeck was the first to offer an independent as well as self-contained contribution on the 'essence of Judaism'.

In the following section an attempt is made to mark out to what extent he took up the elements of the argument that have been dis-

---

39. Cf. Hans-Joachim Kraus, *Geschichte der historisch-kritischen Erforschung des Alten Testaments*, 3rd edn (Neukirchen-Vluyn, 1982), pp. 309–14; Agnes von Zahn-Harnack, *Adolf von Harnack*, 2nd esp. edn (Berlin, 1951 [1936]), pp. 263–67; Eschelbacher, *Das Judentum*, pp. 22–7.

40. Regarding the public debate on Delitzsch, cf. *AZdJ* 67 (1903), nos. 4, 5, 9, 22, 28 and *JJGL* 6 (1903), pp. 23–5.

41. Cf. Schreiner, *Die jüngsten Urteile*, p. 159; Ackermann, *Judentum und Christentum*, p. 28.

42. Eschelbacher, *Das Judentum*, pp. 165f.; and the corresponding passage in Harnack (1985), p. 175.

cussed before. It will also become obvious how decisively he was able to strengthen the Jewish position. The aim is to underline Baeck's specific contribution in his apologetic endeavour against Christianity, both liberal and conservative.

Leo Baeck's Response to Harnack's *Essence of Christianity*

The first Jewish reaction to Harnack's *Wesen des Christentums* appeared in 1901. It was a review written by Leo Baeck, at that time a young rabbi in the Silesian city of Oppeln who was still totally unknown.[43] Baeck's critique focused on two points: (1) Harnack's lack of consideration of Jewish scholarship and literature, resulting in a misrepresentation of Judaism at the time of Jesus, and (2) the apologetic intention of Harnack's presentation as a whole: '... a work that was of purely apologetic character stepped before us, claiming to offer pure history'. [44]

Based on the second point, Baeck's criticism of Harnack is primarily methodological. According to Baeck, Harnack is guilty of confusing the – of course, unavoidable – value judgment of a historian with the unbiased significance of the historical fact within its actual historical context. Baeck views this as replacing the reporting of history with the constructing of history, perpetuating the errors of the Ritschl School. Harnack projects his own personal view of Christianity onto the historical origin of the Christian religion.[45] According to Baeck, such a 'modernisation'[46] – and here the Jewish theologian paradoxically supports Christianity against its own interpreter – falsifies the Gospel by reducing the radical character of its moral imperative.[47]

Baeck feels that Harnack's comparison (based on Wellhausen's theories) of Jesus' Gospel proclamation with the entire Talmud, instead of just the ethical narrative parts, is methodologically incorrect, since the entirety of Christian literature includes much more than simply Jesus' proclamation of the Gospel.[48] Jesus was, according to Baeck, a genuinely Jewish personality. He sees Harnack's rejection of the Jewish identity of Jesus as the typical case of scholarly special treatment of Judaism.[49]

43. The page numbers in the following correspond to the first edition of Baeck's Harnack critique 'Harnack's Vorlesungen' in *MGWJ* 45 (1901), pp. 97–120.
44. Ibid., pp. 118, 97.
45. Ibid., pp. 98f., 100.
46. Ibid., p. 103.
47. Ibid., pp. 103f.
48. Ibid., pp. 106f.
49. Ibid., p. 118, incorporating an appropriate quote of Abraham Geiger; cf. also p. 111; cf. Peter von der Osten-Sacken, 'Rückzug ins Wesen und aus der Geschichte–

In spite of the very sharp method of argumentation, Baeck deliberately calls on the support of other Protestant scholars against Harnack, such as E. Schürer and C.H. Cornill,[50] leading the critique to a possible consonance between Christianity and Judaism, in connection, specifically, with taking up Harnack's general comments on religion from the concluding section of his lectures.[51] This 'external motivation' through the confrontation with Harnack, remained a hermeneutical determinant throughout Baeck's entire life regarding the inner context of his thinking, focusing on the question of the relationship between Judaism and Christianity or more precisely: liberal or culture Protestantism and liberal Judaism.[52]

In 1905, Baeck's own response to Harnack was published. Of the many writings responding to Harnack's lectures, Baeck's was the only one that aimed at presenting an alternative draft from a Jewish perspective.[53] It had the logical title *Das Wesen des Judentums (The Essence of Judaism)*. Baeck did not include his own earlier critiques of Harnack in his two volumes of essays published in the 1930s, since he viewed the work of 1905 as the answer to Harnack.[54]

Antijudaismus bei Harnack und Bultmann', in *Wissenschaft und Praxis in Kirche und Gesellschaft* 67 (1978), pp. 106–22, esp. pp. 113ff.; Marquardt, 'Unabgegoltenes', pp. 173ff., interprets this methodical approach of Baeck's critique explicitly as ideology-critical.

50. Cf. Baeck, 'Harnack's Vorlesungen', p. 108, note; pp. 109, 113.

51. Ibid., pp. 118f..

52. According to Reinhold Mayer, *Christentum und Judentum in der Schau Leo Baecks*, Studia Delitzschiana, 6, (Stuttgart, 1961), p. 13; Reinhold Mayer, 'Leo Baeck', pp. 113f., in *Theologische Realenzyklopädie, 5*, G. Krause and G. Müller (eds) (Berlin/New York, 1980), pp. 112–15; Karl-Heinrich Rengstorf, 'Leo Baeck als Theologe und im theologischen Gespräch: Rede zur Gedenkfeier in Frankfurt am Main am 16.12. 1956', p. 128, in *Worte des Gedenkens für Leo Baeck*, Eva G. Reichmann (ed.), published for the Council of Jews from Germany–London, (Heidelberg ,1959), pp. 104–24; Hans Liebeschütz, *Von Georg Simmel zu Franz Rosenzweig*, (Tübingen, 1970), p. 57; cf. Franz Rosenzweig, *Kleinere Schriften*, (Berlin, 1937), pp. 31–42, here p. 34; in this sense, Rosenzweig fundamentally defined Jewish thought on Judaism as apologetic.

53. Although there is no evidence that Baeck and Harnack ever met, we may see from a letter of Baeck to the widow of Harnack on occasion of his death that Baeck respected Harnack as a scholar. Because the letter has not yet been published, we cite it in full: 'Hochschule für die Wissenschaft des Judentums / Das Lehrerkollegium / Berlin N24, den 13. Juni 1930 / Artillerie-Strasse 14 / Euer Excellenz / bitten wir es aussprechen zu dürfen, dass auch / wir in aufrichtigem Empfinden an der Trauer um / das Hinscheiden Ihres Herrn Gemahls teilnehmen. / Sein Lebenswerk ist ein Werk auch für die Arbeit / und die Aufgabe geworden, die uns anvertraut ist. / Auch wir dürfen ihn Lehrer und Meister nennen. / In innigem Beileide / Das Lehrerkollegium / der Hochschule für die Wissenschaft des Judentums / Baeck' (property of the Staatsbibliothek Preußischer Kulturbesitz Berlin, Handschriftenabteilung, Harnack-Nachlaß, Kasten 26).

54. Cf. Liebeschütz, *Von Simmel zu Rosenzweig*, p. 64; on the influence of Baeck's doctoral supervisor, W. Dilthey, on 'Das Wesen des Judentums', cf. Otto Merk,

Baeck definitely sees his task as an apologetic one,[55] although the tone of his exposition is generally nonpolemic. It is quite intriguing that Harnack is not even mentioned specifically by name in Baeck's text except in the footnotes.[56] However, there is a clear reference to Harnack's *Wesen des Christentums*, regarding the content, obvious through Baeck's borrowing of certain phrases and key terms from Harnack.

According to Baeck, the essence of Judaism lies in the ethical monotheism of the prophets, which confirms the special status of Israel in the history of religions and the lasting religious significance of Judaism: 'Judaism is not merely ethical, but ethics is its basic principle, its essence.'[57]

Tracing the essence of Judaism back to the appearance of the prophets is characteristic of liberal Jewish theology as compared to the traditional Orthodox interpretation of the origin of the essence of Judaism as a whole in the Sinai Revelation. This shift already reflects very well the influence of Protestant historical criticism of the Biblical writings on liberal Judaism.[58] For Baeck, the incompleteness of the line of prophets also determines the incompleteness of the historical development as a component of the essence of Judaism; in other words, the identity of Judaism is explicitly conveyed through history: 'Every system of the Jewish religion is necessarily a history of the Jewish religion. Only in its historical totality can Judaism truly

---

'Judentum und Christentum bei Leo Baeck', in *Traditio–Krisis–Renovatio aus theologischer Sicht: Festschrift Winfried Zeller zum 65. Geburtstag*, Bernd Jaspert and Rudolf Mohr (eds) (Marburg, 1976), pp. 513–28, here pp. 514–16.

The major and real reaction to Baeck's *Das Wesen des Judentums* first came with the publishing of the second edition in 1921, which included historically relevant and motivated characteristic changes and additions. Cf. here Ernst Simon, 'Geheimnis und Gebot: Über Leo Baeck (1948)', *Brücken: Gesammelte Aufsätze* (Heidelberg ,1965), pp. 385–92, here 387–9; Alexander Altmann, 'Leo Baeck and the Jewish Mystical Tradition', in *Essays in Jewish Intellectual History* (Hanover, NH/London, Engl., 1981), pp. 293–311, here pp. 298–302; Altmann sees the change primarily in Baeck's new positive assessment of mysticism. In the following, however, the first edition will be used as the basis because of its relationship to the Harnack debate.

55. Cf. Baeck (1905), p. 28; cf. also the introduction to the notes, p. 162, wherein Baeck does not justify the large number of Talmud quotes primarily because they comprise the 'Wesen des Judentums', but because of the 'Geschichte seiner Verkennung' (history of the underestimation of the Talmud); cf. Simon, *Brücken*, p. 386.

56. Cf. Baeck (1905), pp. 162–6. Of the three comments on Harnack, two of them refer to 'die Mission und die Ausbreitung des Christentums in den ersten drei Jahrhunderten' (Leipzig 1902), and only one refers to Harnack's *Wesen des Christentums*, namely, the description of Greek Catholicism, cf. Baeck (1905), p. 5.

57. Cf. ibid., p. 39; cf. also pp. 18ff.

58. Cf. Liebeschütz, *Von Simmel zu Rosenzweig*, p. 67.

be comprehended'.[59] Incompleteness is a necessary characteristic of a still continuing process of historical development. The inner continuum of this development is expressed through the Hebrew Bible, based, as it were, on ethical monotheism, with its twofold character of being a preserving authoritative tradition and of being for faith, the ever-present word of God.[60]

Through the practical moral character of the message of the prophets, religion and life are, according to Baeck, closely tied to one another in Judaism, not as an experienced *(erlebte)* religion, as Harnack claimed, but explicitly as a lived *(gelebte)* religion.[61] The fundamental ethical dimension, that is, the general nature of the moral imperative in Judaism has, according to Baeck, a twofold integrative function:

1. It ensures the general character and the unity of the religious content; Judaism does not involve a dogma-forming subject or any strict sense of dogma at all. For this reason, Baeck also sees the Reformation as a return to Judaism.[62]
2. The fundamental ethical dimension of Judaism is the warrant for its capacity for becoming universal as a world religion, although the national limitedness and, in this context, the ceremonial law were a 'fence around the law, only a condition of the historical conservation of the idea of ethical universalism.[63]

In his further analysis, Baeck portrays, at times using Harnack's exact wording and key terms, all the qualities that Harnack claimed for the appearance and preaching of Jesus, as implications of ethical monotheism. In this way, ethical monotheism explains the incomparable value of each human soul through the idea of humanity's being created in God's image which Baeck interprets as the moral autonomy of human beings.[64]

Through the close interconnections between religion and life in Judaism, the duty to 'love thy neighbour' is expressed directly, whereas even Baeck considers the mindset *(Gesinnung)* as the inner criterion of ethical action.[65]

Finally, ethical monotheism is even capable of justifying, first and foremost, the moral concept of world history *(sittliche Begriff der*

---

59. Baeck (1905), p. 9; cf. also pp. 27f.; cf. Harnack's reference to total induction of the history of Christianity in determining the essence of Christianity, in Harnack (1985), p. 18.
60. Cf. Baeck (1905), pp. 9–11.
61. Cf. ibid., pp. 21f., 36.
62. Cf. ibid., pp. 31f., 34ff.
63. Cf. ibid., pp. 47, 50f., 151f.
64. Cf. ibid., pp. 93f., 80.
65. Cf. ibid., pp. 108f.

Weltgeschichte[66] on the basis of the ethicisation of the concept of the Kingdom of God.

Like his Jewish contemporaries Baeck was, in his *Essence of Judaism*, primarily concerned with providing a justification for the existence of modern Judaism by constructing a historical continuity with the Judaism of the Hebrew Bible and the subsequent era. The decisive difference is that Baeck does not attempt to prove this primarily through exegetical and historical arguments or by producing evidence of the identity of theological content beyond the post-exilic epoch of Judaism. Rather, he integrates the very notion of a historical continuity as a constitutive element into the concept of the 'essence of Judaism'.

Harnack's appeal was that Jesus' Gospel proclamation represents the original, pure and now partially buried starting point to which modern Protestantism, including the total development of the strengths of its Reformation insights, should return. Baeck opposes this with the concept of the continuum of the Jewish tradition, within which ethical monotheism represents both norm and structure.[67] According to Baeck, the 'universal mission' of Judaism consists in expressing the moral principle of the minority in the world history. In this sense, it is also the measure of the realisation of the destiny of humanity.[68]

In the linking of religion and humanity as a goal of human development, Baeck also sees the possible consonance between Judaism and Christianity – this, however, always in the sense of a historically grounded priority of Judaism as 'the messianic religion of the world'.[69] Judaism was first to include the ethical concept of the Kingdom of God both as a goal of historical development and as a moral task.[70]

It became obvious that Baeck was arguing along the lines of Harnack. His postulate, though, is the superiority of Jewish tradition as the universal Messianic religion. Having secured this, Baeck is able to offer a view of harmony and coexistence with Christianity.

In the following chapter an attempt will be made to step back from the argument itself and try to understand the intrinsic links of liberal ideology within Judaism and Christianity.

---

66. Ibid., p. 135; cf. also pp. 141ff.
67. Cf. ibid., pp. 13f.
68. Ibid., pp. 158f.
69. Ibid., pp. 143f.
70. Cf. ibid., p. 146.

Chapter 5

THE ESSENCE DEBATE AND ITS PARADIGMATIC SIGNIFICANCE FOR JEWISH-CHRISTIAN RELATIONS

The Structure of the Debate: Convergence and Antagonism Between Liberal Theology and Liberal Judaism

Up to this point, liberal theology mainly of culture Protestantism and liberal Judaism as such has been discussed in a relatively undifferentiated manner. Within the parameters of the debate, Harnack's *Wesen des Christentums* is to some degree considered a perfect representative of liberal theology. This is substantiated through the form and the intensity of the Jewish reception, for which Harnack's lectures demonstrated exactly this *pars pro toto* nature. In addition, certain basic elements of the Christian essence debate of Harnack's will be referred to in the following discussion, although they will not each be elaborated upon in detail here.

The intensity of the essence debate, from a Jewish as well as from a Christian perspective, is based upon some fundamental common aspects. Apart from the particular historical situation of Judaism at that time, there was a general atmosphere of 'crisis' around the turn of the century, characterised by the intellectual strands of empiricism and value relativism, cultural pessimism, anti-intellectualism, growing pseudo-romanticism etc.[1] Furthermore, in view of the religious

---

1. Cf. specifically Pinchas E. Rosenblüth, 'Die geistigen und religiösen Strömungen in der deutschen Judenheit', in *Juden im Wilhelminischen Deutschland*, Werner E. Mosse

indifference within their own ranks, liberal theology and liberal Judaism each attempted to forge a reasonable new expression of their respective religious traditions which would be compatible with the conditions of modern society and culture.

Both also demonstrated a historical reference, emphasising the concept of development, the rejection of the irrational, authoritative or dogmatic elements of inflexibility in their respective traditions, and an explicitly ethical understanding of religion and the emphasis of the significance of cultural historical development for the present. In terms of such an openness for modernity directed towards an ethical secular liberalism,[2] one can speak of a 'liberal' theology on both sides. Therefore, the core of the essence debate pertained to the identity of those concerned,[3] whereby a consciousness of possible consonance, as demonstrated in the Jewish writings on the subject, did indeed exist and was even aspired to.

From the Protestant side, Paul Fiebig, a scholar of the New Testament and the Talmud, and others, also referred to the expression of this 'consonance'. In his review of J. Eschelbacher's *Das Judentum und das Wesen des Christentums*, Fiebig stressed the agreement between Eschelbacher and Harnack in the 'real religious and ethical positions'.[4] This agreement could be further analysed and sustained only through a two-sided 'distillation' process concerning the Greek elements of Christianity and the legalism of Judaism.[5] Fiebig also emphasised the necessity of knowing the rabbinical writings and the science of Judaism in order to study early Christianity adequately.[6]

On the basis of commonality in terms of the limitedness and intention, however, the debate also became the context for discovering the material differences of both sides.[7] In terms of the structure

---

(ed.) (Tübingen, 1976), pp. 549–98, here pp. 549–58, ; Tal 1976, 'Theologische Debatte', pp. 623f.

2. Trutz Rendtorff, 'Das Verhältnis von liberaler Theologie und Judentum um die Jahrhundertwende' (Manuscript of a lecture given at the 'Internationale Seminar der Friedrich-Naumann-Stiftung', held in cooperation with the Leo Baeck Institute of London, on the subject of 'Juden im deutschen Liberalismus' from 20–23 May 1986 in Königswinter b. Bonn), *Das deutsche Judentum und der Liberalismus: German Jewry and Liberalism*, edited by Friedrich-Naumann-Stiftung (Sankt Augustin, 1986), p. 2.

3. Cf. Tal, '*Theologische Debatte*', p. 600.

4. Paul Fiebig, 'Rezension von J. Eschelbacher "Das Judentum und das Wesen des Christentums"', in *Theologische Literaturzeitung* 30 (1905), cols 418–21, here col. 420.

5. Cf. ibid., col. 421.

6. Cf. ibid.; cf. also Paul Fiebig, 'Jüdische Gebete und das Vaterunser', in *Die Christliche Welt* 5 (1891), cols 313–21; 368–75, here cols 368f.

7. This is the basic thesis in all of Uriel Tal's works; cf. Tal, 'Theologische Debatte', p. 632; Uriel Tal, 'Liberal protestantism and the Jews in the Second Reich 1870–1914', pp. 34ff., in *Jewish Social Studies* 26 (1964), pp. 23–41; Uriel Tal, *Christians and*

of the discussion, a significant asymmetry makes this apparent.[8] The negation of Judaism became constitutive in a certain respect for Harnack's historical determination of the essence of Christianity, opening up his opinions to Jewish criticism. On the other hand, the Jewish determination of the essence referred more strongly to Christianity than the converse, which is reflected in the Jewish emphasis on the identity of the essential theological content on both sides.

As shown in the analysis of the Jewish writings on the essence, however, dealing with the theory of the decline of post-exilic Judaism theologically led to increased reflection on the historical uniqueness of one's own religion, with the goal of reintegration and positive reformulation. This addition of substance to the *Essence of Judaism* was also definitively motivated by the historical and intellectual period of upheaval for Judaism at the turn of the century, as discussed above. This required a more specific expression of identity.[9]

The theological ambivalence between liberal theology and Judaism is intensified by the fact that, from a Jewish perspective, the debate in theology was always related to the current status of the 'Jewish question', as shown by the sensitive and ambivalent perception of Harnack in the Jewish press. The theological similarities of Harnack's views to the content of the Biblical Jewish faith made his *Wesen des Christentums* interesting to Jewish intellectuals and, conversely, his total opposition to Judaism, at the same time, made him seem like an enemy to the Jewish public.

On the whole, Jewish apologetics seem to have overestimated the status of Judaism in the Protestant essence discussion,[10] for the Protestant reaction to the Jewish discussion, starting with Harnack himself, is rather limited. In addition, the known reviews refer to the Jewish response as being overly sensitive regarding alleged Christian 'attacks' on Judaism.[11]

Harnack defined the essence of Christianity by means of important discontinuities, while the Jewish response pointed to the corresponding continuities in order to establish a historical connection. If this was the case, then the ethics, often expressed in exactly the same way, that were

---

Jews in Germany: Religion, Politics and Ideology in the Second Reich (Ithaca/London, 1975) p. 220.

8. Cf. Tal, 'Theologische Debatte', p. 605.

9. Cf. Tal, 'Liberal Protestantism', p. 40, in which he understands this as the result of the Jewish polemics against Protestant liberalism, which was increasingly considered fraternisation from a Jewish perspective (cf. ibid. pp. 25, 33).

10. Cf. Tal, 'Theologische Debatte', p. 605.

11. Cf. Georg Hollmann, 'Sammelrezension zu "Leben und Lehre Jesu"', including a short discussion of L. Baeck's Harnack review in *MGWJ*, p. 204, in: *Theologische Rundschau* 7 (1904), pp. 197–212; Holtzmann, 'Besprechung', p. 46.

considered, primarily by the Jewish side, as the envisaged point of accord between the two religions, must lead to certain difficulties.

As Leo Baeck clearly showed, this becomes obvious in the conflict concerning claims of priority, as justified on the basis of 'history'.

We may sum up thus.

The relationship between liberal theology and Judaism at the turn of the century must be regarded as ambivalent.

Tension exists between the common, essentially accepted basic ethical theological concepts, on the one hand, and their various methods of 'historical' justification and the non-universality of religious and historical uniqueness, on the other. As far as this represents the fundamental problem of a 'liberal' theology, the Jewish-Christian essence debate takes on a representative character.

This also applies to the particular historical conditions under which the debate took place, since Harnack's *Wesen des Christentums*, as discussed above, served as a catalyst for the intellectual and scholarly self-formation of (liberal) Judaism. As he wrote to his student Ernst Rolff in 1928, Harnack later believed that he should have named his lectures simply 'Introduction to Christianity',[12] in order to avoid the discussion concerning the concept of essence that was sparked off by them. Nevertheless, it was the concept of essence that was in part responsible for the actual reception of Harnack's lectures, and that gave them a paradigmatic significance for the relationship between liberal theology and Judaism.

Stephen Sykes has rightly pointed out that this concept of essence should rather not be used because of the misunderstandings associated with it.[13] Leo Baeck later translates his 'essence' notion and speaks of 'Jewish Existence'. It is, therefore, necessary to test the significance of 'essence' in the following section.

'Norm and History': the Paradigmatic Significance of the Concept 'Essence'

The understanding of the present from its process of becoming ... the historical training of our way of thinking that grows from this and the guidelines for the future that can be gained from this: that is the meaning of history.[14]

12. Cf. Ernst Rolffs, 'Adolf von Harnack und die Theologie der Krisis', in *Die Christliche Welt* 52,2 (1938), cols. 61–65, here col. 61.
13. Cf. Stephen W. Sykes, 'Note to "What does Essence of Christianity mean?"', in *Ernst Troeltsch: Writings on Theology and Religion*, Robert Morgan and Michael Pye (eds) (London, 1977), pp. 180–181.
14. Ernst Troeltsch, 'Was heißt 'Wesen des Christentums'?', in *Gesammelte Schriften*, vol. 2: *Zur religiösen Lage, Religionsphilosophie und Ethik* (Tübingen, 1962 [1913]), pp. 386–451, here p. 425.

Ernst Troeltsch wrote this in his contribution to the essence debate. It marked a decisive point in the discussion, for it was the first time that the methodological assumptions and implications of the essence concept were explicitly mentioned.[15]

The preceding analysis of the Jewish-Christian essence debate should have demonstrated that in the context of the essence debate any reflection regarding one's own historical origin was also considered as a method of expressing some understanding of one's own exostence in modern times. In the following this meaning of the essence concept will be analysed more precisely using Troeltsch's exposition of the 'essence of Christianity'. Reference will be made back to those elements that, as a result of the fundamental problems posed by the essence concept, appear to be transferrable to Judaism.

According to Troeltsch, the basic methodological assumption in the determination of the essence is the process of 'historical abstraction', that is, the overall view of the extent to which individual historical phenomena contributed to the development of an idea, an essence, a concept, etc. If 'historical abstraction' is an integral part of how essence can be determined, then the general principles of critical historiography have to be employed: causality, analogy, probability judgments, critique of tradition. In this sense, the determination of the essence is 'purely historical' and right at the transition from an empirical inductive history to a philosophy of history.[16]

This pertains to the essence concept in three ways:

1. Essence as *criticism:* 'Separation of that which corresponds to the essence and that which contradicts it'[17]
2. Essence as *development,* whereby the origin must be maintained as a priority,[18] not in the sense of a given, unchangeable concept, but rather as essence and unfolding principle that releases new ideas in its development.[19]
3. Essence as *a concept of the ideal,* a standard according to which the future should be formed.[20]

For all three aspects of the essence concept, Troeltsch sees it as indispensable to determine the validity of essence according to personal

15. On the changes and differences with respect to content between the versions of 1903 *(Christliche Welt)* and 1913 *(Gesammelte Schriften),* cf. Stephen W. Sykes, 'Ernst Troeltsch and Christianity's Essence', in *Ernst Troeltsch and the Future of Theology,* John P. Clayton (ed.) (Cambridge, 1976), pp. 139–171; and Sykes, 'Note to "What does Essence of Christianity mean?"', pp. 180f.; in the following, quotes will correspond to the *Gesammelte Schriften II* version.
16. Ibid., p. 398.
17. Ibid., p. 407.
18. Cf. ibid., p. 413.
19. Ibid., p. 418.
20. Cf. ibid., pp. 426ff.

rejection or acceptance. The connection between the – objectively speaking – purely historical perspective and the subjective judgment in the present regarding the validity of the 'essence', takes place as an act of creation. 'Any determination of the essence is historical re-formation.'[21]

The essence concept receives paradigmatic meaning for the search by both liberal Jewish and Protestant theology to express anew the relation between norm and history.

The subjective moment, as emphasised by Troeltsch, in the determination of the essence as a re-formatting of essence is, then, the profound reason for considering the spirit of the time.

The examination of the difficulties of the Jewish-Christian essence debate shows that in the way that 'norm' and 'history' were positioned in relation to each other, it was also determined which possibilities and chances for dialogue with the other side existed for each faith. The particular historical and intellectual relationships of the time intensified this structure.

The great danger of the essence concept lies in its potential for misunderstanding as a concept of a standardised ideal rather than a chance for development. Transforming 'essence' into 'identity' may help future generations to free themselves from the limitations of the essence idea.

The following chapter will attempt to show that such a change of perspective is absolutely indispensable for Jewish theology as a contextual way of thought.

21. Ibid., p. 431.

Chapter 6

JUDAISM AND CHRISTIANITY BETWEEN DIVISION AND AFFINITY

Modern Jewish Theology as Contextual Way of Thought

In the preceding chapter we have seen the analogous endeavours of both Christianity and Judaism to adapt their traditional materials by historical thought. This 'liberal' approach demands a constant search for the essence of a religious tradition relative to the tasks of the time. Before we discuss Baeck's own position and his contribution to Jewish theology we must first give a survey of modern Jewish theology as a whole.

Jewish theology has always been determined by the distinctive social environment in which it developed its particular character. Especially in times of open cultural interchange one can detect a self-conscious act of intellectual reflection on the content and character of Jewish faith. During the centuries of its biblical and Talmudic development the sort of reflective abstraction and intellectual questioning that are characteristic of philosophy and theology may be less pronounced. But even then intellectual modification of some sort was a necessary tool to preserve continuity and at the same time allow certain changes.[1] Eugene Borowitz rightly points out that 'Jewish theology is the product of social hybridization'.[2] The definition of what 'religion' as a term could mean for a specific faith at a specific

1. See for example: Walter Homolka, *Ein dem Untergang naher Aramäer war mein Vater* (Egelsbach/Köln/New York, 1993) on the Seder ritual for Pessach.
2. Eugene B. Borowitz, *A New Jewish Theology in the Making* (Philadelphia, 1968).

time is therefore heavily dependent on the sociological climate in which the theological task is set: 'society' and 'religion' are in a state of interaction; Jewish theology is highly contextual.

In order to assess Baeck's contribution to the theological thought of his age I shall attempt to look at the development of Jewish theology in the nineteenth and twentieth century. By concentrating on some of the major trends I will try to present a picture which communicates something of the contextuality of German Jewish theology as a whole and Leo Baeck in particular and the interaction that occurred between Jewish and Christian thinkers from the Age of Enlightenment until after the Second World War. We have pointed out before that Leo Baeck can be considered as the great theologian of modern Jewish thought. As a leading figure of Western European and American Jewry his contribution towards a developing Jewish understanding of Christianity was very important. He and Claude G. Montefiore might be considered to be pioneer workers in this field, which had been touched on by only a few other serious Jewish scholars before the turn of the nineteenth century.[3]

Baeck's analysis of the Jewish elements of Christianity from early times on was to be followed by other students; it has led to some extent to a greater understanding of Christianity by Jews. However, difficulties cannot be denied when one takes a critical look at Baeck's views with regard to Christian thought. As we have seen in the essence debate polemicism and typology are methods whose usage enabled Baeck only a restricted view at the heart of the matter. Therefore, Baeck's intellectual environment and the presuppositions going with it will have to be more closely examined in order to understand the great restrictions and dependencies which form a part of the theological picture that Baeck is able to draw so eloquently.

His interpretation of Martin Luther and Lutheranism will serve as a last example to show where Baeck puts his emphasis when dealing with Christianity: it is not the authentic reception of Martin Luther's theology but the postulate of enlightened superiority against a state church Lutheranism (see chapter 8, 'The Lutheran State Church').

Continuity and Change: a Jewish-Christian Problem of the Enlightenment Age

It can be claimed that the dramatic changes in the aftermath of enlightenment and emancipation of European Jewry created a sort of social hybridisation to a much more radical extent than ever

3. Cf. Walter Jacob, *Christianity through Jewish Eyes: The Quest for Common Ground* (Cincinatti, Ohio, 1974), p.161.

before.[4] By opening the gates to its environment, itself in the process of intense transformation, the emancipation period had put an end to the Jewish Middle Ages, when through centuries the impact of time and circumstance on the Jewish spirit could be considered as only marginal. Liberal theology amongst nineteenth-century German Jewry was mainly concerned with theological reflection on the integration of Judaism into the framework of modern culture.[5] Legal emancipation presented one paramount task: to prove that the religious value of Judaism was sufficiently strong and unique in character to justify Jewish non-conformity.

The efforts of all Jewish theological enterprise to prove this value, however, will have to be judged by two criteria if the enterprise is to succeed. Theology has to give answers within the modern social context in which it arises. Therefore, it can be expected to show certain affinities to the prevalent thought-forms and determinative ideas of its non-Jewish surroundings. Yet the Judaism so conveyed must also remain authentic enough to merit the description 'Jewish'. Determining what is acceptable in modernity and yet remaining authentic Judaism turned out to be a substantial task in any Jewish theology which intended to be modern in its time. The first great theoretician of modern Jewish thought, Moses Mendelssohn, provides us with a good example of the apparent tensions that are created by this task.

The content of Mendelssohn's faith is fully modern in its emphasis on the universality and rationality of the human spirit. Yet he also affirms a particularistic and supernatural revelation of the law at Sinai – on which his apparent orthopraxis seems to be based – that would not allow any changes of the boundaries defined by tradition. The need for integrity makes this approach to truth on two parallel levels unacceptable, since those two levels cannot be harmonised. Once Kant had published the first of his great critiques, humankind's thinking about the spirit and soul had changed in such a revolutionary way that Mendelssohn's conception no longer seemed to make sense. The belief in supernatural revelation was no longer accepted and the ability of proving religious truth by metaphysics was negotiated.[6] The majority of Jews of later generations

---

4. See Robert Weltsch, ' Die schleichende Krise der jüdischen Identität', and Pinchas E. Rosenblüth, 'Die geistigen und religiösen Strömungen in der deutschen Judenheit', both in *Juden im Wilhelminischen Deutschland: 1890–1914*, Werner E. Mosse (ed.) (Tübingen, 1976).

5. Hans Liebeschütz, 'Jewish Thought and its German Background', in *Leo Baeck Institute Year Book*, 1 (1956).

6. See Julius Guttmann, *Die Philosophie des Judentums*, 1st edn of the reprint (Wiesbaden, 1985), p. 317.

adapted their Jewish observance in an attempt at continuing their affirmation of Judaism during the transition from the ghetto to the social realities of modern life.[7] Despite the departure from tradition they still felt that they were remaining faithful to their Jewish past. Their modernisation of rite and practice stood in conscious opposition to those Jews who adopted Christianity.

In an acceptable Jewish theology, however, this strategy would have to be explained. In this way the demand for an authentic Judaism within changed social and political conditions called for a standard of legitimate modification of the old without losing the link to the religion of their ancestors. To sum up: Jewish liberal theology in the nineteenth century did face the challenge of integrating Judaism into the framework of modern culture. Jewish society was no longer limited to a more or less separated life in the ghettos but was offered the chance to take part in all aspects of social, cultural and economic life of Christian society. This process of overcoming traditional social limits demanded a new interpretation of Jewish religious life. Jewish nonconformity had to be justified by proving the religious value of Judaism. It was liberal theology which was concerned with this task: Jewish scholars who used contemporary scholarship to reinterpret Jewish tradition in a modern way.

'Wissenschaft des Judentums' and the Hegelian 'Idea'

The earliest strategy for the accomplishment of the end of the Jewish Middle Ages was the 'Wissenschaft des Judentums' as a historical science.[8] In their programme for the new learning Zacharias Frankel[9] and Heinrich Graetz had attempted to establish a history of Jewish law and custom, critical in its methods and based on the model of contemporary scholarship, but essentially positive in the appreciation of Jewish tradition. It was hoped that once the development of the Jewish 'idea' as a historical process had been grasped, its essence

7. Moritz Lazarus, *Ethik des Judenthums* (Berlin, 1904), vol. 1, § 87: 'Every age is justified in disregarding, more, is in duty bound to disregard, the written law whenever reason and conviction demand its nullification' (and also § 52). See also Nathan Rotenstreich, *Jewish Philosophy in Modern Times: From Mendelssohn to Rosenzweig* (New York et al., 1968), p.45 ff.

8. Kurt Wilhelm, 'Zur Einführung in die Wissenschaft des Judentums', and Sinai Ucko, 'Geistesgeschichtliche Grundlagen der Wissenschaft des Judentums', both in *Wissenschaft des Judentums im deutschen Sprachbereich*, 2 vols, Kurt Wilhelm (ed.) (Tübingen, 1967).

9. Frankel is widely respected as the founder of the conservative Jewish movement. The legacy of his teaching is preserved at the Jewish Theological Seminary, New York.

would clearly emerge, freed from the bonds of tradition that seemed to impede the entrance into the world of modern Europe.[10]

However, it can be said that this approach did not succeed in tracing the historical reality of Judaism to the extent that it was guided by a preconceived idea of what Judaism ought to be, in order to meet the standards of nineteenth-century religious thought. In well-known Hegelian fashion the historical process was seen to culminate and reach its consummation in the concepts of classical Reform with its 'fathers' Samuel Hirsch, Samuel Holdheim, Salomon Formstecher, Ludwig Phillipson, and above all, Abraham Geiger.[11] In spite of his professed interest in history, Abraham Geiger's reading of Jewish history was dominated by the motives of his own age. The rise of the modern world which was seen as opening up for Jewry many contacts with its environment, had created in Geiger's view the possibility that Judaism could become the classical representative of a religion which was rational and therefore universal. In his idea of an abstract doctrine, the standard according to which Geiger had assessed the epochs of Jewish history, his theology seems – as some critics have said – somewhat unhistorical and dominated by the spirit of enlightenment.[12]

Geiger's intention and that of his allies was to reduce nonconformity as far as it was based on the coincidence of religious and national differences ('Dejudaisierung'). The main theme stayed the same as in Mendelssohn's age: how to retain a distinctive Jewish identity while at the same time attempting to acculturate to a country that defined itself increasingly in national terms.

In the late nineteenth century the naive belief that history manifested the inevitable progress of the 'Idea' became more and more problematic and doubtful. This has many reasons. Perhaps the most significant is that Ranke, Sybel and Niebuhr introduced a new methodology of historiography which revealed the failure of former historico-philosophical constructs to do justice to the requirements of historical science. Owing to the romantic emphasis on individuality it also became quite common to declare that abstract ideas cannot describe particulars. This downfall of the Hegelian metaphysics of history[13] did very much to discredit the classical Jewish Reform theology of the kind represented by Abraham Geiger.

10. For many Jews the 'entrance ticket' to this world seemed to be baptism, as Heinrich Heine comments on his own decision to convert to Christianity.
11. Hans Liebeschütz, 'Wissenschaft des Judentums und Historismus bei Abraham Geiger', in *Essays presented to Leo Baeck on the occasion of his eightieth birthday* (Festschrift) (London, 1954).
12. Emil L. Fackenheim, *Encounters between Judaism and Modern Philosophy: A Preface to Future Jewish Thought* (Philadelphia, 1973), p. 130.
13. This downfall was by no means that complete if one looks at the Hegelian influences within neo-Kantianism; see Siegfried Marck, ' Am Ausgang des jüngeren

Geiger and his contemporaries had erred in projecting their own 'fundamental idea' *(Grundidee)* of Judaism into their reconstruction of history. However, they were at least guided by a more or less philosophical concept of Judaism and avoided the pitfalls of historicism by bringing to the study of Jewish history a clear, albeit somewhat arbitrary, conception of the ultimate goal and nature of Judaism. Nonetheless, they did not endeavour to derive a concept of Judaism from a reading of history but read history in the light of a preconceived 'idea'. The inner connection between 'Wissenschaft des Judentums' and the new theology of Judaism as Geiger had conceived it was no longer felt to be self-evident.

In its later developments 'Wissenschaft des Judentums' lost its sense of purpose and direction, spending its energies in detailed research without being guided by a vision that could impart a unity to such efforts.[14] And theology, bereft of a philosophical principle to underpin it, ran the risk of a moral breakdown. In contrast to such an intention, the Breslau conservative programme, which combined traditional Jewish law and freedom of research, was designed to obtain real contact with the contemporary world without the sacrifice of genuineness. Leo Baeck should be seen in this line of thought.

Liberal Jewish Theology and the Jewish Neo-Kantian Revival

As we will see later an important aspect of the Jewish philosophers' and theologians' task was to draw a line at which assimilation had to stop. By this they created a peculiar and ambivalent context for the relationship between Jewish and Protestant thought in the decades around 1900. The affinity of Jewish thought towards the Protestant spirit of the time created a general problem. In Imperial Germany the Protestant section of the population was considered to represent the more advanced tendencies in cultural, technical and political life. This strongly attracted the sympathies of Jewish intellectuals.[15]

Neukantianismus', in *Materialien zur Neukantianismus-Diskussion*, Hans-Ludwig Ollig (ed.) (Darmstadt, 1987); p. 19.

14. For a critique of 'Wissenschaft des Judentums' see Ismar Elbogen, 'Neuorientierung unserer Wissenschaft', in *Monatsschrift für Geschichte und Wissenschaft des Judentums* 62 (N.S. 26) (1918) and by the same author *'Ein Jahrhundert Wissenschaft des Judentums'*, in Festschrift zum 50 jährigen Bestehen der Hochschule für die Wissenschaft des Judentums in Berlin (Berlin, 1922).

15. Cf. Uriel Tal, 'Liberal Protestantism and the Jews in the Second Reich 1870–1914', in *Jewish Social Studies* 26 (1964), pp. 23–41, here p. 24.

It was for this reason that the theological argument to preserve Jewish separatism had to be established mainly against Protestantism, which exercised great influence among the educated Jewish middle class *(Bildungsbürgertum)* at that time and, by that, encouraged the fear of many Jews of losing people to Christianity. Beyond this vital yet tactical question lay the deeper difference that theological thought derived from Martin Luther's emphasis on faith. This did not foster sympathy with a people shaped and preserved by a belief in an everlasting divine commandment.[16]

The Jewish Neo-Kantian Revival

There was, however, a certain amount of overlap in the conscious connection of values of faith with the human activities in this world. Conservative Neo-Lutheranism claimed its spiritual inheritance as the very root of culture and civilisation.[17] And one result of this tendency to bring faith into the modern world was the interpretation of Kant's autonomous ethics as a specifically Protestant teaching.

Interestingly enough, it was usually Jews, in philosophy as well as in politics, who argued in favour of a return to Kant.[18] During the seventies of the nineteenth century, when neo-Kantianism in philosophy and Protestant theology was only in its beginnings, the Breslau rabbi and teacher at the Theological Seminary[19] Manuel Joel declared the Königsberg thinker's critical philosophy to be the given basis for the theoretical understanding of monotheistic religion.[20]

The Search for 'Essence'

In this critical situation Hermann Cohen had attempted on the intellectual stage to carry out this programme philosophically, and – in Jewish terms – to restore the 'infinite' gap between ideality and reality, *noumenon* and *phenomenon*. Due to his influence twentieth-century Jewish theology in Germany was able to liberate itself from a sterile historicism, and recovered the almost lost domain of the absolute, of truth and faith in a truth by allying itself to the revival of Kantian thought.[21] It must be kept in mind, though, that Cohen did not primarily intend to offer an apology for religion. He must be seen as a

16. In contrast to this the reformed church showed less antagonism towards this part of the legacy of the Hebrew Bible.
17. See Friedrich-Wilhelm Graf, 'Konservatives Kulturluthertum', in *Zeitschrift für Theologie und Kirche*, 85 (1988), especially p. 45 ff.
18. To paraphrase Otto Liebmann's famous saying.
19. In Breslau Joel became the successor of Abraham Geiger, by far the most important representative of Protestant influence on Jewish theological ideas.
20. Manuel Joel, *Religionsphilosophische Zeitfragen in zusammenhängenden Aufsätzen besprochen* (Breslau, 1876), p. 3ff. and 55 ff.
21. Fackenheim, *Encounters*, p. 132f.

philosopher for whom intellectual and academic concerns were paramount. This makes his achievement for a new philosophy of Judaism even more remarkable.

Cohen continued and elaborated the Kantian concept that ethics provide the key to understanding human beings and organising society. Duty itself, not its fulfilment, is at the heart of humanity's existence. It is an eternal task whose accomplishment grows steadily in reality yet remains infinitely distant and incomplete.[22] Nevertheless that task must be carried out in the real world. Otherwise it would remain on a purely conceptual or imaginative level. If the ethical task is to be accomplished, however, the ethical domain has to be linked to nature.

Continuity is achieved only if the system contains an idea which transcends both the realm of ethics and the realm of nature so that they can maintain their respective integrity and individual structures, yet is comprehensive enough to relate both realms harmoniously to each other. This makes the idea of God a rational necessity for Cohen's system: a God who is one and unique and has primary significance for humankind by being the foundation and rationale of ethics.

In *Religion der Vernunft aus den Quellen des Judentums*[23] the permanent ingredients of Judaism can thus be identified: its ethics and its understanding of God are considered to be the lasting and unique characteristics. Judaism is presented as the classic representation of the religion of reason. Cohen recognises the need for ceremony and ritual, that is, the bulk of non-ethical commandments of the tradition *(Ritualgesetze)*. But certainly any such acts are of lesser importance when compared to ethical duty. Ethics, according to the neo-Kantians, enabled humankind to order life according to an a priori system of principles.

Cohen's criterion of continuity in change becomes apparent: the ethical duty is paramount while non-ethical activities might be valuable or useful, but not permanently or absolutely obligatory. Judaism's uniqueness is based on the importance that ethical monotheism enjoys. Defining ethical monotheism as the centre of Jewish faith also opens up the possibility of declaring Judaism superior to Christianity. God's unity and uniqueness appear to be compromised by the Christian doctrines of the Trinity and the Incarnation. And although Christianity certainly incorporates a specific morality it seems to have been marginalised by the predominant emphasis on faith.[24]

---

22. Hans Joachim Störig, *Weltgeschichte der Philosophie* (Stuttgart et al., 1985), p. 543.
23. Hermann Cohen, *Religion der Vernunft aus den Quellen des Judentums* (Leipzig, 1919) (The Religion of Reason out of the Sources of Judaism).
24. Uriel Tal, 'Protestantism and Judaism in Liberal Perspective', in *Christians and Jews in Germany: Religion, Politics and Ideology in the Second Reich* (Ithaca/London, 1975), p.187.

At the end of the nineteenth century the executive committee of the Rabbinerverband Deutschlands (the association of non-orthodox rabbis in Germany) put it this way:

> As long as liberal Protestants continue to adhere to the tradition of the Incarnation, the redeeming power of Jesus, and the abolition of the law as a fundamental spiritual and ethical principle ... Christianity will not be free of elements that cannot meet the scrutiny of reason ... and it is our task to contribute freely from the storehouse of pure monotheism – and hence the storehouse of the purest morality – to human culture in general and to our German culture in particular.[25]

To sum up: neo-Kantian revival was quite successful in the minds of Jewish theologians at the turn of this century and beyond. It was considered a proper way of defining the Jewish faith within the new environment of the Second German Empire with its growing nationalistic ideology that expected uniformity more than anything else. The implicit attack on the concept of individual responsibility and each other's ability to shape his or her life did not foster sympathy with a people preserved by a belief in an everlasting divine commandment.

It was considered by many to be the task of German Jewry to uphold the concept of individualism and a rational-critical outlook that gives credit to the insights that equality is not at all synonymous with homogeneity and egalitarianism and that freedom cannot mean total assimilation to the surrounding national culture. For modern Jewish theology it meant a twofold reorientation: firstly, a regeneration of the old apologetics under new conditions and, secondly, for the first time, a historico-critical investigation into the origins of Christianity with the intention of relativising it as a historical phenomenon.[26]

Liberal German Jewry and Culture Protestantism – Affinity and Rivalry

Jewish Affinity Towards Protestant Zeitgeist

It will be useful to have a glance at the links that existed between Christian and Jewish thought in the nineteenth century, especially between culture Protestantism[27] and progressive Judaism. In the aftermath of their emancipation the task of Jewish philosophers and

25. Martin Rade, *Die "Mission" der Deutsch-Evangelischen Kirche* (Berlin/Leipzig, 1890), pp. 2–4.
26. For an overview see Jacob, *Christianity*.
27. See Graf, 'Konservatives Kulturluthertum'. And Friedrich-Wilhelm Graf, 'Kulturprotestantismus: Zur Begriffsgeschichte einer theologiegeschichtlichen Chiffre', in ABG 28 (1984), pp. 214–68.

theologians was to draw a line beyond which assimilation could not proceed. Nonetheless, it is interesting to note the tremendous influence that explicitly Protestant thought had on Jewish theology, as we have seen before. It seems paradoxical that the conflict between German Judaism and Protestantism derived from a shared set of values and common political goals, a rather similar sense of aesthetics and a common way of life. This created a peculiar and ambivalent situation in the decades around 1900, when the affinity of Jewish thought towards Protestant 'Zeitgeist' appeared to be symptomatic for liberal Judaism in general and included close friendships between representatives of both camps.[28]

It has been noted already to what extent Leo Baeck was indebted to the moderate wing of the German Jewish Reform movement. To what extent, however, was he influenced by the Protestant thought of his time?

Friedrich D. E. Schleiermacher

From the end of the eighteenth century to the beginning of the nineteenth, liberal Protestantism was essentially an ethical-theological movement and a school of historical theology under the leadership of Friedrich Daniel Ernst Schleiermacher, Christian Baur and later within the framework of the 'Jüngere Tübinger Schule'.[29]

F.D.E. Schleiermacher is most certainly one source of influence on Jewish theology.[30] In his *Glaubenslehre* in 1821 he had laid down the fundamental principles by which the greater part of later liberal Protestant thought developed its method. He sought to portray the contents of Christian belief as expressions grounded in a human being's religious consciousness of redemption through Christ. Schleiermacher interpreted religion not in terms of practical reason, but in terms of man's self-consciousness, particularly the type of self-consciousness that Schleiermacher identifies as religious consciousness. This reliance upon religious experience made the conception of the immanence of God the main focus of nineteenth-century theologies.

In the later nineteenth century the theology of Albrecht Ritschl showed less interest in metaphysics, but stressed conquest of nature by

28. See Trutz Rendtorff, 'Das Verhältnis von liberaler Theologie und Judentum um die Jahrhundertwende', in *Das deutsche Judentum und der Liberalismus: German Jewry and Liberalism* (Sankt Augustin, 1986), pp. 96–112; Max Wiener, *Jüdische Religion im Zeitalter der Emanzipation,* (Berlin, 1933); David Bronsen, ed., *Jews and Germans from 1860 to 1933: The Problematic Symbiosis* (Heidelberg, 1979).
29. Uriel Tal, 'Liberal Protestantism and the Jews in the Second Reich 1870–1914', in *Jewish Social Studies* 26 (1964), p 23.
30. Leo Baeck takes great pains to ensure that his reliance on the sense of religious consciousness is not confused with that of Schleiermacher, which is a good reason to think he was not unaware of his debt (see footnote 12, chapter 7).

the spirit and emphasised the moral content of faith as an essential key for theology. Thus liberal theology allied itself with the ethical aspirations of nineteenth-century liberal doctrines of historical progress, and the need for social reconstruction. Schleiermacher and Ritschl had separated theology from philosophy as natural theology so that theology became 'autonomous', but at a high price. Once the principle of the independence of faith from reason was affirmed, a historical theology developed which was then confronted with the crisis of historicism.

Wilhelm Dilthey

Another influence is the decisive impulse and direction from Dilthey's *Verstehende Psychologie*, which seeks to enter sympathetically into the patterns of thought that underlie the literary creations of the past. It is directed towards understanding (rather than explaining) the vital connection *(Lebenszusammenhang)* in the elements of the whole and to relive the spiritual struggles of former epochs: comprehension, not judgment is the aim.

It would be an exaggeration to say that Baeck was actually a pupil of Dilthey's. Nevertheless, in one important aspect the interests of both coincide: their thought concentrates on the human mind in its search for the relation between time and eternity. By means of a comprehensive picture both tried to overcome the positivistic limitation of historical knowledge to the collection and knowledge of facts. Dilthey's kind of approach was needed in order to do justice to Judaism as a historical entity. Baeck felt it to be important to see Judaism as a complex whole characterised by continuity. Even more, he wanted to approach it with a comprehensive and sympathetic vision.

Das Wesen des Judentum sets out to accomplish this. Three characteristics can be underlined: its sense of morphological unity, its feeling for morphological unity *(Gestalt)*, and the determination to allow Judaism to describe itself as far as the inevitable intrusion of the subjective element permits it. Those subjective elements have been examined. Nevertheless, a critical note should be added here: it may well be argued that Dilthey's theory of interpretation based on self-identification with the historical sources seems to say more about the person him- or herself than about the character of the tradition that person tries to understand.

More importantly, it can occur that the interpreter is insufficiently aware of his/her subjectivity and thus less able to guard him/herself and the reader against its excesses. So Baeck's vision of an 'essence of Judaism' makes him appear almost authoritarian in his practice of ignoring or even suppressing contradictory material.[31]

31. The visionary and idealistic character of Baeck's *Essence of Judaism* was stated as

It is difficult for the reader to determine to what extent the given data are representative with regard to the essence of a tradition. And quite generally it is a matter of further investigation whether the rather static concept of 'essence' is at all capable of dealing with dynamic historical developments.[32]

Though he does not mention this, Baeck may also have been influenced by Rudolf Otto's well-received book *The Idea of the Holy*. It appeared in 1917 and gave new vigour to the notion of religion arising from a unique level of consciousness.

Liberal Protestantism, the Jews and the National State

In the period of the Second Empire, however, liberal Protestantism saw a profound change.[33] Both the institutional framework of the church and social organisations saw a decline in dedication as well as quantity. Nevertheless, liberal Protestantism became an important pillar of Imperial Germany's nationalism. And it shaped the way of life of the intelligentsia and the upper-middle class *(Bildungsbürgertum)*.[34] Rudolf von Bennigsen, the leader of the Protestant League (Protestantenverein) and one of the leaders of the National Liberals described this new orientation:

> As originally conceived, Protestantism was separate from political life. It became clear as early as Luther's time that just as the German states could not exist without Protestantism, so this religion could not exist in a political vacuum.
> Now, since the formulation of the spiritual foundations of liberal Protestantism, it has become even more evident that Christianity is not merely a matter of sermons ... it is a part of the 'personality-idea' *[Persönlichkeitsidee]* inherent in the concept of German national citizenship ... [35]

At the turn of this century, Martin Rade, one of the liberal Protestant leaders of the Second Reich and editor of their main weekly *Christliche Welt*, could define Liberal Protestantism critically as a system of opinions and beliefs that had turned from a religion into a sci-

---

early as 1923 in Friedrich Niebergall's review on the second edition: ' ... der Titel des Buches müßte genauer heißen: Das Ideal des Judentums ... ', in *Christliche Welt* 37 (1923), col. 27.

32. Against the use of 'essence' in Horst Bürkle, ' Das europäische Christentum und die nichtchristlichen Kulturen', in *Zeitschrift für Missionswissenschaft* 1 (1985). See Hans-Werner Gensichen, 'Das Christentum im Dialog der Kulturen: Kontextualität und Universalität', in *Zeitschrift für Missionswissenschaft* 1 (1985).

33. See Karl Kupisch, *Zwischen Idealismus und Massendemokratie: Eine Geschichte der evangelischen Kirche in Deutschland von 1815–1945* (Berlin, 1955).

34. L. Mueller, 'Die Kritik des Protestantismus in der russischen Theologie und Philosophie', in *Hamburger Akademische Rundschau*, 3 (1948/49) no. 1, pp. 45 ff.; Salo W. Baron, *Modern Nationalism and Religion* (New York/Philadelphia, 1960).

35. Bennigsen, Rudolf von, *Der liberale Protestantismus* (Berlin, 1888), p. 1.

entific attitude and then into a secular theology that was well capable of serving as the main support of the new German nationalism.

> Liberal Protestantism has been transformed from a religion to a secular ideology with a religious aura, and from a framework for the beliefs of individuals to a framework for a national culture with an aura of holiness ...
>
> Today this is the ideology of the German nationalist, of the German intelligentsia and of all who rise up against atheistic socialism on the one hand, and against conservative clericalism on the other ... [36]

This also meant a profound change of perspective within the organised Jewish community in the Second Empire. From the beginnings of liberal Protestantism until the 1880s, many German Jews had believed that this movement safeguarded the realisation of Jewish legal and social emancipation.[37]

Rabbi Joseph Eschelbacher expressed this attitude even as late as 1884 when he stated that:

> the conservative Protestants constitute at once a social, political, economic and religious bloc that is closed to the social integration of German Jewry ... whereas the liberal Protestants ... together with the Jews of Germany ... are proponents of the constitutional state [*Rechtsstaat*] founded upon the principle of natural and secular law, upon that rationalism that is shared by all mankind ... and upon the equality of all men, an equality not dependent upon ethnic origins or the religious faith of the individual ... [38]

The Protestant section of the population was considered to represent the more advanced tendencies in cultural, scientific technical, and political life. For obvious reasons this attracted the sympathies of Jewish intellectuals very strongly. This is the reason why the theological argument in favour of preserving Jewish separatism had to be established mainly against liberal Protestantism. It was Martin Philippson, another major Jewish spokesperson, who asserted in 1903 that liberal Protestantism was likely

> ... to prove extremely dangerous to the continued existence of a Jewish community seeking to attain full integration within German society, without, at the same time, ceasing to be Jewish ... for, following in the footsteps of Professor Theodor Mommsen, they demand of us that we give up our Jewish distinctiveness, both spiritual and communal ...

36. Symposium der Freunde der Christlichen Welt (Berlin 1899), pp. 14–18.
37. Schleiermacher's 'Briefe bei Gelegenheit der politisch-theologischen Aufgabe und des Sendschreibens jüdischer Hausväter, von einem Prediger außerhalb Berlin' already show the intention of liberal Protestantism to establish an independence of civil liberties from baptism into the Christian church. See Kurt Nowak, *Schleiermacher und die Emanzipation des Judentums am Ende des 18. Jahrhunderts in Preußen* (Berlin, 1984).
38. Joseph Eschelbacher, *Der konservative Protestantismus und das Judenthum*, Verband für Jüdische Geschichte und Literatur (VJGL), (Berlin, 1898), p. 2.

Furthermore, from their viewpoint, equality *[Gleichheit]* does not mean that all men are of equal value and consequently have the right to be different from one another ... [but rather] for the liberal Protestants and the liberal nationalists, equality means equalisation *[Gleichmacherei]* ... and, moreover, equalisation within the framework of Christian society. This is a framework that threatens us as a new Leviathan.[39]

After Adolf von Harnack published his lectures 'What is Christianity?' at the beginning of the twentieth century[40] the leaders of German Jewry came to realise that the liberals' insistence upon the separation of church and state by no means indicated any willingness to dispense with the establishment of an authoritative Christian ethic and publicly Christian conduct.[41]

Harnack and Ernst Troeltsch claimed that it was the great achievement of the Lutheran Reformation and, to an even greater degree, modern Protestantism, including pietism, to encourage the view that the Gospel provided no straightforward answers to the problems of everyday politics.

The state operates within its own moral framework. This morality, however, was seen as rooted in Christianity, so that the nationalism of the Second Empire could appear to be essentially Protestant nationalism, and even the glory of the fatherland could be seen as essentially Christian in character.[42]

The Jewish answer was clear: such a liberalism would be a despotism of unification and could definitely lead to the suppression of individualism and freedom of religion and conscience. It would encourage the individual to abandon individual ethical values, until finally a 'political-social mush of the masses' *(politisch-sozialer Brei aus den Menschenmassen)* would result.[43]

39. Martin Phillipson, *Konservative und liberale Protestanten: ein Wort über die Ritschelsche Schule!*, Verband für jüdische Geschichte und Literatur, (Berlin, 1903), pp. 4–14.
40. Adolf von Harnack, *Das Wesen des Christentums* (Leipzig, 1900).
41. Uriel Tal, 'Protestantism and Judaism in Liberal Perspective', in *Christians and Jews in Germany* (Ithaca/London Allgemeine Zeitung des Judenthums (AZdJ), 1872, no. 23, p.42.n, 175), p. 221.
42. Ernst Troeltsch, *Die Bedeutung des Protestantismus für die Weiterentwicklung der modernen Welt* (Munich/Berlin, 1906), p. 32. In 1889 Martin Rade declared: 'Through knowledge und understanding of, and belief in, the life of Jesus, and ... the first three Gospels, as illuminated by scholarly, philological and historical research, ... we will be able to build ethical lives in the spirit of the German nation ... ' (Martin Rade, *Die 'Mission' der Deutsch-Evangelischen Kirche* (Berlin/Leipzig, 1890), p.1). For an overview of the situation in the Weimar Republic turn to Kurt Nowak, *Evangelische Kirche und Weimarer Republik: Zum politischen Weg des deutschen Protestantismus zwischen 1918 und 1932* (Göttingen/Weimar, 1981).
43. *Allgemeine Zeitung des Judentums* (AZdJ), 1872, no. 23, p. 42.

Affinity and Division of Liberal Judaism and Liberal Protestantism

What is striking is the affinity of thought within both movements as has been indicated before.[44] The nature of the dialogue between these two closely related groups was not what it had been during the first parts of the nineteenth century. Hegelianism no longer provided the basic framework for ideological debate between liberal Protestants and liberal Jews. Rather, historical research and the neo-Kantian ethics laid the foundation for both a new convergence and a new rivalry between the two camps. Both groups sought to reinterpret their religious traditions, using reason and scholarly investigation as their criteria. Nevertheless, both clothed their new interpretations in traditional garments and cited traditional authorities to support their claims.[45]

1. Both liberal Protestants and liberal Jews sought a way of combining tradition with the liberal concept of history as a conscious progression toward ethical perfection and monotheism, which provided both a ritual framework for daily life and a cognitive framework for humanism and rationalism.
2. Both liberal Protestantism and liberal Judaism vehemently repudiated those elements of their respective faiths which they considered irrational. They attacked particularly belief in miracles and what they called paralysis by dogma as well as 'primitive' and 'unaesthetic' rites.
3. For both groups, the central focus of religion was now the human being, either as the 'spirit of the nation' *(Volksgeist)* or the 'soul of the nation' *(Volksseele).*[46]

What intrinsically divided them were the two main issues that I referred to at the end of last section: the superiority of either Judaism or Christianity as a religion, and the question of Jewish attempts to gain equality and emancipation within a Protestant Christian state.

It is worth looking at this Protestant-Jewish affinity in more detail. Leo Baeck as one of the great Jewish theologians of this century would seem to be a good choice, if we want to see the interrelationship in Christian and Jewish thought and the interaction of 'society' and 'religion' in general more clearly. In the following I shall present his theology at some length since he provides one of the main theological pillars of Jewish thought today.

---

44. Courth, Franz, *Das Wesen des Christentums in der liberalen Theologie,* (Frankfurt am Main/Bern/Las Vegas, 1977).
45. With regard to Baeck see Eugene B. Borowitz, *A New Jewish Theology in the Making* (Philadelphia, 1968), p. 86.
46. It was Herder who coined those terms.

Chapter 7

IDENTITY BETWEEN TWO POLES – LEO BAECK'S SYSTEM OF POLARITY

Jewish Theology as a 'Reflection' of its History

Baeck expressed his own view of the legitimate possibilities of a Jewish theology in an essay entitled 'Theologie und Geschichte' ('Theology and History')[1] in 1932. The liberal theology of the historical school culminating in Harnack's account of Christianity had left a spiritual void and called forth the 'theocentric theology' of Erich Schaeder, Tillich's doctrine of 'Kairos', and the 'Dialectical Theology' of Karl Barth and Friedrich Gogarten. Dialectical theology deeply undermined the liberal concept of religion as one of the elements of culture *(Kulturprotestantismus)*. It expressed the view that the crisis of modern humankind resulted from the absoluteness with which it had invested culture. In place of human-made culture it put the Word of God.

This radical questioning of culture constituted a challenge to both liberal and orthodox Jewish theology. In Jewish thinking a belief in the religious value of human culture had been deeply ingrained. Hence, it became necessary to examine this question posed by dialectical theology from a Jewish point of view.[2]

Turning to the particular project of a Jewish theology Baeck warns against transferring to Judaism theological concepts, terminology

---

1. In *Bericht der Lehranstalt für die Wissenschaft des Judentums*, XLIX (1932), pp. 42–54.
2. See Alexander Altmann, 'Zur Auseinandersetzung mit der "dialektischen Theologie"', in *Monatschrift für Geschichte und Wissenschaft des Judentums*, 79 N.S. 43 (1935), pp. 349ff.

and methods peculiar to Christianity.[3] These will undoubtedly distort any description of Judaism. Just as Adolf von Harnack, his contemporary, had pointed out in dealing with the Catholic church and Gnosticism, 'to encounter our enemy's thesis by setting up others one by one, is to change over to his ground'.[4]

For Baeck, the two elements of revelation and church constitute the nature of theology in Protestantism. Critical reflection upon the word that constitutes the church is interpreted as the main function of theology. Baeck insists that this notion has no comparable validity in Judaism. Since Judaism does not know dogmas in the accepted sense of the word, Jewish theology has to be undogmatic.[5] It can only be a theology of its teachers, not the theology of a church administering the symbols of the faith. Hence Baeck's definition of a Jewish theology interprets it as 'reflection' *(Besinnung)* not upon the word of revelation but upon the history and tradition of Judaism. The concern of a Jewish theology is not recourse to revelation but to the Jewish idea, the eternal task, the way, the future.

In this sense, Baeck claims, Judaism can remain true to its history and can nevertheless overcome the pitfalls of historicism. This approach avoids historicism by seeking the abiding element, the specific character, the essence and idea of Judaism. Moreover, it does full justice to history by discovering this idea in the actual field of history and tradition. Baeck uses the formula: 'The teaching of Judaism is its history, and its history is at the same time its teaching.'[6]

Franz Rosenzweig's thesis 'The history of the Jewish people is God's revelation'[7] shines through.[8] But it should not surprise us too much; Baeck shares quite a few analogies of thought with the existentialist branch of Jewish neo-Kantianism. Both can be traced to the same root: Hermann Cohen. Leo Baeck's cast of mind is in many ways different from Cohen's, yet bears the unmistakable vestiges of Cohen's influence.[9]

Baeck's addition of a new principle of explanation like religious consciousness to complement the ethical does not, however, strengthen

---

3. Leo Baeck, 'Theologie und Geschichte', in *Aus drei Jahrtausenden* (Tübingen, 1958), p. 37. See also the 'Babel und Bibel' controversy.

4. Adolf von Harnack, *What is Christianity?* (Philadelphia, 1986), pp. 207ff.

5. Leo Baeck, 'Besitzt das überlieferte Judentum Dogmen?', in *Monatsschrift für Geschichte und Wissenschaft des Judentums*, vol. LXX, p. 225-36.

6. Baeck,'Theologie und Geschichte',in *Aus drei Jahrtausenden* (Tübingen, 1958), p. 39.

7. See Friedlander, *Leo Baeck* (1968) p. 50.

8. Baeck opposes, however, any traditional notion of chosenness. All human beings can know God and some everywhere do. The Jews are chosen only in the sense that when they selected to be confronted with God's command to be human as all people are, they chose to respond as a people. See Borowitz, *New Jewish Theology*, p. 88ff.

9. Tal, *Protestantism and Judaism in Liberal Perspective*, p. 188.

the neo-Kantian line. Once anything beyond the Kantian sense of the legitimately rational is admitted as a basis for consideration and judgment the sufficiency of the neo-Kantian explanation is repudiated. Cohen himself felt a warm friendship for Baeck and saw in him the appropriate successor of his work. Indeed, no other Jewish theologian among Cohen's disciples shows a comparable understanding of what Cohen's idea of the 'eternal task' means in terms of religious thinking. It is the axis around which Baeck's own highly personal thinking revolves. Nonetheless, to the devout, there remains an unbearable distance between what philosophy says religion ought to be and what religion knows as its reality.

From the neo-Kantian background Baeck now introduced the subjective level of religion as experienced and interpreted by Jewish believers into his explanation of Judaism. Whether he ever openly admitted this major methodological departure will have to be separately investigated.[10]

Baeck was not capable of joining the existentialists under Rosenzweig's leadership and of going along with their audacious and, at times, risky explorations. He remained too much indebted to Cohen for that, but he nevertheless transcended Cohen's conceptuality in utilising Schleiermacher's category of religious self-consciousness.[11]

> Divine love, this all-embracing divine attribute, is paralleled within man by a basic religious feeling which the inmost source of all faith and all religious sentiment, all receptivity and openness toward God. It is humility, which is nothing else than the awareness of the immeasurable Divine love. ... It combines apparent opposites ... the feeling of standing before God as little and insignificant, and without merit; but also the firm personal confidence that one is God's child in Whom one has the rock and support of existence; that one can always hope for His kindness – to be unutterably insignificant before God and yet also unutterably great through him.

Religious experience testifies to what lies beyond the ethical, to the God who has the right to issue imperatives and make them categorical. Reason cannot reach such a realm, as powerful as it may be in all other ways.

It should therefore not be surprising that paradox and dialectic are major motifs in Baeck's thinking. In Baeck's dissociation from Schleiermacher's religion 'as absolute dependence'[12] Cohen's ideal-

---

10. Ibid., p. 190.
11. Leo Baeck, *Das Wesen des Judentums,* 1st edn (Berlin, 1905), p. 71, in Friedlander (1968), p. 64.
12. Baeck, *Wesen des Judentums,* p. 80: 'Das ist der große Mangel in Schleiermachers Begriff der Religion, daß er ihr Wesen ausschließlich in dem Gefühl der Abhängigkeit von Gott findet und das ebenso wesentliche Freiheitsmoment in ihr außer Acht läßt ... '

Leo Baeck as army rabbi during World War I

Leo Baeck
with his fiancé,
Nathalie b.
Hamburger, in
Oppeln

Leo Baeck with Albert Schweitzer

Leo Baeck with the President of the Federal Republic Theodor Heuss

Leo Baeck in his daughter's garden in London

Hebrew Union College Cincinnati (Ohio) 1951
From left to right: J. J. Petuchowski (rabbinical student),
Wolfgang Hamburger (rabinnical student), Leo Baeck, Alexander Guttmann
(Professor of Talmud), Franz Landsberger (Director of the Jewish Museum and
Professor of Jewish Art), Samuel Atlas (Professor of Jewish Philosophy),
Albert H. Friedlander (rabbinical student)

ism lives on most strikingly.[13] But for Baeck ethics without this mysterious root in God is mere moralism. Reason cannot touch this root, but it is nevertheless present in the consciousness of the faithful believer. Baeck also evokes this tension between the feeling of dependence and the feeling of ethical forces shaping the world by the juxtaposition of the terms 'classical' and 'romantic'.

The Typology of 'Classical' and 'Romantic' Religion – an Attempt to Define the Relationship between the Church and the Synagogue

Before we turn to the typology of 'classical' and 'romantic' religion in detail it will be necessary to analyse Baeck's inner development and the methodology of his inquiry over the decades. One will have to investigate his dependence on the intellectual climate of his time will as well as the criteria of selection that shape Baeck's idea of Protestantism and Christianity as a whole.

Cabbala and Mysticism as 'Romantic' Elements Within Judaism

During the 1920s a growing scholarly interest in mysticism is to be noticed. In order to clarify the position which Baeck actually held with regard to mysticism this section offers a more precise evaluation of his position.

Even before Gershom Scholem, Baeck discovered the significance of the mystical element in Judaism. It gives evidence for the depth of Baeck's commitment to Judaism that he, a liberal rabbi, felt increasingly drawn toward this strand in the Jewish tradition that had suffered almost total disregard in the period of emancipation. It is, however, an awareness that had to grow step by step. This process occurs in parallel with his estimation of Christianity. Baeck's scholarly work lay, above all, in the interpretation of Midrashic literature. Baeck opened himself to the world of Cabbala only after much initial reluctance. In his doctoral dissertation of 1895,[14] he spoke of the cabbalistic teaching of the seventeenth century as a 'mental delusion' *(Irrwahn)*.[15]

Heinrich Graetz, who had been a lecturer at the Breslau Rabbinic Seminary, which Baeck attended from 1891 onwards, had been even more outspoken in denouncing Cabbala. Baeck had learned from Heinrich Graetz's system of voluntarism, the living process of ethical action and rational thought that also enclosed within itself romanti-

---

13. Borowitz, *New Jewish Theology*, p. 79.
14. Baeck, *Spinozas erste Einwirkungen auf Deutschland* (Berlin, 1895).
15. Ibid., p. 71.

cism. But he did not share Graetz's harsh judgment and prejudices against Eastern Judaism and Hassidism.[16]

Baeck's attitude had hardly changed when ten years later, in 1905, he published *The Essence of Judaism.* Opposition to all mysticism, including its Jewish variety, is evident throughout the first edition of the work. The reason for this seems to have been more than the then common attitude towards Cabbala. The book, after all, had a particular purpose: the vindication of Judaism in the light of reason and ethics.

Like his intellectual predecessors Baeck was in sympathy with the theological trend of the period. However, he abhorred the intellectual antisemitism that prevailed in the Protestant theology at that time. Schleiermacher had described Judaism as 'dead', a mere 'imperishable mummy', and a 'sad legacy'[17] after its prophetic element declined and its Holy Books were closed. Adolf von Harnack, too, had come close to repeating this judgment in his celebrated lectures on the 'Essence of Christianity',[18] which presented Pharisaic Judaism in a picture of utter gloom (see chapter 3, 'The Essence of Christianity'). Leo Baeck rose to the challenge in a review[19] and blamed Harnack for having projected an idealised modern concept of religion upon the historical Jesus, who had been far more in accord with his native environment than Harnack wanted to admit. In his book *Das Wesen des Judentums,* which was his full-scale counterattack, Baeck no longer engaged in direct polemic but offered a portrayal of historical Judaism as the religion of ethical monotheism as such.

Considering the intellectual climate of the time as it has been described above, it is not surprising to find that this presentation of Judaism shows little awareness of the importance of mystical tradition. Baeck suggests that the harshness of historical reality gave rise to mystical yearnings at certain times. This theory of Jewish mysticism as a product of deep anxiety has been rejected, and rightly so, by Gershom Scholem.[20] *In Essence of Judaism* Baeck shows the polarity of Jewish religious experience: the oscillation between 'mystery' and 'commandment' *(Geheimnis und Gebot),* God's distance and nearness, freedom and strict order, oneness and otherness. In this 'tension' Baeck sees the very nature of Judaism and the deepest root of its vitality. God is experienced as ground of both the mystery and the commandment. Even more: the commandment itself bears witness to the mystery.

16. See Albert Friedlander, *Leo Baeck: Teacher of Theresienstadt* (London, 1973), p. 121.
17. Friedrich Schleiermacher, *Über die Religion* (Hamburg, 1958), p. 159.
18. Adolf von Harnack, *What is Christianity?* (Philadelphia, 1986).
19. Adolf von Harnack's 'Vorlesungen über das Wesen des Christentums', in *Monatsschrift für Geschichte und Wissenschaft des Judentums,* vol. XLV, p. 97–120.
20. Gershom Scholem, *Major Trends in Jewish Mysticism* (New York, 1946).

At the same time Baeck emphasises the primacy of the ethical element in Judaism. With Cohen he stresses the fact that Judaism is not merely ethical but that ethics constitute its very essence. The revelation of God and the revelation of the ethical task are one. In the act of revelation it is not the nature of God that is revealed but His will. Although Baeck agrees with Schleiermacher in giving feeling and sentiment a place in religion, he insists with Cohen: religion is no religion unless it is ethical. The Jewish religious experience is that of 'ethical sentiment'. In this combination, Baeck argues, that the autonomy of religion – as Schleiermacher had claimed it – can be safeguarded.

Myth is therefore categorically excluded from the Jewish realm. For Baeck, Judaism is the only religion that has produced no mythology proper inasmuch as myth imparts something about the fate of the gods and hardly anything about the duty of humankind. Even in Cabbala the main concern is the way of man and the doing of God's will.

One has to remember that around the turn of the century German Protestant theology was dominated by the school of Albrecht Ritschl. He rejected the mystically inclined theology of Schleiermacher as a relic of romanticism, and the Hegelian type of thinking as the imposition of an alien metaphysics upon theology. Ritschl and his followers pleaded for a return to Kant's view of religion as a non-mystical, non-metaphysical, purely practical and thus ethical concern.[21] This outlook greatly appealed to Leo Baeck, influenced as he was by Hermann Cohen.

In order to understand Baeck's reluctance with regard to mysticism one also has to be aware of the disruptive power of mystical thought and its tendency to question and destabilise identity. Baeck's concept, which has ethical monotheism at its heart, will inevitably run into problems with an approach that seeks an immediate link between God and human being rather than dividing the two and then providing the connecting element of ethical conduct.

The Concept of 'Essence'

Baeck's early attempts to explain Jewish mysticism certainly imply that mysticism is not by itself a part of the essence of Judaism. In fact, mystical movements are characterised as transient phenomena of relatively short duration. Baeck understood the essence of Judaism to have remained constant, rather than being subject to transformation. The curve of the essence may have fluctuated between high and low extremes but the essence never changed. So Baeck describes a process of regeneration rather than mutation *(Gestaltwandel)*. Besides

---

21. Karl Barth, *Protestant Thought: From Rousseau to Ritschl* (New York, 1959).

this, Baeck's concept of essence first of all involves the idea of a norm according to which all historical phenomena have to be judged.

In this connection the influence of his supervisor at Berlin university, Wilhelm Dilthey, seems to have been of decisive significance[22] (see chapter 6, 'Wilhelm Dilthey'). According to Dilthey the inner life of religion can be apprehended more deeply if one follows its development in the course of history through identification and experiential participation *(Erlebnis und Verstehen).* [23]It may perhaps be said that Troeltsch and Harnack follow this path to some extent.

By building up a comprehensive picture both Dilthey and Baeck tried to overcome the positivist restriction of historical understanding to the accumulation of material data. Dilthey's kind of approach was needed in order to do justice to Judaism as a historical entity. Baeck wanted to approach it with a comprehensive and sympathetic vision that would enhance its stability. *Das Wesen des Judentum* sets out to accomplish this aim. Two characteristics can be identified: its sense of morphological unity *(Gestalt)* and the determination to allow Judaism to describe itself as far as the inevitable intrusion of the subjective element permits it.

The search for the underlying essence of intellectual constructions came to Baeck through Dilthey as much as his recognition of the definite limitations of the psychological approach.[24] One starts off with the individual experience, but then moves on beyond it: 'The history of civilization and history of philosophy demonstrate how man's experiences with himself, this picture that the realms of his self seemed to show him, were the first creation, and how only from here a picture of the community and of the cosmos were built up.'[25] We have criticised this approach before: Dilthey's theory of interpretation based on self-identification with the historical sources seems to say more about oneself than about the character of the tradition that one tries to understand. The interpreter may not be aware of his/her subjectivity and thus unable to safeguard the reader against its excesses. What are the criteria to distinguish between the essential on the one side, the unessential and secondary on the other? The reader cannot tell whether or not the data presented represent the essence of a tradition. So Baeck's vision of an 'essence of Judaism' makes him appear almost authoritarian in his practice of

22. H.A. Hodges, *Wilhelm Dilthey: An Introduction* (London, 1949); John L. Mebust, *Wilhelm Dilthey's Philosophy of History* (Philadelphia, 1974).

23. Clara Misch (ed.), *Der junge Dilthey* (Leipzig, 1933), p.40.

24. Friedlander, *Leo Baeck,* pp. 63f.

25. Leo Baeck, 'The Psychological Root of the Law' (Wingate Lecture at the Hebrew University 1951), Hebrew University Garland, Norman Bentwich (ed.) (London, 1952), p. 13.

suppressing counter-evidence or ambiguities. It is here that Scholem made a radical break with the very concept of the 'essence of Judaism'. He held the position that a rather static concept of an 'essence' is not capable of dealing with a historical development.[26]

The way in which Baeck understood 'essence' both in a normative and total *Gestalt* sense reflects Troeltsch's discussion of the methodological problems raised by Harnack's *What is Christianity?*[27] One may ask, does Baeck take up Troeltsch's advice to develop the question of 'essence' into one of 'identity'?[28] In order to describe in a methodologically adequate way a dynamic process of the growth of tradition, Baeck later found a possible way out of the dilemma: in his second great work he speaks of 'Jewish existence' as the determining factor in a constant God-people relationship.[29]

To conclude: Baeck's research in the field of Jewish mysticism commands respect, but his chief merit lies in his effort as a theologian to integrate an awareness of Jewish mystical tradition into the very fabric of modern Jewish thought.

Before we look at Baeck's achievements in forming a distinct contribution to a modern Jewish theology we have to investigate his polarity model further. The poles of 'mystery' and 'commandment' can be identified as the root of the polar notions that sum up Baeck's view of man's basic religious questions.

The Polarity of Mystery and Commandment

The 1920s were an exceedingly creative period in Baeck's life. His most important essays were written in this time. In three lectures at the Darmstadt *'Schule der Weisheit'* ('School of Wisdom') under the chairmanship of Graf Hermann Keyserling Baeck presents most compelling philosophical statements bearing on Judaism. The conferences that were organised at the 'Schule der Weisheit' intended to discuss philosophical and ethical issues in the light of different cultural and religious

26. Against the use of 'essence' see Horst Bürkle, 'Das europäische Christentum und die nichtchristlichen Kulturen', in *ZfM* 1 (1985). See Hans-Werner Gensichen, 'Das Christentum im Dialog der Kulturen: Kontextualität und Universalität', in *ZfM* 1 (1985).

27. Ernst Troeltsch, 'Die christliche Welt', in *Gesammelte Schriften*, vol. II. (Tübingen, 1913).

28. In his essay 'Theologie und Geschichte' Baeck discusses Troeltsch's position seen against the rising reaction of dialectical theology. It is clear from this exposition that the driving force behind Troeltsch's system had remained alien to Baeck, who held the position that Judaism's essence had always kept its original character despite a rhythmic change of periods. See Stephen W. Sykes, 'Ernst Troeltsch and Christianity's essence', in *Ernst Troeltsch and the Future of Theology*, John Powell Clayton (ed.) (Cambridge, 1976), pp. 139–71.

29. Leo Baeck, *Dieses Volk: Jüdische Existenz*, 2 vols (Frankfurt am Main, 1955 and 1957).

backgrounds.[30] Baeck was invited as a Jewish thinker to enrich the variety of religious views. Two of his lectures are of special importance for our task. In the first lecture, called 'Geheimnis und Gebot'.[31] he declares that the polarity of mystery and commandment precluded any opposition between mysticism and ethics. Baeck obviously presumed a correlation to obtain between mysticism and mystery.[32]

What is even more interesting is the shift in the basic structure of the lectures. The one essence that manifests itself in the many historical forms of Judaism is now defined in the formula 'mystery and commandment' *(Geheimnis und Gebot)*, a concept of polarity that goes beyond Cohen's mere ethical monotheism. Cohen's 'correlation' of God and human being, if it is more than the correlation between ideas, leads to a tension in the religious life that Baeck could ultimately resolve only through this polarity of mystery and commandment. In response to this polarity human beings have to preserve a balance. They must neither submerge themselves in the mystery nor become mere keepers of the law. Both concepts have an intrinsic link. For the commandment proceeds from the ultimate ground of being, and the mystery appears in the unconditional 'thou shalt'.[33] It is here that Baeck stepped outside of Cohen's system.[34] It would seem that Baeck's sort of typology is bound to incur a certain formalisation which does violence to the fullness of historical variety.

In certain respects Baeck idealises Judaism and fails to take full account of the more erratic elements that can be found in certain strata of Jewish mysticism. Furthermore one could say that Halachic tradition is not given its due prominence. In contrast to other attempts to systematise Jewish theology in a slavish imitation of the Protestant model, Baeck's work appears nevertheless as a genuine presentation of authentic Judaism.[35]

30. Graf Hermann Keyserling, who also founded the 'Gesellschaft für freie Philosophie', doubted the European set of values and wanted to enrich European thinking by adding Chinese, Indian and other cultural traditions. See *Reisetagebuch eines Philosophen*, (Munich, 1913), enlarged edn (Munich, 1919). Further details given in Barbara Garthe, 'Über Leben und Werk des Grafen Hermann Keyserling' (unpublished dissertation, University Erlangen-Nuremberg, 1976).
31. Leo Baeck, *Wege im Judentum* (Berlin, 1933), p. 33–48.
32. See Baeck, 'Theologie und Geschichte', in *Aus drei Jahrtausenden*, p. 38. There, 'mysticism and ethics' is juxtaposed with 'mystery and commandment' (die Verborgenheit und die Forderung), which implies that mysticism corresponds to the mystery.
33. For a discussion of the concept of 'Geheimnis und Gebot', see Friedlander, *Leo Baeck: Teacher*, pp. 158–66.
34. Friedlander, *Leo Baeck: Teacher*, p. 154. For Tillich's affinity to the neo-Kantian correlation concept: Gunther Wenz, *Subjekt und Sein* (Munich, 1979), p. 20f.
35. See Kaufmann Kohler, *Grundriß einer systematischen Theologie des Judentums auf geschichtlicher Grundlage* (1910), reprinted (Hildesheim/New York, 1979). Besides

It is not surprising that Baeck deals with the theological concepts of Judaism not dogmatically or in the abstract but as expressions of human experience. In this approach he is following the Schleiermacher–Dilthey tradition. This means that he prefers to speak not of God but of the Jewish faith in God. Baeck is a psychologist of religion in the deep sense in which Dilthey understood the term as 'empathy' *(Verstehende Psychologie)*. In describing faith, he does not expound doctrine but shows how faith arises from a concern with the meaning of life. In discussing revelation, he again does not proceed doctrinally but deals with the prophetic experience as such. 'Not passages are to be interpreted but men are to be understood.' Do we hear some critique of traditonal Judaism here? At any rate we can feel a certain flexibility in Baeck's thought, which shows a shift of opinion about how the essentials of religion can be defined: by taking seriously the experiences of the individual within a community of faith and summarising the development that took place. Such a concept of de-dogmatisation is not without the danger of reducing everything to a humanist level. In his understanding of revelation Baeck has certainly links with Abraham Geiger, and bears an affinity to Franz Overbeck's concept of *Urgeschichte* as the breaking forth of some new vision unaccountable in terms of 'development'.[36] This does not necessarily abolish the 'mystery' of revelation but refrains from expressing it in traditional terms.

The second Darmstadt lecture dealt with 'polarity and tension'.[37] Two fundamentally disparate types of civilisation are defined: the Greek, which is fixed upon timeless perfection on the one hand, and on the other hand the Biblical view, which experiences the tension between the infinite ground of its being and the infinite task of perfecting the world.

Here Baeck lays the ground for his distinction between 'romantic Christianity' and 'classic Judaism'.

Classical and Romantic Religion

Christianity and the eastern religions are able to arouse a romantic interest. Geiger had characterised Christianity as the 'Mother of Romanticism', and Leo Baeck contrasted Judaism and Christianity as 'classical' and 'romantic religion' respectively. His basic attitude towards Christianity is best expressed in his long polemic essay

---

Baeck this is the other prominent attempt at a 'systematic theology of Judaism', which had exercised a lot of influence within the American Reform movement.

36. See Alexander Altmann, 'Zur Auseinandersetzung', p. 349 ff.

37. Originally 'Die Spannung im Menschen und der fertige Mensch' in *Der Leuchter*, IV (1923). The title is changed in *Wege im Judentum* (Berlin, 1933): 'Vollendung und Spannung'.

'Romantic Religion'.[38] In this essay Baeck differentiates two types of religion, the classical and the romantic. Judaism as classical religion in its ethical monotheism is contrasted to Christianity as romantic religion in its mystical, emotional faith. As the most important representatives of romantic religion, the contributions of Paul and Luther to romantic aspects of Christianity are discussed in detail as we will see later.

For Baeck romanticism derives from a sense of the indistinct Infinite to which the world is not *'Bild'* but *'Sinnbild'*, pointing to an inner life in nature and history beyond the grasp of reason. Symbolic form is therefore the very medium in which Romanticism expresses itself.

> Feeling is supposed to mean everything: this is the quintessence of romanticism ... Its danger, however, which it cannot escape is this: the all-important feeling culminates eventually in vacuity or in substitutes, or it freezes and becomes rigid. And before this happens, it follows a course which takes it either into sentimentality or into the phantastic; it dodges all reality, particularly that of the commandment, and takes refuge in passivity when confronted with the ethical task of the day.
>
> Empathy makes up for much and gives a freedom which is really a freedom from decision and independence from inner obligation.[39]

Baeck's essay 'Romantische Religion' was not so much concerned with purely theological views. It shows, however, his awareness that moral decisiveness was sadly missing in many German theologians. Baeck also uses the typological method in this context and identifies two types of religious experience. The one – called the classic – is positive, outgoing, spontaneous, ethical, social, action-orientated, rational. The other – the romantic – is passive, receptive, individualistic, self-centred, inward, concerned with faith and its content, confirming itself in emotions, emphasising grace.[40] Of course, such pure types exist only in abstraction, but to Baeck's mind history documents religions that are outstanding representatives of these possibilities. Judaism is described to come closest to the classic type while Christianity is the most conspicuous example of romantic religion.[41]

38. In *Festschrift zum 50 jährigen Bestehen der Hochschule für die Wissenschaft des Judentums* (Berlin, 1922).
39. Leo Baeck, 'Romantic Religion', in *Judaism and Christianity* (New York, 1958), p.290.
40. For a discussion of the general terms see Richard Benz, *Die deutsche Romantik: Geschichte einer geistigen Bewegung,* (Leipzig, 1937); Franz Schultz, *Klassik und Romantik der Deutschen,* 2 vols (Stuttgart, 1934/1940). Recently the antithetical polarity between romanticism and enlightenment has been disputed in favour of the more oscillating model of an 'intended perfection'; see Helmut Schanze, *Romantik und Aufklärung* (Nuremberg, 1976), and Wolfdietrich Rasch, 'Zum Verhältnis der Aufklärung zur Romantik', in *Romantik,* Ernst Ribbat (ed.) (Königstein/Taunus, 1979). Kurt Nowak, *Schleiermacher und die Frühromantik* (Weimar, 1986).
41. See Fritz Strich, *Deutsche Klassik und Romantik oder Vollendung und Unendlichkeit,* 1st edn (Munich, 1922). Strich not only identifies Christianity with romanticism

Baeck surveys the whole range of the Christian experience, Catholic as well as Protestant, so as to present what, from the viewpoint of the religion of reason, are its most undesirable features. He draws on the complete arsenal of polemic that had been built up by the Jewish apologists of the preceding century, particularly his neo-Kantian forebears. He continually contrasts the ethical monotheism of Judaism with the mysticism of grace in Christianity, to the obvious discredit of the latter.

Ultimately Baeck confronts here the German Lutheran church. The programmatic formula 'Sola fide' ('By faith alone') is interpreted as making the righteous human, being the creation of divine grace and not of his own moral actions. The faith of Paul, as seen again in Luther, is the decisive opposition to ethics: 'vitam sinas esse terram et doctrinam coelum'.[42] Doctrine and human life are strictly distinguished. For Luther, according to Baeck, actions whether moral or immoral cannot strengthen or take away the purity of doctrine.

In *The Essence of Judaism* Baeck had distinguished world religions as representing two basic types, the world-affirming and the world-rejecting. Judaism he considers the classic example of the former type and he calls it a religion of ethical optimism. Religions of all kinds, even of the other basic type such as Buddhism, can have ethical teachings. Their essential attitude towards the world, however, is withdrawal from it. Once this distinction is made, Baeck's more extensive polemic is carried out against Christianity which would seem to share Judaism's basic faith in God and the emphasis on the centrality of ethics. However, Baeck finds Christianity's self-understanding to be radically different from that of Judaism. In his opinion the ready subservience to power of his Christian contemporaries could be traced to the romanticism inherent in Pauline Christianity.[43]

Subjectivity is the problem of all seemingly 'objective' typologies, and Baeck's tendency to resort to private value judgments dominates the whole of his argument.

Why are there just two types, why are these the romantic and the classic, why are Judaism and Christianity the chief representatives, how would one have to assess the counter-evidence in both religions? For Baeck the answers to all these questions can simply be presupposed. Baeck does admit that Judaism has romantic elements

---

but also delineates a theory of polarity close to Baeck. See also Friedlander, *Leo Baeck*, p. 125.

42. *D. Martin Luthers Werke: Kritische Gesamtausgabe* (Weimar, 1883 onwards), vol. XIV, p. 464. Baeck quotes this in 'Romantische Religion', *Festschrift zum 50 jährigen Bestehen der Hochschule für die Wissenschaft des Judentums in Berlin* (Berlin, 1922), p. 38.

43. See Liebeschütz, *Von Simmel zu Rosenzweig*, p. 80.

and Christianity classical ones, but he does not investigate this to see how much his typology is likely to be mistaken or simplistic. Moreover, Baeck speaks of Judaism in terms of Reform Jewish theology as an ethical and rational faith. He does not, however, contrast this with a similar interpretation of Christianity but with a more traditional Protestantism and Catholicism, rather than, say, Harnack's interpretation which is so closely linked with Baeck's own roots. One could say that it remains doubtful whether Baeck was capable of presenting the church-synagogue relation satisfactorily.

Christianity within the Framework of Baeck's System of Polarity

Leo Baeck never dealt with Martin Luther exclusively. His analysis of Luther seems to be always integrated as part of his thoughts on Christianity as a whole. For this reason I believe it is important to understand Luther's teachings – as Baeck sees them – in the wider context of the framework of Baeck's system of polarity. We shall attempt to find possibilities of a structured approach to Baeck's critique and want to extract its underlying principle.

'Romantic' and 'Classical' as poles

According to Leo Baeck, Christianity, as well as Judaism, is a religion of historical revelation. They both appear to have the starting point in mystery and refer to an event from the past in order to determine and explain the further course of truth.[44] However, Baeck makes a fundamental distinction between the two religions: Judaism explains a beginning that continues beyond the present, relating also to the future; that is, it incorporates a Messianic component. The dawn of Christianity, on the other hand, represents the absolute goal in itself and the achievement of final redemption. To Baeck's mind the church sees the life and death of Jesus Christ as the sum total of all essential events. It is quite clear, then, that everything else in history can be judged only in relation to this: how it corresponds to this unsurpassable experience. Based on this assumption, Baeck assigns two terms to Judaism and Christianity, defining them as a 'classical' and a 'romantic' religion, respectively. We will have to analyse more precisely the origin of those terms and Baeck's intention when he introduces them.

Both types of religion have a 'foreboding knowledge of the irrational'[45] in common. But the way in which the irrational is experi-

---

44. Baeck, *Aus drei Jahrtausenden,* part I: 'Romantische Religion' (pp. 42–120), p. 65.
45. Ibid., p. 120. Parallels to Rudolf Otto's work seem obvious.

enced in this two types of religion is definitely different. Whereas in a romantic religion the self drowns in the ocean of irrationality, however, for the classical religion, the being, the real, the commanded, are revealed by the irrational. In this way, the irrational in Judaism becomes the basis for the real and the ideal, in the encounter of Creator and Creation.

It is Baeck's belief that every religion exhibits certain romantic elements. Each religion has a 'religious ideal' from which sensation, mood, subjectivity and joy exist ends in themselves.[46] But romantic religions seem to lack two characteristics of a classical religion: the will to master life through morality; and obedience to the commandments of practical reason. According to Baeck, though, a religion in which the romantic and classical elements are not balanced is dangerous.

Christianity as a 'Romantic Religion'

In Baeck's works the terms 'romantic' and 'classical' correspond to 'mystery' and 'commandment'.[47] Judaism exists in the tension between both experiences. Christianity, however, seems to have shed the commandment and to consist solely of the mystery, the mysterious. With this, the first moment in which one opens oneself to faith appears to represent the epitome of human life and at the same time a human being's salvation. For Baeck, there is no room in this idea for individual achievement in life. An attitude of faith seems to replace for him aspiration and striving; individuals can simply experience this faith, and can consider themselves complete.[48] To Baeck, this represents faith for faith's sake. And he makes it very clear to whom this statement refers, namely Paul, whom Baeck considers a mere Hellenistic thinker under the influence of Greek mys-

---

46. Ibid., p. 47.
47. For the identification of Christianity with 'mystery' see for example Baeck, 'Romantic Religion' in *Judaism and Christianity*, p. 189f.: 'Tense feelings supply its content, and it seeks its goals in the now mythical, now mystical visions of the imagination. Its world is the realm in which all rules are suspended.' For Judaism's characterisation by 'commandment' see for example Baeck, *The Essence of Judaism*, (Frankfurt 1930), p. 5 '... actions procuring salvation and gifts of grace are unknown to Judaism; it possesses no such effective actions to bring heaven down to earth. It has always kept within certain limits of sobriety and severity; it demands even more than it gives. That is why it adopted so many commandments, and refused sacraments and their mysteries ... Thus there was no necessity to create and to hand down any decisive formulas or creeds to guarantee stability and security... . In Judaism articles of faith never attained such importance; they were never a condition of salvation, and did not imply that if you accepted them you had all, if you rejected them you had nothing.'
48. Baeck, *Aus drei Jahrtausenden*, pp. 110–11.

tery religions.[49] It is Paul who stands in opposition to the Gospels and Jesus, whom Baeck assigns to the Jewish sphere.

Consequently, Baeck opposes everything in the church which seems to be influenced by Pauline thought. This applies to Augustine, as well as to Luther, both of whom Baeck considers as part of Pauline thought and as further developments of Pauline shortcomings. Baeck's 'romantic' religion is above all 'Pauline' religion. The traces of Judaism and the Biblical-Jewish traditions present in the Christian church are the voices of 'classical' religion.

A characteristic distinction is made: the active, ethical element of Judaism, with its emphasis on the personal on the one hand, and the passive, magical sacramental element of Pauline belief, with its transformation of the individual into the metaphysical, on the other.[50] The religion of the romantics is understood to be solely receptive. Because their faith is always passive, it is simple for them to feel 'complete'. The religion is not based upon the appealing or commanding laws of God, but rather is persistent in the expectation of the gift of God's grace. 'Activity fights for everything, passivity has everything ... The only activity of a genuine romantic person is self-congratulation on his state of grace.'[51]

For this reason, Baeck claims, romantic religion loses the ability to develop an ethic. Ethics were abandoned with the receiving of the commandment.[52] With regard to Protestantism, Baeck declares that an ethic could not be part of the essence of the religion, but is merely added on to it.[53] Classical religion, however, constantly urges believers towards God's commandments as the ultimate goal, uniting all humanity.[54] 'In classical religion man is to become free

---

49. Paul as a Hellenist, cf. Baeck, ibid., p. 50ff. (1922); Paul as a Jewish apostle, cf. Baeck, *Dieses Volk: Jüdische Existenz*, vol. II, p. 190.

50. Baeck, *Aus drei Jahrtausenden*, part II: 'Judentum in der Kirche' (pp. 121–40), p. 132.

51. Baeck, 'Romantic Religion', in *Judaism and Christianity*, pp. 210f. The polarity of 'activity' versus 'passivity' in the form presented seems striking to me. Even more so, as its underlying Kantian root does not really foster Baeck's extreme position. In order to make this more clear I would like to replace those terms by 'spontaneity' and 'receptiveness'. According to Kant any active work of cognition is fundamentally based on receptiveness, which explicitly does not include or presuppose any theoretical perception of God.

However, a harmonious balance between activity and passivity is something that Baeck himself would quite like to assume for Judaism. We may thus conclude that his system of polarity merely hints at theoretical extremes that are really not applicable to reality.

52. Baeck, ibid., p. 269.

53. Baeck, 'Das Judentum in der Kirche', in *Aus drei Jahrtausenden*, p. 135.

54. Baeck, 'Romantic Religion' in *Judaism and Christianity*, p. 292.

through the commandment; in romantic religion he has become free through grace.'[55]

Baeck describes the development of Judaism as the path gradually to overcome the miraculous notions of 'childhood'.[56] On the contrary, Christianity as romantic religion revived the faith in miracles and made it a constant and a central concept of religion.

In summarising, the following picture emerges: Christianity, as far as it corresponds to the romantic-Pauline ideology of religion, demonstrates absolute dependence. Freedom is granted to humanity out of mercy, and each person remains on the receiving end. Such faith, however, means a totally static position, which cannot allow any development beyond it.

On the other hand, in classical Jewish religion, freedom is the goal to be achieved through the commandments. Individuals must actively develop themselves. Although they are always bound by their being God's creation, they nevertheless play an active role in the relationship between God and humanity.[57] Faith is an individual's life work: to work[58] for 'goodness' on earth for the sake of God's honour.[59]

Baeck's system of opposing types of religion has consequences for the faith of the individual. In the following chapters we will analyse the constitution of the individual before God in Lutheranism and in Judaism, as Baeck presents them in quite a particular way.

---

55. Ibid., p. 211.
56. Ibid., p. 227.
57. Ibid., p. 284.
58. Ibid., p. 211.
59. Baeck, *Wege im Judentum*, part 5: 'Heimgegangene des Krieges. Über den preußischen Staat', pp. 382–400 (1919), here p. 387.

Chapter 8

DIFFERENCE CREATES IDENTITY – LEO BAECK AND MARTIN LUTHER'S THOUGHT

The Debate on the Constitution of the Individual before God

Leo Baeck's Exposition of the Teachings of Martin Luther

The following paragraphs are intending to give a structured outline of Baeck's understanding of Martin Luther's thoughts. It must be kept in mind that Luther did not present a systematic theology in the ordinary sense that would cover the *theologoumena* that are touched here without being misleading; there is also no doubt that my summary will in itself bear an interpretation of what I think that Baeck understood when he refers to Luther's words. In any case, I shall try to remain faithful to Baeck's wording in order to make my reconstruction as accurate as possible.

The Individual and Original Sin

According to Baeck's interpretation of Luther's views, original sin stands above the abilities of an individual. It is in his understanding the determining force and the unyielding definition of humankind. Sin is not in the person, but rather the person is within original sin. Neither the individual nor humanity as a whole caused the original sin, nor do they have the ability to remove it. Mortals are powerless, at the mercy of original sin. Because sin is so integral to the nature of humankind, only an act beyond this realm of nature – that is, a miracle – can eliminate sin. Thus, sin is overcome through God's grace, through a redeemer.[1] In this interpretation, however, it seems to Baeck that the individual is condemned to a totally passive role. It is not the individual who seeks and strives, wins or loses; rather, the struggle takes place in and for the individual. In this way, religion becomes redemption from the will and liberation from the deed.[2]

Commandment and Grace

It is somewhat awkward that Baeck refers to Matthew 5:18 and Gal. 3:24 when he attempts to explain the Pauline understanding of the law. The law as the principle of the Bible remains valid up to the moment of redemption. Because Paul sees Christ as the redeemer, redemption has taken place and is present in faith and baptism. However, to postulate any further obligatory nature of the laws would then be to deny that this salvation had taken place.[3] However, Paul and Luther did not merely oppose something ceremonial. 'Law' is for them any valuation of human activity, even the most moral. 'Whoever expects the good from the fulfillment of the commandments and duties, still lives under the yoke of the Law.'[4]

Whereas earlier, only darkness surrounded the spirit, now divine grace guarantees to show the light that guides humankind to its prescribed goal: to become perfected individuals.[5] But the commandment is lifted for the complete and perfect individual. Those who judge themselves as just will find themselves on the path leading away from justice. To Baeck's mind Luther expresses it as follows: to 'befoul oneself' with the law.[6]

The law is lifted through faith in Jesus Christ as the Redeemer.[7] For Baeck, this signifies the rejection of moral freedom which makes goodness, as realised by the individual, possible for the individual.

Righteousness Solely on the Basis of Faith

Christian righteousness flows from faith in the son of God ('Justitia christiana est fiducia in Filium Dei')[8] and is not to be identified with

1. Baeck, 'Romantic Religion', in *Judaism and Christianity*, pp. 243f.
2. Baeck, *Aus drei Jahrtausenden*, p. 123.
3. Ibid., p. 205.
4. Baeck, 'Romantic Religion', in *Judaism and Christianity*, p. 249.
5. Ibid., pp. 206, 210.
6. Ibid. p. 242, quoted from Erl.,WA 17 I, p. 111. 'Also das ein rein hertz haben nicht allein heisse nichts unreins gedencken, sondern wenn durch Gottes wort das gewissen erleucht und sicher wird, das sichs nicht besuddelt am gesetz. Also das ein Christen wisse, das yhm nicht schadet, ob er es halte odder nicht, und thuet wol, das sonst verbotten ist, odder lessit, das sonst geboten ist, ist yhm keins suënde, Denn er kan keine thun, weil das hertz reine ist.'
7. WA 40 I, p. 672: 'Quare credentibus in Christum tota lex abrogata est'.
8. WA 40 I, p. 366: 'Christiana iustitia coram deo est credere in filium. Sic Abraham

righteous action.[9] This is because Christ fulfilled the law for human-kind.[10] And the Gospel is a doctrine which does not allow for any law: 'Est ergo evangelium doctrina talis quae nullam legem admittit.'[11] This is what Baeck reads in Luther, drawing the conclusion that by conscious referral back to Paul, Luther taught unconditional original sin,[12] the totality of divine grace,[13] corresponding to complete passivity on the part of humanity.[14] The individual does not recognise God, God merely recognises him, Baeck says.[15] And in the certainty of salvation, Luther seems to deny any value to work and human action and reduces everything to a dependence solely on grace and faith: there is no room left, Baeck claims, for individual moral action and the duty of shaping the world.[16]

Salvation on the basis of faith seems not to be achieved through specific acts, but to be received solely through that which was determined in the beginning.[17] Morality itself remains void of any religious meaning. Baeck cites Luther:

> I live as I live; that does not make the doctrine false. We must not consider and judge the life, but the doctrine. Even if the life is not so pure, the doctrine can remain pure nevertheless, and one can be patient with the life.[18]

'By faith alone' could mean only the following for Luther: without action, even anti-action:

---

in semen. vel fides est fiducia cordis per Christum in Deum.' Baeck quotes from Erl-Irmischer I, p. 334: '... christianam justitiam proprie ac diserte sic definire, quod sit fiducia in filium Dei, seu fiducia cordis per Christum in Deum.'

9. Baeck, 'Romantic Religion', in *Judaism and Christianity*, p. 244; WA 1, p. 84

10. WA 1, p. 105.

11. Erl-Irmischer II, p. 113. However in WA 40 I, p. 141: 'Ideo Evangelium solum revelat filium Dei. Est ergo doctrina vel cognitio in qua nulla penitus lex est.'

12. Baeck, 'Judentum in der Kirche', in *Aus drei Jahrtausenden*, p. 134; 12. WA 42, p. 106

13. WA 24, p. 244. 'Es mus von hymel und allein aus gnaden komen, das Gott durch die verheissung des Euangelions das hertz trifft, das es fuelet und muesse sagen, das es vor nye bedacht odder ynn synn genomen habe, das yhm solche gnade solt widderfaren.'

14. WA 6, p. 530; WA 2, p. 420; cf. Leo Baeck, *Epochen jüdischer Geschichte* (Stuttgart, 1974), p. 119. 'Recte ergo dixi, oportere ergo hominem de suis operibus diffidere et velut paralyticum remissis manibus et pedibus gratiam operum artificem implorare.'

15. Baeck, 'Romantic Religion', in *Judaism and Christianity*, p. 204.

16. Baeck, *Wege im Judentum* (Berlin, 1933), p. 385.

17. Baeck, 'Romantic Religion', in *Judaism and Christianity*, pp. 203f., cf. p. 85; WA 24, p. 18: 'Denn ein solch mensch mus allen dingen gestorben seyn, dem guten und bösen, dem tod und leben, der hell und dem hymel und von hertzen bekennen, das er aus eygnen krefften nichts vermag.'; DB 7, p. 23: 'Zu Rom. 9–11 'leret er von der ewigen Versehung Gottes, Daher es ursprunglich fleusset, wer gleuben, oder nicht gleuben sol, von suënden los, oder nicht los werden kann. Damit es je gar aus unsern henden genomen, und alleine in Gottes hand gestellet sey, das wir frum werden.'

18. Baeck, 'Romantic Religion', in *Judaism and Christianity*, p. 252; WA 24, p. 607 (falsely cited by Baeck as p. 606).

You do not owe it to God to do anything except believe and profess. In all other matters he releases you and leaves you free to do as you please without any danger of conscience.[19]

This reads as though the more sin there is, the more opportunity for God's divine grace exists to prove its strength. In this context Baeck sees Luther recommending the famous 'fortiter pecca' ('sin bravely') in 1521 to Melanchthon. To him it appears to be by no means ironic, but, on the contrary, deeply imbued with Pauline doctrine.[20]

We may question here whether or not Luther's concept is really identical with Paul's. Christian Luther studies have for decades tried successfully to present us with a considerably more differentiated picture of the two. However, Baeck's fervour may again be a product of his highly structural confrontation of classical and romantic elements within religions. In any case, Luther himself may have rightly pointed out what he explained about action, for example in his *Sermon von den guten Werken*. Truly, humankind's only viable action in its relationship to God can be faith. This faith, however, constitutes the freedom to act in whatever way is requested.

It is thus quite important to note the priority of conscience within the acquired state of faith. In some respects Baeck and Luther may not even be so far apart in their approach to everyday moral behaviour as it would seem at first sight. Strictly speaking, the dividing line really emerges when the question of redemption arises: whether or not God had to bring Jesus Christ as the driving force of humankind's salvation, and whether or not the old path of biblical commandment could retain its validity. This question is at the heart of Judaism's identity crisis since Paul. Baeck enters the Jewish-Christian battlefield armed with enlightenment thoughts when he focuses on the value and priority of moral action based on an individual free will.

Free Will

To Baeck it is obvious: the faith of those who must wait as a lame person awaits healing is not an expression of deep conviction and of certainty which emerges from seeking and researching. According to Baeck, Luther's true insight works *within* the individual, rather than being brought into existence *by* the individual.[21] And, as there is no active choice for faith and healing in Christianity, there is no choice concerning the will, for the will of the individual is always the

19. WA 12, p. 131; cf. WA 17 I, p. 111 (cf. footnote 20).
20. Baeck, 'Romantic Religion', in *Judaism and Christianity*, p. 252.
21. WA 10 I 2, p. 29. 'Darumb lerne hie auß dem Euangelio, wie es tzugehet, wenn gott ansehet uns frum tzu machen, und wilchs der anfang sey, frum tzu werden. Es ist keyn ander anfang, denn das deyn konig tzu dyr kome und fahe ynn dyr an...'

will to sin.[22] The human being can do nothing but sin.[23] There is no allowance for a gradual approach to the truth. The flow of grace alone gives the individual the sum of knowledge and total insight.[24] So romantic religion really asks for the sacrifice of the intellect. To say it with Luther: 'In all who have faith in Christ reason shall be killed; else faith does not govern them; for reason fights against faith.'[25] With this, knowledge must make itself subordinate to faith, 'credo quia absurdum' – 'I believe because it is absurd.'

At the instant of receiving faith, the individual is like a mere tool of a higher power.[26] Life is heteronomy and at the same time, the omniscient and the blind face each other irreconcilably.

Salvation to a State of Grace through Word and Sacrament

If one follows Baeck's approach, it is quite logical that happiness or grace is made to be the epitome of a fulfilled Christian life, the rhyme and reason of being. This state of grace clearly comes from divine grace and not as a result of moral action. Faith which does not require the completion of any tasks set by God refers back to the self and, therefore, becomes a yearning for bliss.[27] The individual asks selfishly if, when and how redemption will be granted. This leads to a 'sentimental brooding about sinfulness',[28] as often seems typical of Protestantism, making it, according to Baeck, a doctrine of the salvation of the self. The sacraments offer this self-assurance, creating the individual's state of grace.[29] Bread, wine and holy water become supernatural substances, through which faith flows and the individual is transformed, purified and renewed.[30] On the other hand, Baeck cites the Reformer Kaspar Schwenckfeld, who reproaches Luther, saying that he 'will not let anybody become blessed without an external thing'.[31]

In Baeck's eyes baptism and holy communion are, for Luther, not symbols, but rather supernatural realities. And the same is the case

22. However, cf. Kant's 'You can because you ought to' in Baeck, 'Romantic Religion', in *Judaism and Christianity*, p. 254.
23. WA 10 I2, p. 29. "... du kanst nichts denn sundigen, thu wie du wilt. ... unnd must sundigen, wo du alleyn wirckst auß freyem willen.'
24. Baeck, 'Romantic Religion', in *Judaism and Christianity*, p. 205.
25. Ibid., p. 207; see WA 47, p. 328 (quoted from Erlangen edn).
26. Baeck, 'Romantic Religion', in *Judaism and Christianity*, p. 208.
27. Ibid., p. 285f.
28. Ibid., p. 278.
29. Baeck, 'Romantic Religion', in *Judaism and Christianity*, p. 225.
30. WA 6, p. 538: 'Sicut enim verbum dei potens erst, dum sonat, etiam impii cor immutare, quod non minus est surdum et incapax quam ullus parvulus, ita per orationem Ecclesiae offerentis et credentis, cui omnia possibilia sunt, et parvulus fide infusa mutatur, mundatur et renovatur.' (falsely cited by Baeck as p. 539).
31. Baeck, 'Romantic Religion', in *Judaism and Christianity*, p. 226.

with the 'word of God'. This 'word' does not merely *mean* something, it is significant and effective in itself and solely by being preached. 'That you should hear and receive the word is not by your strength, but by the grace of God which makes the gospel bear fruit in you that you may have faith in it.' [32]

As constitution of faith, the 'word' descends upon humanity; and without any action on their part, human beings are brought to accept it. Through 'word' and sacrament, they are taken and placed within the realm of salvation, no longer asking what tasks they are to do, but whether redemption has already been granted.

Baeck's View of the Constitution of the Individual before God

As demonstrated in the previous chapters the individual's constitution before God according to Luther's teachings is viewed by Baeck as a state of passivity, as a mere awaiting of God's grace. This contradicts Baeck's concept of responsibility of a human being and his concept of life. According to Baeck, the meaning of life consists of two spiritual experiences that are joined together in Judaism: the mystery and the commandment.[33] In the mystery, the individual is shown the deeper reality which is hidden below the surface of one's life.

> he becomes conscious that he was created, brought into being – conscious of an undetectable and, at the same time, protective power. He experiences that which embraces him and all else. He experiences, in the words of the ancient metaphor in the Blessing of Moses, 'the arms of eternity.'[34]

While the mystery raises the question of the meaning of life, the commandment raises the question of its goal. The commandment is the unconditional demand that grasps humanity totally.[35] Pressuring, victorious, absolute and independent, the commandment passes from generation to generation on into the future.[36] It is grounded in the being, the eternal, the unfathomable, and appears to humanity as that which blesses, is creative and is fertile.[37] 'The realm of the commandment is a realm of revelation and as such a realm of grace.'[38]

It is Baeck's firm belief that both mystery and commandment come from the one God and neither can exist without the other.

32. Ibid., p.225. Luther's Works, Erlangen edn., 10 (2), 12.
33. Leo Baeck, 'Geheimnis und Gebot' in *Wege in Judentum* (Berlin, 1933), part 1: Geheimnis und Gebot, pp. 33–48 (1921–22); cited in the English form 'Mystery and Commandment', in *Judaism and Christianity*, pp. 171–85.
34. Ibid., p. 171.
35. Baeck, 'Zwischen Wittenberg und Rom', in *Wege in Judentum*, pp. 270–87 (1931), here p. 280.
36. Baeck, 'Mystery and Commandment', in *Judaism and Christianity*, p. 178f.
37. Ibid., p. 179.
38. Baeck, *Dieses Volk*, vol. 1, p. 103.

Without the certainty of the mystery, there can be a moral structure consisting of teachings of wisdom and counsels of reason, but the unchangeable and categorical nature of the commandment would remain unfathomable for humanity.[39] The mystery and the experience of faith is that which gives birth to a religion. But it still is not all of religion, any more than birth is equivalent to life.[40]

Faith and freedom in Judaism, according to Baeck, do need the tension of the polarity of mystery and commandment, for the infinite appears in the finite, and whatever is finite bears witness to the infinite.[41] Such a relationship between mysticism and ethics is not one of conflict, but represents a necessary combination on the way to God. For Baeck the goal of life is righteousness before God: through work and achievement, through the fulfilment of one's duty and the struggle for the commandment. Rather than creating a clear conscience, religion should constantly unsettle and challenge it. Only then can it really be religion. It must be able and determined to offer resistance to every power possible, in the name of defending the eternal.[42]

To Baeck, the religious consciousness is moulded by the experience of closeness to God, not by a special status relative to God which some individuals hold out of divine grace.[43] Human beings live with humility before God, in full knowledge of their absolute dependence and with a reverence for the ethically superior that demands and directs,[44] speaks and requires a reply – man's decision – and brings them joy.[45]

According to Baeck, human life exists in the tension between desire and duty. 'Ye shall be unto me a kingdom of priests and a holy nation' is a phrase that has acquired in Judaism the character of a religious confession.[46] Faith does not turn away from the world. It does not await salvation from the world and its days. On the contrary, it is faith in the world and the certainty that all possible opposites will be reconciled. It is redemption not from the world, but in the world. This world should be sanctified and therefore, raised up to the Kingdom of God.

'Holy' and 'profane' are, therefore, inseparably joined. In essence, there is no mundane life; nothing is 'the mere world', God is in everything,[47] He permeates the whole of life. All future is a future of the commandments – a future in which it is realised and

39. Baeck, *Wege im Judentum*, p. 280.
40. Baeck, 'Romantic Religion', in *Judaism and Christianity*, p. 210.
41. Baeck, 'Mystery and Commandment', in *Judaism and Christianity*, p. 175.
42. Baeck, 'Zwischen Wittenberg und Rom', in *Wege in Judentum*, p. 287.
43. Leo Baeck, *The Essence of Judaism*, 6th edn (London,1936), p.44f.
44. Baeck, *Wege im Judentum*, part 1, p. 34.
45. Baeck, *Dieses Volk*, vol. 1, p. 57.
46. Baeck, Leo, *The Essence of Judaism*, (1936) p. 45.
47. Baeck, 'Mystery and Commandment', in *Judaism and Christianity*, p. 292.

fulfilled,[48] which thrives through the path it takes, not through miracles, myth or fate. In the days of the Messianic age, the spirit of God will live unchallenged in the hearts of humanity. At that time all commandments and obligations will cease to exist, for duty will have become part of the innermost nature of the individual. God's will will become our own and in that sense, our will will become one with the divine will.[49]

Religion and the State

The Lutheran State Church

To understand Baeck's critical views on Luther's teaching of the 'two kingdoms' and the 'kingdom of God', we first have to give a short survey of the Lutheran church in Prussia as experienced by Baeck. Leo Baeck sees the 'police state which makes all decisions for the people' as a direct development from Lutheranism. Coining the term, Baeck says it has become the 'Prussian religion', combining an inflexible sense of authority and subject with a Christian world view, relegating ethics, however, to the private sphere.[50]

With its church state and state church, the ruling sovereign of the state being at the same time the *summus episcopus* (highest bishop) of the Protestant church, Lutheranism had a decisive influence in Prussia and represented the conservative, one is even tempted to call it 'destructive', power. Opposition against this development during the same time period was the driving force of the Enlightenment and Kantian philosophy.[51] Through such a connection to the state, Lutheranism neglected to represent a universal message, not taking advantage of the chance to become a world religion. The idea of the kingdom of God took on a secondary role to the confessional state.

Baeck refers quite simplistically to Ernst Troeltsch's term 'Christian society' as the goal of Protestant efforts, which had actually been used far earlier by F.J. Stahl and the conservative 'Kreuzzeitung'.[52] However, with the church being taken over by the state, a beginning of protest took on a rather non-Protestant end.

Baeck sees the period following the First World War as a turning point of Protestantism. The revolution of 1918 was an unexpected shock for the Protestant church.[53] Not only did the alliance with the

48. Baeck, 'Romantic Religion', in *Judaism and Christianity*, p. 120.
49. Ibid., p.241.
50. Baeck, *Wege im Judentum*, p. 386.
51. Ibid., p.384.
52. Baeck, 'Volksreligion und Weltreligion', *Wege im Judentum*: pp. 195–207 (1931), here p. 204. See also Richard Rothe's works in the second half of the nineteenth century.
53. See Hans-Walter Krumwiede, *Evangelische Kirche und Theologie in der Weimarer*

state fall apart, the Protestant church had to come to an agreement with the new democratic or even revolutionary powers of the new democracy. The Protestant church lost its state support and at the same time, a living piece of its certainty and ideals.[54]

The state as the purpose of history (Hegel), Baeck claims, never represented a doctrine of faith nor a justification.[55] Following the collapse of the old meaning of the state,[56] it seemed to Baeck that Protestantism needed not only a new means of support, but also new content. But how did this connection between throne and altar develop? Leo Baeck sees the roots in Luther's teachings of two kingdoms.

On Luther's 'Two Kingdoms': The Individual between Church and State

The teaching of the 'two kingdoms' is one of the most important and at the same time one of the most disputed aspects of Lutheran Protestant theology. Its importance derives from focusing on the basic distinction of law and gospel. This, however, fosters the tendency of isolating areas that actually belong together and, by this, isolating political life from ethical norms.[57] It is my intention to give a short introduction to the doctrine of the 'two kingdoms' and then focus on Baeck's interpretation.

In a classical sense, Augustine had already divided the living sphere of human beings into two realms. Through birth, the individual is placed into the world of the mundane, the '*civitas terrana*', a world determined by calculating, counting and weighing. Solely through the unfathomable grace of God can the individual enter the '*civitas dei*', the sphere of God. But only the few are chosen; the masses, the '*massa perditionis*', are condemned to eternal death. The human being is relegated in this view to the earthly sphere, and only through the passive fact of being chosen can the individual be lifted beyond this sphere by God's hand. The two kingdoms stand in opposition and only the miracle of divine election can raise an individual from the lower to the higher realm.[58] Baeck sees Luther as directly dependent on Augustine. In his view Luther appears to be primarily Augustine's student and successor.[59] Luther even, so he

---

Republik, Grundtexte zur Kirchen- und Theologiegeschichte 2 (Neukirchen-Vluyn, 1990), p. 10.

54. Baeck, *Wege im Judentum*, p. 271.

55. Ibid., pp. 271f.

56. Ibid., p. 383.

57. A complete discussion of the teaching of the 'two kingdoms' is given in Heinz-Horst Schrei (ed.), *Reich Gottes und Welt: Die Lehre Luthers von den zwei Reichen*, Wege der Forschung 108, (Darmstadt, 1969); here p. IX.

58. Leo Baeck, *Epochen jüdischer Geschichte* (Stuttgart, 1974), p.118f.

59. Baeck, 'Judentum in der Kirche', *Aus drei Jahrtausenden*, p. 133: 'die katholische

assumes, intensifies the teachings of the individual's total dependence on the mercy of God '*sicut cadaver*': the individual must await
the grace of God passively, like a corpse. Where election lies outside
the realm of human decision and freedom, where the individual is
condemned on the basis of original sin unless touched by God's
grace, there the human community must be based on social constraints. According to Baeck, there is no motivation,[60] not even the
opportunity for independent, free moral action.

Baeck cites a well-known quotation from the Middle Ages: '*homo
est animal bipes quod vult cogi*' – the individual is a two-legged being
that needs to be subjected to force.[61] This world of the lost and the
rejected can be ruled only by violence. Even on the basis of its own
assumptions, Lutheranism was, according to Baeck, never in the
position of creating a system of ethics founded on religion.[62] For
Baeck, Luther's secular world is the place for morality. As the '*custos
utriusque tabulae*',[63] the ruling sovereign within his disciplinary powers had the responsibility to enforce matters of morality. In this way
the individual was assigned to two spheres. On the one hand was the
'spiritual individual' who had faith, and on the other hand was the
'civil individual' who kept the commandments. Baeck saw this division as the inherent religious and ethical weakness of Luther's doctrine. Morality is that which the authorities demand.

> Moral demands are thus no longer commandments or categorical imper-
> atives, but mere directions: either decrees of the constituted authorities or
> 'counsels of the conscience' of those who have heard a call. The doctrine
> of morality becomes a doctrine of individual cases, and the study or sci-
> ence of it approximates jurisprudence and becomes a matter of interpre-
> tation and legality.[64]

But that is not all. Luther established his church with the assistance of the secular rulers, and it became more and more based on
the authority and the protection of the state.[65] A visible church and
state are joined in Lutheranism.[66] This sort of religion cannot exist
without the state, for the authority of the state and of the church lie
in the same hands. The ruling sovereign is at the same time the head

---

Kirche dagegen "kam doch immer wieder zu einem duldenden Einvernehmen
mit einer Art von Semi-Pelagianismus.'"
60. Baeck, *Wege im Judentum*, p. 385.
61. Baeck, *Epochen*, p. 120.
62. Baeck, *Aus drei Jahrtausenden*, p. 135f.
63. An expression used by Melanchthon, cf. Baeck, *Wege im Judentum*, p. 386 and
Dieses Volk, vol. 1, p. 103.
64. Baeck, 'Romantic Religion', in *Judaism and Christianity*, p. 267f.
65. Baeck, *Wege im Judentum*, pp. 384f.
66. Leo Baeck, 'Helfer und Lehrer. Über Mittelalter und neue Zeit', *Wege im Judentum*,
pp. 401–22 (1927), here p. 403.

of the church. With that, the state is granted absolute rule.[67] 'Let every soul be subject unto the higher powers', for they reign by authority of God's commandment.[68]

Luther appears to be filled with a deep pessimism regarding the world in its sinful state.[69] This corresponds to an inflexible and fatalistic sense of subservience, of subordination of social classes as a divine institution. The human being must be resigned in accepting the life and work circumstances he or she is born into. One is not allowed to tamper with the rigid barriers of caste and guild. Dependence and class as willed by God represent strict Lutheran thought.[70] The motivation for social drive is lacking, and work and cultural life are devalued.[71] The principle of being 'complete' discourages any advancement.

Baeck denounces Luther's lack of optimism as the most significant evil in his interpretation of the individual between state and church. If the Messiah has already come and salvation has already been granted, then any hope for the future loses its meaning, to a large degree, and any urge to shape and better the world lacks a goal.[72]

'The Kingdom of God' according to Leo Baeck

In view of the Lutheran state-church alliance, Leo Baeck poses what he considers the highest questions of truth and freedom: does religion assist in achieving a 'clear conscience' by making a pact with all forms of power, even evil ones, for the sake of the demands of present? Or is religion capable of resisting and determined to resist for the sake of eternity?[73]

Baeck refers to the two realms and says that they do not oppose each other, but are intertwined, for 'the one realm should penetrate the other, influencing and determining it'.[74] The higher realm con-

---

67. Baeck, *Aus drei Jahrtausenden*, p. 136.
68. Leo Baeck, *Spinozas erste Einwirkungen auf Deutschland*: Inaugural Dissertation (Friedrich-Wilhelms-Universität Berlin) (Berlin 1895), p. 8; and Baeck, 'Romantic Religion', in *Judaism and Christianity*, pp. 213f. This is almost a quote from Romans 13:1.
69. Baeck, *Wege im Judentum*, p. 387.
70. Baeck, 'Romantic Religion', in *Judaism and Christianity*, p. 213; and Baeck, *Wege im Judentum*, p. 385.
71. Only the rejection of monastic idleness moved Luther to show some esteem for secular work.
72. Baeck, 'Romantic Religion', in *Judaism and Christianity*, pp. 285f.; and Baeck, *Aus drei Jahrtausenden*, p. 136.
73. Baeck, *Wege im Judentum*, p. 287.
74. Baeck, *Epochen*, pp. 119ff. See more closely Luther's idea of 'Königsherrschaft Christi' (Christ as King of both heavenly and earthly spheres); Ernst Wolf, 'Die Königsherrschaft Christi und der Staat', in Werner Schmauch and Ernst Wolf, *Königsherrschaft Christi: Der Christ im Staat*, Theologische Existenz heute N.S. 64 (Munich, 1958), pp. 20–61.

tinually enters the lower one in, the form of the commandment to touch humankind. The commandment includes goodness, devotion, selflessness, faith and reconciliation. 'Being chosen' is not passive, being chosen by divine grace, but an acceptance of God's call: 'Now if you obey me fully and keep my covenant, then out of all nations you will be my treasured possession. For mine is the whole earth.'[75]

This depicts the freedom of the individual very clearly. Each person has the ability to grasp or to waive the chance to be chosen, according to his or her own will. The commandment grasps individuals in the earthly realm and assists them in lifting themselves to the higher one. Both worlds are connected to each other, as expressed in the second section of the 'Amidah' prayer: '... to order the world through the Kingdom of the Almighty'. The kingdom of God, therefore, enters the earthly realm, so that the realm to come can begin for the people in the here and now. The dawn of the future starts in the present. The way to the higher realm, however, must be made by each individual, wherever he or she is at that moment. Deutero-Isaiah appeals for this in his call 'Clear the way!'[76]

All action should be taken for the sake of God and not the state. Absolute independence of religion from the state is to Baeck's mind extremely significant. The Lutheran Reformation, however, placed religion in the hands of the state.[77] It is not difficult to note that in the context of the Weimar Republic Baeck's view is concentrated on conservative Lutheranism with its mentality of perseverance and grievance over the abdication of the monarchic system. The full picture emerges only when one includes culture Protestantism, which must be considered as quite a notable minority in the Protestant spectrum of the Weimar Republic with influences on the German church up until now.

Representatives such as Otto Baumgarten, Martin Rade or Hermann Mulert welcomed the revolution of 1918 and the emerging Weimar Republic as an opportunity for the church to liberate itself from the alienating alliance with the state. The theological and ecclesiastical consequences gave a chance for redirection towards the 'actual' goals of Protestantism.

Analysis

Leo Baeck: Representative of Jewish Theology?

Leo Baeck's picture of Judaism comes, on the one hand, from the spirit of rabbinical tradition and, on the other hand, from the pat-

75. Ex. 19:5.
76. Isa. 40:3; Baeck, *Epochen*, p. 124.
77. Ibid., p. 100.

terns of thought of his time. It is particularly conspicuous how often Baeck uses the terminology of Immanuel Kant in the continuation of Jewish neo-Kantianism.[78] He speaks of 'moral action' *(sittliches Handeln)*,[79] of 'heteronomy' *(Heteronomie)*,[80] of striving for 'bliss' *(Glückseligkeit)* as an antithesis to 'morality' *(Sittlichkeit)*,[81] and of 'advice for the conscience' *(Gewissensratschläge)*,[82] the 'commandments of practical reason' *(Gebote der praktischen Vernunft)*[83] and the 'categorical imperative' *(kategorischenr Imperativ)*.[84]

All in all, Jewish neo-Kantianism seems to conflict with the thought and background of the Christian Reformation. It is hoped, however, that previous arguments and examples show how rarely Baeck touches the reality of Reformation thought, which is much more complex and full of dialectics. The tensions of Luther's terminology are not sensitively received by Baeck. This also raises the question to what extent Baeck is really arguing in full accordance with Jewish tradition, though he must first be cleared of the accusation that he argues simply in the philosophical manner of the Enlightenment. Rather one could say that he uses this system of contemporary thought and its terminology in order to present his Jewish standpoint.

Leo Baeck's Assumptions about Luther

Leo Baeck presents a picture of Lutheran theology from a Jewish perspective that appears quite intriguing, especially for the Jewish intelligentsia he was trying to convince. Nevertheless, I have indicated before that one might well be right in posing the question to what extent he was able to present Martin Luther's intentions fairly and even whether this was what he wanted. One has to keep in mind

78. For another example of Jewish-Kantian synthesis see Friedrich W. Niewöhner, 'Isaac Breuer und Kant: Ein Beitrag zum Thema "Kant und das Judentum"', in *Neue Zeitschrift für systematische Theologie und Religionsphilosophie*, 17 (1975), pp. 142–50 and 19,2 (1977), pp. 172–85.
79. Immanuel Kant, *Kritik der Urteilskraft*, § 29 Allgemeine Anmerkung.
80. Immanuel Kant, *Grundlegung zur Metaphysik der Sitten*, 2. Abschnitt, also *Kritik der praktischen Vernunft*, 1. Teil, 1. Buch, 1. Hauptstück, § 8, Lehrsatz IV
81. Immanuel Kant, *Kritik der reinen Vernunft*, Methodenlehre, 2. Hauptstück, 2. Absatz, also *Kritik der praktischen Vernunft*, 1. Teil, 1. Buch, 1. Hauptstück, § 8, Anmerkung II and ibid., 1. Teil, 2. Buch, 2. Hauptstück, V, also *Die Religion innerhalb der Grenzen der bloßen Vernunft*, Vorrede zu 1. Aufl., 1. Anmerkung and ibid., 1. Stück, Allgemeine Anmerkungen, 2. Anmerkung, also *Metaphysik der Sitten*, Einleitung II.
82. Immanuel Kant, *Metaphysik der Sitten*, Tugendlehre, Einleitung XII b.
83. Immanuel Kant, *Kritik der praktischen Vernunft*, 1. Teil, 1. Buch, 1. Hauptstück, § 7 and ibid., 1. Teil, 1. Buch, 1. Hauptstück, § 7, Anmerkung.
84. Immanuel Kant, *Kritik der praktischen Vernunft*, 1. Teil, 1. Buch, 1. Hauptstück, § 1, also ibid., 1. Teil, 1. Buch, 1. Hauptstück, § 7, also *Grundlegung zur Metaphysik der Sitten*, 1. und 2. Abschnitt.

that Baeck was not really interested in Luther himself or in the historical situation which Luther had to face when he developed his ideas. Luther appears as merely a part of the dispute with Christianity in the post-Enlightenment environment, when historico-critical questioning shattered the basis of Bible and tradition as well as the old concept of a Christian occident.

Therefore, this representation of Christianity is more a sign of deliberate and schematic polemic than the attempt to give the opposing view due credit by a very differentiated presentation.[85] Elucidating the contrast between Judaism and Christianity by describing them, respectively, as classical and romantic religions is characteristic: it obviously uses contemporary German philosophical schemes.

An objective perspective will not be able to avoid the insight that Baeck's polarised model of 'mystery' and 'commandment', probably works much better within one single faith tradition than in the comparison of two different ones. Baeck's constructs of polarisation make it difficult to evaluate fairly the actual developments and schools of thought in Christianity as well as Judaism. There is room to argue whether or not this was Baeck's intention. There seem to be clear indications of an intended and conscious one-sidedness of ideas and positions for the sake of apologetics and critique.[86] The separation of influences on the church – the Jewish-biblical tradition on the one side and Hellenistic influences on the other – appears to be especially doubtful. Baeck's equation: 'Gnosticism is Christianity without Judaism and, in that sense, pure Christianity'[87] is open polemic. The church may not always have liked the various influences united in its tradition. However devastating Christian scholarly judgement was, its inheritance from Judaism was rarely ever disputed and was even acknowledged by Paul as its root.[88] Furthermore one has to be aware of the dispute that broke out over the issue of Gnosticism, which was under fierce attack by mainstream Christian theology, especially by Irenaeus of Lyons in his book *Adversus Haereses* (against the dissenters) (c. AD 180).[89] Baeck's theory of 'Judaism in the Church' becomes even more problematic when he tries to distil this Jewish foundation from Christianity in order to create an 'objective' image of it.

85. On Baeck's limited aproach to Christianity see Reinhold Mayer, *Christentum und Judentum in der Schau Leo Baecks*, Studia Delitzschiana 6, (Stuttgart, 1961), pp. 44–9.
86. Mayer, *Christentum und Judentum*, pp. 48–9.
87. Baeck, 'Romantic Religion', in *Judaism and Christianity*, p. 250.
88. Rom. 11:18.
89. On the rejection of Gnosticism by Irenaeus see Carl Andresen, 'Die biblische Theologie des Irenäus von Lyon', in *Handbuch der Dogmen- und Theologiegeschichte*, vol. 1: *Die Lehrentwicklung im Rahmen der Katholizität*, Carl Andresen (ed.) (Göttingen, 1988), pp. 79–98, here pp. 80, 81, 97 and 98.

It is striking, yet highly questionable when Baeck includes Jesus and
the Gospels in this Jewish foundation, and further examines the history of Christian theology in order to extract Jewish influences on the
one hand, genuine Christian (i.e. non-Jewish) influences on the other.
Baeck defines two paths in the Christian history of religion, namely, a
Jewish one reaching from Jesus via Pelagius and Duns Scotus to
Calvin, and a Christian one starting with Paul and leading to Augustine and Luther. However, Christianity is only properly received as
this mix of various influences. Just as Judaism is. This rough division
makes it easy to assume that Baeck was really less interested in the theological questions of the time than in presenting a highly stylised view.

Nevertheless, I do not see that Baeck wants to exploit this 'Jewish
strand' in Christian theology for his own purposes. If we consider the
discussion with Harnack, we might see Baeck's motivation: in opposing Christian ignorance, which despicably rejects Judaism as a faith of
the past, and declares Christianity to be the 'absolute religion', Baeck
issues the explicitly polemical warning[90] not to underestimate the
vividness and actuality of the Jewish faith. After all, early historical
Bible criticism was also not very concerned whether or not to eliminate text passages in the Old Testament that seemed 'unchristian'.

Baeck's polemic emerges from two methods of analysis: first,
everything he values in Christianity is carefully extracted and then
attributed to Judaism.[91] In this way, Jesus and the Gospel – as
opposed to Paul – can suddenly end up in the 'Jewish camp'. Baeck
uses this principle all the way through when dealing with the church
tradition. It culminates in the development of his polarity model: the
Pauline-romantic and the Jewish-classical religion. At this point, the
portrayal of Judaism as well as Christianity becomes ahistorical, with
Baeck fully accepting this.

On the other hand, parallel phenomena in both religions are
viewed positively in Judaism and judged negatively in Christianity.
For example, 'grace' in Judaism joins happily with the positive term
of 'commandment'. In Christian terms, however, 'grace' becomes
the very basis of 'passivity' and 'egocentricity'.

All this makes the conclusion likely that Baeck had only limited
access to the complex and perhaps somewhat unsystematic world of
Luther's thinking. And we also have reason to believe that such
understanding was not at the centre of his endeavour. Nevertheless,
it has to be accepted that Baeck recognised the key points of Luther's

---

90. Walter Jacob entitled his essay on Leo Baeck 'Modern Polemic'. To him, Baeck
    represents *the* contemporary prototype of this genre. Walter Jacob, *Christianity
    through Jewish Eyes: The Quest for Common Ground* (Cincinnati, Ohio, 1974), pp.
    137–161, notes: pp. 261–263.
91. Mayer, *Christentum und Judentum*, p. 87

teaching. The following chapter will have to evaluate whether or not they received fair treatment by Baeck.

Leo Baeck and Martin Luther in Conflict

The Doctrine of Justification

Leo Baeck focuses on the systematic duality of 'grace' and 'freedom' when he criticises the assumption that justification solely by faith *(sola gratia)* devalues moral action and forces humankind into passivity. Baeck is generous enough to overlook the differentiation here which Luther[92] is eager to make; he distinguishes between outward and inward righteousness. The one refers to human beings as part of society regarding their behaviour against their fellows – *coram hominibus.* The individual acts justly in his contact with fellow individuals by fair action. Before God, however – *coram deo* – only purity of the heart counts. This inward justice cannot be achieved through action – as Baeck has also rightly pointed out – but is freely given as the gift of faith in Jesus Christ by grace alone.

Sinful humankind can never actively achieve this righteousness, for it is merely ascribed without merit and dignity *ex gratia* (Rom. 3:28). With his teachings on the truly instilled faith *(fides vere infusa),* Luther deliberately distances himself from scholastic theology, which thinks it possible to prepare for such a gift of faith by pious action. However, the significance of good deeds is not lost with the *sola fide* principle. In this respect Leo Baeck's objection has to be toned down, in real life faith and action are interlinked and not divided. Faith cannot exist without action or deeds. Whoever has faith in Jesus must also act according to it.[93] In John 6:36, 'faith' and 'emulation' are always used in parallel senses and in John 1:35–51, the terms are used interchangeably. The imperative 'follow me'[94] does not contradict Deutero-Isaiah's call for action 'clear the way', which Baeck emphasises.[95] Dietrich Bonhoeffer expresses this explicitly:

Cheap grace is the deadly enemy of our church. We are fighting today for costly grace.... .

... Grace is represented as the church's inexhaustible treasury, from which she showers blessings with generous hands, without asking questions or fixing limits. Grace without price; grace without cost! ...

Cheap grace means grace as a doctrine, a principle, a system. It means

---

92. See Joachim Rogge and Helmut Zeddies (eds.), *Kirchengemeinschaft und politische Ethik: Ergebnis eines theologischen Gesprächs zum Verhältnis von Zwei-Reiche-Lehre und Lehre von der Königsherrschaft Christi* (Berlin, 1980), pp. 12–14

93. See lecture of E. Wolf in *Unter der Herrschaft Christi*, Beiträge zur evangelischen Theologie 32 (Munich, 1961), p. 76.

94. Mark 1:17, 2:14; Luke 5:1–11; 1 Cor. 11:1.

95. Isa. 40:3.

forgiveness of sins proclaimed as a general truth, the love of God taught as the Christian 'conception' of God ... . The church which holds the correct doctrine of grace has, it is supposed, ipso facto a part in that grace. In such a church the world finds a cheap covering for its sins; no contrition is required, still less any real desire to be delivered from sin ... .

Cheap grace means the justification of sin without the justification of the sinner. Grace alone does everything, they say, and so everything can remain as it was before.[96]

Cheap grace is grace without discipleship, grace without the cross, grace without Jesus Christ, living and incarnate.

... grace is *costly* because it calls us to follow, and it is *grace* because it calls us to follow *Jesus Christ*.

Luther is impelled to emphasise: actions do not have any value or influence in order to gain the state of righteousness in the eyes of God, faith alone is the decisive factor. But no faithful Christian will fall short in his striving for ethical conduct and active discipleship.

Leo Baeck would not agree with that. To his mind the possibility for community with God flows from the fulfilment of the commandment. The Jew can prepare for faith through action, guided to faith through the fulfilment of the Halacha. And Halacha is actually more than 'the commandment'; it is a way of life. Action on the part of the individual is a prerequisite to experiencing closeness to God in the Jewish tradition of faith.

Apart from this controversy concerning Luther's alleged denigration of social and moral action, Baeck's fear is unfounded. Actions or deeds remain an important component of human existence even in Protestant theology. The Lutheran doctrine made a decision with regard to the question of which comes first: faith or deeds. The one does not exclude or outrule the other.

On the basis of the church's teaching of original sin Luther, however, makes a decision about the sequence of the two: corrupted humankind can overcome its state of sin because God chooses to enable it to do this – but only by faith in Jesus as the human presence of God in the world; and only after accepting that no righteousness can be achieved by keeping the commandments. An attempt to keep them would lead to frustration at not being able to do so and would be sinful in itself. Once this corrupted status is accepted God may enable his creation to act justly by granting faith in Jesus. This experience of faith, love and hope is then the very root of social action.

The Doctrine of Original Sin

According to Luther, having insight into the constitution of the world and its order of creation and grace is a prerequisite for just action. This

96. Dietrich Bonhoeffer, *The Cost of Discipleship*, (London, 1949); cited by John de Gruchy, *Dietrich Bonhoeffer - Witness to Jesus Christ* (London, 1987), p. 157.

insight is *ex gratia* (given by grace), it must 'enlighten', for the human being is in a state of sin. By this Luther means the fundamental sin of not having faith and of renouncing God. As 'original' sin, this not only destroys the original community with God, but represents a real corruption of the entire person, the entire human creation. This *corruptio naturae* determines the status of the individual and is passed on from generation to generation. In this way, the individual cannot recognise his or her own sinful behaviour. Reason is blinded by the corruption of human nature and cannot understand what belongs to the spirit of God.[97]

Baeck contrasts this to the Jewish standpoint. Here, the individual is not prevented from understanding the constitution of the world because of an 'original sin'. Everybody in Jewish terms has the free will to be either good or evil. Through the gift of 'grace of the commandment', God makes the path to righteousness readily available to everybody who is willing to take it.

Luther's standpoint cannot be reconciled with this view. Here we find definite controversy between the anthropologies of Judaism and Christianity, which, of course, is taken up by Baeck. This is even more so as Luther attacks what he calls 'semi-Pelagianic' tendencies of church doctrine, which in turn are objects of Baeck's respect.[98]

Free Will and the Commandment

The teaching of original sin has far-reaching consequences for Luther's entire theological thinking. Free will represents the highest ideal for Baeck, for the capacity to act is given by God but the direction which our deeds take is up to man's free will. Luther holds that no individual has a free will with regard to redemption or eternal salvation.[99] In 1525, in his book *De servo arbitrio*, he clearly expressed this in the course of his debate with Erasmus of Rotterdam. Luther speaks of man as an animal that carries a burden. If God were to sit on its back it would take the course directed by God. In case the devil rode on it – it would follow the devil's direction.[100] In the same way a human being is not free to choose the rider that is going to direct him/her. Rather God and the devil battle to hold on to the donkey or to take possession of it.[101]

With this, the commandment is clearly given different value. Baeck is wrong in claiming that Christianity abolished the law. However, the term that it is 'fulfilled' by Christ gives an idea of the different interpretation of its function. Nevertheless, in the dispute on

97. Bernhard Lohse, *Martin Luther: Eine Einführung in sein Leben und sein Werk*, 2nd edn (Munich, 1982), p. 167.
98. Baeck, *Aus drei Jahrtausenden*, pp. 129, 131ff.
99. WA 18,661,29–662,7.
100. WA 18,635,17–22.
101. Ibid.

antinomianism, Luther had claimed: who abolishes the law abolishes the gospel. He thereby emphasised the idea that the law is necessary for its judging and condemning character in order to make the sinner aware of Christ as fulfiller of the law.[102] According to Luther, the commandment achieves two tasks. Firstly, the commandment tells the individual how to behave in order to be just to his or her fellow human beings. The *usus legis civilis* is to support the good and to prevent evil. However, the commandment also demonstrates the sinfulness of human beings by plaguing their consciences and leading them to Christ and the Gospel in order to seek forgiveness for their sins.

The *usus theologicus seu spiritualis* of the commandment supports the view that individuals are not righteous before God because of their righteous action, but for the sake of Christ's suffering for humanity. The purpose of the commandment is not to appeal to the free will of the individual; just the opposite, its purpose is to expose the powerlessness of the individual (Rom. 3:20). Finally, the *tertius usus legis* supports the view that there exists a certain relation between faith and law. Faith enables 'joy and love for the commandment'.[103] This approach of faith to the law of God is interpreted as a demand of the Creator on his creature, a demand which the creature fulfils out of free obedience and without claiming a reward. It is there, in this strong combination of faith and law, that Lutheran thought comes closest to Baeck's intentions and also closest to demanding social action and the political implementation of the Gospel.[104]

'Law' and 'Gospel' both refer to God as the One who judges and who pardons. The law does not mean the Hebrew Bible as opposed to the New Testament, but refers to one of the two ways of community and communication within the entire scriptures.[105]

Thus we may say: 'commandment' is a theological topos of importance and is definitely found in Christianity and specifically in the doctrine of Martin Luther. It is obvious to me, however, that Leo Baeck can hardly be satisfied with this interpretation of the commandment. To Baeck, 'the commandment' is the path leading to God; to Luther it represents a path of admonishment pointing the way to the right path as well as leading astray.

---

102. See Bernhard Lohse, 'Von Luther bis zum Konkordienbuch', in *Handbuch der Dogmen- und Theologiegeschichte*, vol. 2: Die Lehrentwicklung im Rahmen der Konfessionalität, Carl Andresen (ed.), pp. 39–45.

103. See Eilert Herms, 'Die Bedeutung des Gesetzes für die lutherische Soziallehre', in *Von Wittenberg nach Memphis: Festschrift für Reinhold Schwarz*, Walter Homolka and Otto Ziegelmeier (eds.), (Göttingen, 1989), pp. 62–7, here p. 67.

104. Ibid., p. 67. See further discussion of the usus tertius legis in Gerhard Ebeling, 'usus politicus legis–usus politicus evangelii', in *Zeitschrift für Theologie und Kirche* 79 (1982), pp. 323–48.

105. Rogge and Zeddies, *Kirchengemeinschaft und politische Ethik*, p. 20

The Doctrine of Two Kingdoms

It is important to recognise two continually distinguished perspectives in Luther's thought: *coram hominibus* and *coram deo*. Such a distinction is also apparent in the doctrines of the two kingdoms.[106] Baeck can, therefore, accuse Luther of placing the earthly realm at a distance from God. To him a society of sinners seems to function merely on the basis of social constraints; the authorities enforce matters of morality. Thus, for Baeck, morality becomes a purely external quality in Luther's system. Furthermore this could mean a limitation of God's omnipotence and ability of direct interference.[107]

But is Baeck right here? Luther makes it perfectly clear that both kingdoms are ruled by God in the same way when he speaks of the 'Reich Gottes zur rechten und zur linken Hand' ('God's realm to his right and to his left hand').[108] God rules in both orders, for the secular regime is not profane, separate from God. Indeed, the Christian ruler exists and rules under the sceptre of God. By viewing society from two perspectives, Luther can leave behind a theocratic society that gives the church direct political power. This does not mean that God is 'relieved' of the rule over creation, but it makes possible a secular society which can exist in its own right and dignity totally apart from the church.[109]

This involves the fundamental distinction between what is necessary on religious and on social grounds; what makes up the spiritual and the secular realms in the one world of God. I feel that Luther uses precisely this argument in opposing the corruption of the church through power, which Baeck continually refers to.[110] At the same time Luther sanctifies everyday life and therefore takes up one of Baeck's most important values.

It is essential to consider that obedience towards the secular authority stops at the point where it would be directed against God. The *clausula Petri* in Acts 5:29: 'We must obey God rather than men'[111] represents a higher law than the appeal to be a subject to the authority. It justifies, according to Luther, a – passive – right of resistance.[112] It is pre-

---

106. Luther never actually used the term 'doctrine of Two Kingdoms'. It first appears around 1922 in secondary research literature; cf. Lohse, *Martin Luther*, p. 192.
107. The Barmer Theological Declaration expresses similar reservations in Thesis 2.
108. Paul Althaus, *Um die Wahrheit des Evangeliums* (Stuttgart, 1962), p. 265.
109. Matthias Kroeger, *Theologische Klärung unseres Friedensverhaltens: Eine Zweirei-chelehre für den Frieden* (Stuttgart, 1984), p. 70.
110. Walter Jacob, *Christianity through Jewish Eyes: The Quest for Common Ground* (Cincinnati, Ohio, 1974), p. 140: Baeck 'discussed the dangers of corruption through power, which had often occurred within the Church.'
111. Cf. the tension between the statements of Rom. 13 and Rev. 13.
112. Lohse, *Martin Luther*, p. 197; and Bengt Hägglund, *Geschichte der Theologie: Ein Abriß* (Ost-Berlin, 1983), p. 183.

cisely this resistance which Baeck also demanded.[113] In the end it may be a true judgement to say that Luther's distinction between the elements of holiness and profanity prepared the ability for the Protestant church to redefine its position in and reconcile itself with a pluralistic society.

The 'Complete' Individual and Predestination

Baeck implies that Luther claims only those who have been chosen from the beginning will receive salvation on the basis of faith.[114] However, in contrast to Calvin's doctrine of a double predestination, to Luther, *praedestinatio* always means *praedestinatio ad salutem* (to salvation). This does not fit with the image of the passive waiting state of the condemned. Much more, it represents the hopeful affirmation of God's perpetual openness to humanity. God is always willing to offer salvation to the sinner. In this sense, Luther does not have much more in common with Calvin than the use of the term, but rather presents a counterbalance to Calvin's theory of the determination of the individual.

Consequently, Baeck may be overreacting at this point. *Praedestinatio ad salutem* seems indeed very consistent with the Jewish image of covenant and chosen people. God is loyal to the chosen people, Israel, even when they continually violate the covenant, as stated in Lev. 26:42–4.[115] Even Baeck's conception of the 'finished man' is awkward. According to Baeck, the redeemed individual needs no trust in the future, feels no 'Messianic' urge. The 'new individual' of Christianity[116] who, through Christ's act of salvation, is now free from original sin, is called to fellowship and hopes for Christ's second coming. With this second coming, the kingdom of God will dawn.

With reference specifically to the Lutheran doctrine of repentance, it is obvious that Baeck is thinking too functionally here. The dying of the 'old' individual and his/her being blessed with redemption wrought by the cross of Christ, and thus the birth of the new person, is all reflected and actualised in the entire life of a Christian. This transformation into a 'new' individual can by no means be fixed at any specific point in life from which the certainty of redemption could be dated. The individual is placed in the process of transformation by means of baptism and holy communion, and is thereby given a task: to let love become effective through faith.

Luther's essential understanding of word and sacrament is rightly questioned by Baeck, who prefers the reformed doctrine in its form

---

113. Baeck, *Wege im Judentum*, p. 287.
114. Baeck, 'Romantic Religion', in *Judaism and Christianity*, pp. 203f.; and Baeck, *Aus drei Jahrtausenden*, p. 136.
115. The idea that repentance is always possible and that God always awaits the return of Israel to Him is best expressed in the selichoth for the High Holidays.
116. Rom. 5:12–21.

represented by Calvinism. But in the end it is irrelevant for the discussion of Judaism and leads once again back to the problem of commandment and divine grace. In any case, a Christian is not 'complete', but considers him- or herself placed at a new beginning, setting out for a new start.

The Main Problem of Law and Divine Grace

In Baeck's response to Martin Luther, his polarisation of 'mystery' and 'commandment' is conspicuous. Although he generally tries to unite both aspects in a true religion, the impression remains that 'mystery' receives insufficient attention in Judaism. This emphasis might result from the neo-Kantian background of Baeck's reception of the Jewish tradition as presented in his argument with Christianity. In any case, it is not characteristic of Baeck's theology in general.[117] It appears as if an artificial opposition is constructed that does not arise at all within inner-Jewish debate. For example, divine grace cannot simply be assigned to the mystery, as opposed to the commandment. Because to Jewish thought, it is precisely the commandment that is the path of grace which God has prepared. And even further: whether or not this understanding is a viable way has not remained unquestioned even in the Hebrew Bible itself.[118]

Thus both Jews as well as Christians depend on grace, whether the grace of God or the grace of Christ.[119] The conflict arises with the question of whether or not individuals, through action, are able to justify themselves in the sight of God. This refers not to the will of human beings but to their ability. Both Baeck and Luther answer this question explicitly: that which is denied by Luther is vehemently affirmed by Baeck, in the Pharisaic tradition. It must be noted that there is definitely evidence in the Hebrew Bible that indeed questions these convictions of Baeck and Judaism.[120]

Here, justice is not self-evident, as in other parts of the Hebrew Bible, but rather impossible. Being in a state of guilt the individual can live only with God's forgiveness. This is the message given in the Psalms of Repentance[121] and in Job,[122] corresponding to the institution of expiation of the priestly scriptures.

---

117. Baeck, *Dieses Volk*, vol. II (1957) p. 22.67.318.
118. Jer. 13:23, Eccles 7:20, Ps 130:3f. and Ps 51:7–12.
119. Robert Brunner (ed.), *Gesetz und Gnade im Alten Testament und im jüdischen Denken* (Zurich, 1969), p. 78.
120. For greater detail, cf. Werner H. Schmidt, *'Rechtfertigung des Gottlosen' in der Botschaft der Propheten: Festschrift für Hans Walter Wolff* (Neukirchen, 1981), pp. 157–68.
121. Ps. 6; 32; 38; 51; 102; 130; 143.
122. Job 4:17; 9:2; 14:4; 15:14; 25:4 ff.

Chapter 9

FROM ESSENCE TO EXISTENCE – TOWARDS A GENUINELY JEWISH THEOLOGY

Bewilderment and Unrest

In this chapter I will try to present the various endeavours that have been made in the twentieth century towards a genuinely Jewish theology. This background will help in evaluating Baeck's achievements in creating an adequate image of Judaism.

In the early 1930s with the crisis of historicism the call for an authentic Jewish theology became urgent. The period was one of bewilderment and unrest. It was the time when Karl Jaspers wrote his portrayal of the growing uneasiness and alienation of modern humankind.[1] In 1927, Martin Heidegger had published his *Being and Time (Sein und Zeit)*,[1a] the most authentic and compelling document of secularisation, showing a humankind that had lost the sense of eternity, and interpreting existence as 'Being towards Death' ('Sein zum Tode'). Hans Joachim Schoeps expressed this mood of despair in his 'Jewish Faith in this Age' ('Jüdischer Glaube in dieser Zeit').[2] In his negation of human-centred idealism Schoeps looks like a truly

1. Karl Jaspers, *Die geistige Situation der Zeit*, 5th edn (Berlin, 1955).
1a. Martin Heidegger, *Being and Time* (New York 1962); German first edition 1926.
2. Hans-Joachim Schoeps, *Jüdischer Glaube in dieser Zeit* (1932).

Barthian theologian introducing only slight modifications in order to suit Jewish requirements.

The Tasks of the Time

Around the same time in the 1930s Martin Buber convened a meeting of Jewish theologians at the, office of the Reichsvertretung der deutschen Juden in Berlin. There, he submitted a scheme for the publication of an anthology to be entitled *Beiträge zu einer jüdischen Theologie* (Contributions towards a Jewish Theology) – a book that was never written. Alexander Altmann, however, preserved the proposed table of contents.[3]

I. DISTINCTIONS
1. THE PROBLEM OF POWER
THE CLAIMS OF THE STATE. ABSOLUTISM OF STATE AND CHURCH. THE RELATIONSHIP OF JUDAISM AND STATE AND THE CLAIM OF ABSOLUTISM.
2. MESSIANISM AND PROGRESS IN SOCIETY
3. RELIGION AND CULTURE
TRUE AND FALSE UNIVERSALISM. MISSION.
EXCURSUS A: JUDAISM AND DIALECTICAL THEOLOGY

II. ELEMENTS
1. HISTORY AND TRADITION
2. THE DOUBLE ASPECT OF TEACHING AND LAW AND THE ROLE OF THE AUTHORITY OF TRADITION
3. THE SIGNIFICANCE OF THE BIBLE
   (A) BIBLICAL SCHOLARSHIP
   (B) BIBLICAL MESSAGE
4. PRAYER
5. SIN AND ATONEMENT
6. DEATH
EXCURSUS B: THE CONCEPT OF 'SYSTEM' IN JEWISH THEOLOGY

III. PATHS
1. SECTS AND TRENDS IN JEWRY
2. FORMS AND METHODS OF JEWISH EDUCATION
3. THEOLOGY AS A PROFESSION.
4. RELIGIOUS JUDAISM AND ITS PART IN THE SOLUTION OF THE PROBLEMS OF THE AGE

A clear picture emerges especially from the first part – 'Distinctions' ('Abgrenzungen') – as to the state of Jewish theological thinking at that stage. There was, in the first place, the question of the relationship between religion and state. Then there was the problem of Messianism versus the ideology of progress, which is linked with

3. Alexander Altmann, 'Theology in Twentieth-Century German Jewry', *Leo Baeck Institute Year Book* 1 (1956), pp. 193–216.

the problem of religion and culture. Dialectical theology had deeply attacked the liberal concept of religion as one of being culturally infected). It had expressed the view that the crisis of modern humankind resulted from the absoluteness with which it had turned to secular culture. In the place of human-made culture it put the word of God again.

This radical questioning of culture constituted a challenge to both liberal and orthodox Jewish theology. In Jewish thinking a belief in the religious value of human culture had been deeply ingrained. Hence, the urge arose to examine from a Jewish point of view this question posed by dialectical theology.

Jewish Existence: Nation and Peoplehood

As we have heard in the biographical notes on the life of Leo Baeck, Hitler's devastating regime resulted in an serious caesura in Baeck's literary activity between 1941 and 1944. Yet, even in the concentration camp of Theresienstadt, where he stayed from 1943 to 1944, Baeck did not stop working. What emerged were two volumes entitled *This People: Jewish Existence*.[4] In this work the concept of 'essence' is replaced by that of 'existence'. The Jewish religious tradition appears no longer as a mere phenomenon in the history of ideas but as the very expression of the people's uniqueness.

Previously he had pointed out the uniqueness of ethical monotheism as a revolutionary force that broke into the world constituting a 'revelation'. Now he describes the historical appearance of this people as something quite extraordinary, as *'ein Einmaliges'*. A particularistic touch prevails.[5] Only the Jewish people, Baeck points out, has the peculiar gift of embracing both mystery and commandment.[6] They experience the metaphysical as the 'commanding mystery'. Seen from this perspective, Jewish mysticism has now become a

4. *Dieses Volk: Jüdische Existenz,* vol. 1, 2nd edn. (Frankfurt am Main, 1955): vol. 2 (Frankfurt am Main, 1957).
5. It is interesting to note Rosenzweig's criticism of Baeck as uttered in 'Apologetisches Denken', in *Kleinere Schriften,* (Berlin, 1937). Rosenzweig sees the basic dogma of Judaism as the chosenness of Israel. In that he challenges Leo Baeck's position that there are no dogmas at all in Judaism. This dogma, however, has to be experienced, rather than pronounced. Rosenzweig would set this closed-off mystery against the Christological dogmas. One could live within this mystery without systematising it. Contrasted with Baeck's early position one can note that his new existential approach meets with the ideas held by his friend Rosenzweig.
6. In Baeck's theology 'nation' was a part from the very beginning. In his search for the idea in the long succession of generations he counters Harnack's emphasis on the Protestant individual as a wanderer towards a relationship with Jesus.

manifestation of Israel's regenerative power, rather than distorting the regenerative process.[7]

The experience of the Holocaust had changed Leo Baeck's position. His work is a true witness of the development of Jewish theology in the twentieth century: from the denial of the uniqueness and essential otherness of the Jew towards a reaffirmation of Jewish uniqueness in metaphysical terms. It is striking to see how the issue changed: from the 'essence' towards the 'existence' of Judaism.

Evaluation and Outlook

What remains of Baeck's theology that exercises enduring influence?

It is certainly his ethical approach which places humankind and its autonomous creativity at the centre of interest. It is also the preservation and reappreciation of the emotional and mystical forces that work in Judaism despite the neglect they had suffered in the age of enlightenment. And moreover we see a tendency towards moral universalism, a Messianic tendency reaching out to all human beings and all the world.[8]

It is true that the problems of Baeck's age may have changed. The Holocaust has dispelled the rivalry between the two sisters, church and synagogue, and brought them closer in understanding and appreciation. Internationally this has fostered a development of even closer links between modern Jewish theology and other schools of thought.

Baeck's work ends a period of search for the essentials of Jewish faith that had enormous influence on Jewish spirituality in this century. Until quite recently one could be considered a good Jew if one believed in God and led a moral life. Baeck also provided a bridge of deeper understanding between the mystical and the rational elements in Jewish tradition, which could be used by later generations to go back and experience anew what their ancestors had known: there is an existential possibility of knowing God transcending all the sets and systems that could be developed from the institutional side of faith.

Today the task for Reform Jewish theologians remains much the same as it was in the nineteenth century: to find a balance of continuity and change that safeguards the authenticity of Jewish religious life on the one hand and, on the other hand, takes seriously the insight that God makes a journey with his people where there will be new impressions of the relationship between God and his people on the way.

7. See Baeck *Das Wesen des Judentums*, 1st edn (1905).
8. Leo Baeck, 'World Religion and National Religion', in *Mordecai M. Kaplan Jubilee Volume* (New York, 1953).

Chapter 10

IDENTITY AND DIALOGUE – CONCLUSION ON THE JEWISH–CHRISTIAN ESSENCE DEBATE

Leo Baeck – Parent of Jewish–Christian Dialogue

In the first chapter I undertook to show that Leo Baeck can be considered to be one of the most distinguished thinkers of German liberal Judaism in the first half of the twentieth century. Baeck has prepared the ground for the development of the Jewish–Christian dialogue. His virtue lies in his constant interest in Christianity, which not even the events during the Third Reich could weaken, and his change from the search for the 'essence' of Judaism to the concentration on 'existence' and 'identity' of the people of Israel. His interest in the historical Jesus sets an example for various Jewish attempts to understand the teachings of Jesus as an integral part of Jewish tradition and history. His continuing interest in Christianity goes back to the turn of the century, when Baeck became involved in the essence debate with Adolf von Harnack. He is one of those who support the 'reclaiming of Jesus into Judaism' *(jüdische Leben-Jesu-Forschung)*.

Historicism and Liberalism

In order to understand Leo Baeck it was helpful to see the historical background of the Jewish emancipation and antisemitism during the German Empire of 1871. I submit that emancipation is a phenomenon of the post-Enlightenment age, which can be understood in the context of the emergence of rational thought with the development of modern sciences and the social integration of minority groups. For Jews this meant both the loss of autonomy and the emergence of different Jewish denominations. The integration into the bourgeois society was seen more and more as the assimilation into a Christian society. Jewish science and theology reacted to this challenge both by renewed apologetics and a historical approach in research on Christianity. The interest of Jewish society in a science of Judaism increased with the emergence of antisemitism. Along with the influence of the Enlightenment strong anti-Jewish tendencies remained powerful, developing the idea of an anti-Judaism based on racial reasoning, i.e. antisemitism. The Jewish reaction was prompt, increased assimilation into a society dominated by Protestant thought and loss of identity as a Jewish community, which resulted in Jewish religious liberalism.[1]

Up to this point Jewish and Protestant liberalism resembled each other. During the first decades of the Second Reich liberal theology, both Protestant and Jewish, shared the same set of values and the same problems that had to be solved theologically. By the authorities' connecting Christianity to the state, and enforcing the idea of a Protestant Prussian state, Jews were expelled from further identification with liberal ideology. The debate about essence separated them even more. Only the assumption of a historical development of the Jewish ceremonial law enabled any ritual reform. This liberal Jewish thought aimed at modernising Jewish faith and ritual. At the same time it attempted to create some group identity on a new basis.

Harnack's *Essence of Christianity* marks the climax of this Jewish struggle. It was the science of Judaism that provided the tools of an intellectual process for changing the social environment of German Jewry. Baeck as a representative of liberal Jewish theology has to be seen in the same line as the representatives of the *Wissenschaft des Judentums* (science of Judaism). As a result of his studies at the Universities of Breslau and Berlin he was as well educated in the non-Jewish field as in the Jewish.

Harnack's *Essence of Christianity*

Baeck joined the debate with Christianity by writing his *Wesen des Judentums (Essence of Judaism)* as an answer to Adolf von Harnack's

---

1. We could lay down that 'liberal' streams within a theology are considered to be those that try to give answers to the challenges of their period in a reasonable way and provide the people with a contemporary interpretation of their religion.

Wesen des Christentums (Essence of Christianity). This work tries to explain the conservative elements within Christianity by means of the historical method.[2] It aims at developing a Christian way of life that is adapted to the demands of the present era. Harnack presents his notion of Christianity by juxtaposing a polarised view of an individualistic, undogmatic, creative and renewing Jesus with a petrified, 'pharisaic Judaism' clinging to the law.

I have condensed Harnack's idea of the essence of Christianity in the following characteristics:

1. Knowledge of the individuality of each human being
2. A direct relationship between each individual and God
3. Imitation of Jesus by faith and deeds

The term 'essence' is a programme in itself; Protestant theologians since Schleiermacher were searching for a 'formula' that was able to present the inner nature or the most important quality of Christianity according to modern scientific standards. For Harnack this appeared to be essentially an adoption of the ideals of the reformation.

The postulate that an 'essence' must be formulated, however, carries two dangers: first the claim of superiority for one's own religion by means of idealisation; and second, the denigration of other religions. Neither Harnack nor later Baeck escaped this trap. They presented their faiths using as criteria idealistic standards and each tried to justify the superiority of their faith over the other one – as related rivals have a great need to find important differences between one another. The closer the enemies, the more necessity to differ.

Harnack's argument is based on Julius Wellhausen's theory of Israel's having been in a state of decline since the times of the prophets. From there he easily concluded that Israel was a previous and decadent stage of Christianity that lost its legitimacy by the coming of Christ as the Messiah.[3]

2. Troeltsch was the first to analyse more thoroughly this historical method, which is used to develop the idea of essence. This leads to the 'historical abstraction', i.e. the knowledge to what degree historical events influenced the development of an idea, an essence, etc. The basic concept of the 'historical abstraction' is the option of reunderstanding the meaning of essence afresh for each succeeding era instead of maintaining a rather static definition. The method is scientific, the results are subjective (Troeltsch: 'creative deed').

3. Just as modern exegesis of the Hebrew Bible has put its emphasis more on holistic view rather than a pure analysis of sources, an analogous development can be seen in systematics: philosophical bias seems to be succeeded by an interest in the ongoing process of creating an identity of faith through ever new approaches and perspectives to the faith tradition. So the dynamic changes direction from historical retrospective towards an increasing focus on the way God goes with his creation in the here and now.

The Jewish Response – Baeck's *Essence of Judaism*

It was this reappearance of the idea of a Christian superiority over Judaism, now disguised in the question of essence and presented to the general public by a respected academic, that seemed to have led to an apologetic dispute with Harnack. The Jewish side tried to point out the legitimacy and value of Jewish existence, to prevent Jews from deserting Judaism and blending into Christianity. It was principally Felix Perles, Martin Schreiner and Joseph Eschelbacher who criticised the Christian disregard for Jewish research on the life of Jesus, its confusion of Halachic and Haggadic elements, its Christocentric and Germanocentric approach and the neglect of Jewish ethics. But the possibility of reconciliation was never denied.

Baeck's criticism, in particular, seemed to be that Harnack's methodology was not historical in that its views of a philosophy of creation and disintegration in history are assumed to be historical facts. Baeck confronts Harnack's essence of Christianity with his essence of Judaism, which is based on three concepts:

1. The prophets' ethical monotheism
2. The essence of Judaism is revealed by the history of the Jewish people with God
3. The continuity of the Jewish tradition and the ties between ethical monotheism and the commandments

One idea that both Judaism and Christianity have in common is their objective of a correlation between religion and humanity as the goal of human development.

Baeck's Polarity Model and its Apologetic Intention

As an alternative concept to that of Harnack, Baeck elaborated a model of two opposing poles – 'classical' and 'romantic' – to argue the superiority of Judaism over Christianity. Whereas 'classical religion' or Judaism is depicted in terms of Kantian attributes and a high standard of ethics, and is defined by rationalism and fulfilment of the law of God, 'romantic religion' (i.e. Christianity) is characterised by mysticism and emotional faith. This presentation, however, has been seen on close inspection to be a 'black-and-white' description of Judaism and Christianity.

Baeck's apologetic and prejudiced approach to Christianity and Judaism is even more evident in his presentation of the teachings of Martin Luther. Baeck's attack on Martin Luther can be explained partly in terms of the circumstances of the times.

For Baeck the Protestant Prussian established church represented Protestantism as a whole. The content of his attack, however, is primarily centred on the main question of the state of the individual before God. Can any human being, on the basis of individual strength and free will, fulfil the commandments and be righteous in the eyes of God, by being active for better or worse? For Baeck the human being under Judaism has the duty and opportunity to prove him- or herself ethical and righteous by striving to keep God's commandments. Humankind under Christianity is portrayed as being entangled in sin and, therefore, unable to do good works unless faith is granted by divine grace. This faith makes individuals righteous before God and enables them to follow Christ's example in acting well.

Jewish Theology's Search for Identity

Slowly a pattern of contemporary Jewish theology evolved. I described it as a contextual way of thought strongly influenced by its environment. The social changes, to which Jewish society was subject during emancipation, made a reinterpretation of the Jewish religious life necessary. Judaism had to prove its 'value' in a situation of competition with the Christian environment. Every religious reinterpretation had to be up to date and at the same time so close to the Jewish tradition that it still deserved the label 'Jewish'.

The science of Judaism was the secular attempt to found a modern Jewish identity. Its method is historical, the conceptual creator is Hegel, its main representatives are Zunz, Geiger, Graetz, Frankel, the 'Berliner Lehranstalt'; and its consequences a 'de-Judaisation' (cf. Geiger). When Hegel's philosophical view of history was superseded the reform movement lost a considerable part of its strength of persuasion and legitimation. The Breslau Seminary follows a rather more moderate path by combining tradition with modern science. We have seen that Leo Baeck's thought was shaped by this concept. He has to be seen in the context of liberalism in Germany. The open-minded political and social profile of liberalism led to a special affinity between liberals – who were generally Protestants – and Jews. The Jews, however, worried that liberal Protestantism could seduce people to baptism. Though Kantian ethics are generally considered to be related to Protestantism, it was mainly Jewish philosophers such as Manuel Joel and especially Hermann Cohen who tried to understand Kantian philosophy as a key for the analysis of monotheistic religions. In *Religion der Vernunft aus den Quellen des Judentums* ('The Religion of Reason out of the Sources of Judaism') (1919) Hermann Cohen suggested the departure from pure historicism and the redirection towards concepts like 'ethics' and 'truth'. Basing himself on Kantian philosophy Cohen asserts that Judaism is a rational, Kantian religion in its roots. Its essential element is duty, whereas cult and rites are secondary. In comparison, Christianity with its ideas of trinity and divine incarnation then seems a step backwards from 'rational' Judaism. The strong affinity between liberal Protestants and Jews could also be seen in the influence that Scheiermacher and Dilthey exerted upon Jewish liberal thought. However, this affinity was set boundaries by Protestant nationalism and the heat of the 'essence' debate.

Just as in Baeck's 'Theology and History' the historical school explains religion as a part of the culture and emphasises the manmade parts. In opposition to this tendency a dialectical theology develops within Christianity that takes away the emphasis from the culture and stresses again the self-revealing God. Liberal theology has to face this critique and challenge. Baeck rejects this criticism with regard to Judaism. He considers this a specifically Christian problem, as Jewish theology is undogmatic. According to Baeck a Jew does not question God's revelation. Rather, he sees Jewish theology as a meditation on Israel's history and tradition. On this basis he develops his system of polarity with the poles 'classical' and 'romantic' religion. We have seen that Baeck regards Judaism to be the only religion that has not created any mythology. In other religions the mystic seeks an ecstatic encounter with God. In contrast to this Judaism focuses on the fulfilment of God's will. Nevertheless Baeck concedes that even Judaism is hallmarked by the tension between mystery and commandment. It is most important for the life of a human being to establish a balance between those two poles. All in all it can be seen that Baeck attempted to erase all irrational elements from Judaism.

Classical and Romantic Religion

Mystery and commandment correspond to the polarity of classical and romantic religion. To Baeck's mind Christianity and the religions of the East can be considered romantic; Judaism, however, is referred to as classical. Both Christianity and Judaism are described as religions of revelation. Baeck's distinction is that, while Judaism is in a continuous state of creation, Christianity has practically reached its goal. The reason for this is the disproportionate emphasis on mystery as opposed to commandment. The classical religion of Judaism focuses on ethics and activity, the romantic religion of Christianity, however, is passive and faith-orientated. Baeck's assertion is that

Protestant ethics do not genuinely belong to the essence of Protestantism, but are a supplement. I have shown how Baeck attempts to prove this hypothesis. He presents his understanding of Martin Luther's teachings on original sin, grace, righteousness and salvation to underline his polarity model of activity and passivity. His second point of criticism is directed towards the Lutheran state church. Its throne-altar alliance serves him as proof of the hypocritical division between the spheres of politics and religion. This presentation totally neglects the liberal Protestant tendencies after 1918 that reshaped the understanding of Christianity in a secular state.

My analysis of the above facts shows that Baeck's thought arises from a combination of Jewish tradition, neo-Kantian ethics and the concepts of Schleiermacher and Dilthey. Despite Baeck's problematic methodology his theology can be considered an instructive example of bewilderment in the Jewish theology of the thirties. In fact Jewish theology had two objectives at the time. On the one hand it had to define the relationship between religion and state, on the other hand it had to react to the criticism of dialectical theology. As an answer to this challenge Baeck wrote his two volumes This People – Jewish Existence, where he exchanges the concept of essence for the one of existence and also redefines his understanding of mystery and commandment: 'Das gebietende Geheimnis', the mystery that gives birth to commandment. In the end I consider it to Baeck's credit that Jewish theology has overcome the concept of essence in favour of the term 'existence'. Modern progressive Jewish theology has to deal with the same dilemma that its predecessors in the nineteenth century had to face: to balance continuity and change.

A Critical View

This study was an attempt to describe and interpret Leo Baeck's writings on Christianity in the light of post-Enlightenment bewilderment. What is the effect of Baeck's image of Christianity on the Christian-Jewish dialogue? As mentioned above the search for 'essence' did not lead to an understanding of the two religions but distanced them. Searching for the 'essence' of a religion means at the same time to be unable to see the qualities of other religions which might shine through in one's own tradition. Although strengthening Jewish religious self-consciousness, the writings of Leo Baeck on Christianity are like a monologue to a Jewish audience. Being interested in one's superiority results in not being capable to communicate.

Baeck can be sure that his writings helped to strengthen Jewish religious self-consciousness in a time of trial. However, this kind of defence has an instrumental deficiency when communication and dialogue are sought. Baeck's attitude towards the relationship of Judaism and Christianity is a different one in his late writings, with his experiences in America in mind. It is not the view of Christianity or Judaism that changed – Baeck still asserts the contrast between 'classical' and 'romantic' religion₁– but he is later arguing the case for true religious encounter.

It is, then, no longer the 'essence' that is important but the religious self-consciousness or the religious identity of a person that enables a dialogue with members of a different faith to start. Thus, when the social patterns changed, 'essence' gave way to 'existence', the existential search for one's own identity. It was the generation of Baeck, Buber and Rosenzweig that opened the gates for such interreligious encounter in a profitable exchange of the 'I and Thou'. To sum up:

1. Baeck's theology was innovative in its reference to Wilhelm Dilthey's *Verstehende Psychologie (Psychology of Empathy)*, and neo-Kantianism as represented by Hermann Cohen.
2. A development of Baeck's intellectual approach to his theological system can be detected in a change from historicism to existentialism.
3. Although Baeck's understanding of Christianity is limited and often prejudiced one must respect his efforts. He encouraged Jewish scholarly interest in research on Jesus. And, above all, Baeck's interest in Christianity was not weakened even during the Third Reich. After 1945 Baeck supported the Jewish-Christian dialogue, especially in Germany.
4. Baeck is highly regarded as a symbol of German liberal Judaism and as one of the last surviving representatives of German Jewry. Jewish institutions all over the world bear his name. Whereas the remembrance of his person is significant, Baeck's contribution to Jewish theology did not find a successor nor does it seem to exert any great intellectual influence.

I would like to conclude my analysis with a vision of Leo Baeck that may serve as a model to the encounter of different religions:

> Human beings and communities, peoples and religions should understand one other. They should not become the same, and they cannot become the same. To understand means, at the same time, to respect one another, and only those who respect themselves can respect others. Human beings and peoples and creeds will stay separated, they will live on in their individuality, but they will know that they belong together, that they are parts of the one humankind, that they should dwell together on this our earth, seeing each other, understanding each other and, when necessary, helping each other.[4]

---

4. Leo Baeck, *Judentum, Christentum und Islam: Rede gehalten von Ehren-Grosspräsident Dr. Leo Baeck anlässlich der Studientagung der Districts-Gross-Loge Kontinental-Europa XIX in Bruxelles (22. April 1956)*, pp. 18–19.

EPILOGUE
by Esther Seidel

Retrieving the Rationalistic Heritage:
Leo Baeck and Liberal Jewish Theology

> Er lehrte uns, was wesentlich war, er bewies uns, was wesentlich ist und bleibt. (H.G. Adler)[1]
> Der Theologe muss theologisch philosophieren. (A. Geiger)[2]

The exceptional personality of Leo Baeck has been described and appreciated in a number of Festschriften, anthologies and monographs. Seldom has a man's character been assessed so unequivocally as one of untiring diligence, inner independence and genuine humility. In his outstanding scholarship he combined the mastery of classical and oriental philology with philosophy, history and religious studies, and they all bear witness to the vast field of his learning. It has been said that all these qualities together have contributed,

---

1. 'He taught us what was essential; he proved to us what is and remains essential.'
   Hans G. Adler, 'Leo Baeck in Theresienstadt', in *Worte des Gedenkens für Leo Baeck*, Eva Reichmann (ed.) (Heidelberg, 1959), p. 61.
2. 'The theologian must philosophise theologically', quoted in: Samuel S. Cohon, *Jewish Theology*, A historical and systematic interpretation of Judaism and its foundations (Assen, 1971), p. 27. This quotation as it stands in its original language is perhaps deliberately equivocal. In one sense, with the emphasis on 'philosophise', it means that a theologian should present his theology in a philosophical, i.e. coherent and systematic, way. On the other hand, with the emphasis on the adverb, it could mean: what matters now is that the theologian not only philosophises, but that he does so with a demonstratively religious attitude. Presumably, Geiger had the second interpretation in mind, whereas the first was taken to be an obvious requirement.

in the darkest hour German Jewry ever experienced, to his fearlessness and to his grandeur and nobility of spirit. Leo Baeck was a prime example of how a human being, when faced with evil and death, could conduct himself with dignity and self-respect, and yet remain fully responsible for his fellow men. He knew no rest or self-satisfaction and remained the teacher, rabbi, *Seelsorger*[3] and spiritual leader for generations to come.

When we consider Leo Baeck's contribution to Jewish theology, it is noteworthy that he has been celebrated as 'the exponent of the more classical type of religious thought'[4] just as readily as he was said to have 'remained firmly entrenched in the liberal position which his *Wesen des Judentums* had mapped out.'[5]

The purpose of this epilogue is to show that both these statements hold true for Leo Baeck's position. Leo Baeck's theology arose out of the German cultural background of his time and, although firmly anchored in neo-Kantianism, it sought to overcome the 'primacy of reason' by also taking into account the prevalent 'existentialist thinking'. Both these perspectives are represented, as Walter Homolka's study has shown, both in Leo Baeck's earlier work, which had a more idealistic and universal approach (accentuating the essence of Judaism) and then in his later work, in which there is more of an emphasis on the particular and individual and on Jewish identity. However, as befits a thinker whose thought moves between polarities, these two ostensibly different positions do not, in our opinion, indicate a break in Leo Baeck's theology. They merely accentuate the two different focal points of his whole spectrum of thought – each pole reflecting and referring to the different needs of the respective German *Zeitgeist*. Leo Baeck's position remained constant throughout,[6] and both elements have come to fruition amongst his successors who have followed him further along his path towards a liberal Jewish theology.[7]

Before Leo Baeck's theology was influenced by the existentialist discussion and thereafter by the Holocaust, it had its first roots in the classical (rationalistic) philosophical tradition and, although that tradition had become less credible in retrospect when the belief in the

---

3. This most appropriate German term with regard to Leo Baeck means literally somebody who cares for the spiritual welfare of his people (usually translated 'pastor').
4. *Encyclopaedia Judaica* (Jerusalem 1971), vol.15, entry 'Theology', p. 1109. 'Classical' refers here to Baeck's rationalistic position within Jewish thought as opposed to the 'new' existentialist thinking of Buber and Rosenzweig. In his religious practice, Baeck adhered to tradition, combining it with a liberal outlook.
5. Alexander Altmann, 'Theology in Twentieth-Century German Jewry', in *Leo Baeck Institute Yearbook* 1 (London, 1956), p. 202.
6. See Altmann, 'Theology', p. 202.
7. This path is investigated by Albert H. Friedlander in his book *Riders towards the Dawn, From ultimate suffering to tempered hope*, (London, 1993).

noble aims of human reason was shattered through the horror of organised evil, Leo Baeck never completely left the rationalistic path. We wish to consider to what extent some of the challenging questions raised by a rationalistic perspective can be regarded as valuable contributions to a meaningful discussion about the tasks of a liberal Jewish theology today. Leo Baeck combined both the universal with the particular outlook, and it seems that our current period of intellectual uncertainty and self-centredness has lost the link to a more comprehensive, unifying, universal perspective. Therefore, we must retrieve the missing dimension, for we believe with Hans Liebeschütz that 'Earlier or later the search for the "Essence of Judaism", deeply and sincerely rooted both in the ancient tradition and in the modernity of the environment, will become topical again, and in this context Leo Baeck's contribution to Jewish thought will remain indispensable.'[8]

And furthermore, if the continuation of Baeck's influence 'depends on our relationship to the world of thought ... he has left us in his writings',[9] then we must also make the effort to examine the roots of his thought in the German background of his period, not least in order to acknowledge Baeck's spiritual independence and his own Jewish interpretation of concepts and ideas against that background.

Leo Baeck participated in the *Wissenschaft des Judentums*, whose achievements he assimilated and continued.

The concept of *Wissenschaft* as it had emerged in the nineteenth century from the specific German Idealist background and under the influence of Kant and Hegel, had given the Jewish people the opportunity to redefine how they saw themselves and to formulate their own aims.[10] While the results of the *Wissenschaft des Judentums* could lay claim to having re-established Jewish autonomy and, perhaps even more importantly, the significance of the Jewish contribution to mankind as a whole, there was also much criticism: Jewish self-definition, under the influence of speculative philosophy, had remained highly abstract.[11] Geiger's concept of reform, too, had become entan-

---

8. Hans Liebeschütz, 'Between Past and Future: Leo Baeck's Historical Position', in *Leo Baeck Institute Yearbook* 11 (1966), p. 27.

9. See ibid., p. 3.

10. See Richard Schaeffler, 'Die Wissenschaft des Judentums in ihrer Beziehung zur allgemeinen Geistesgeschichte im Deutschland des 19.Jahrhunderts', in *Wissenschaft des Judentums - Chochmat Yisrael. Anfänge der Judaistik in Europa,* Julius Carlebach (ed.) (Darmstadt, 1992), p. 113–31.

11. For the influence of Hegelian thought in that context see the chapter on 'Philosophy of history and the renaissance of the Jewish people', in *Jews and German Philosophy,* Nathan Rotenstreich (New York, 1984), p. 160–9. This chapter shows how Hegelianism, here as represented by Hegel's successor K.L. Michelet, provided a reservoir of ideas for Moses Hess, one of the first theoreticians of the Jewish renaissance and of Zionism.

gled in idealism and historicism and was criticised for having been forced upon Jews by the demands of the *Zeitgeist.* And although the detailed historical research of the *Wissenschaft des Judentums* deserved to be praised, it was alleged that it had been done without a proper 'vision', and worse, it had failed to address religious concerns.

Although it was through Hermann Cohen 'that 20th century Jewish theology in Germany emancipated itself from a sterile historicism',[12] it was nevertheless felt that the impact of Cohen's systematic mind and power of abstraction was too strong[13] and did not seem to have done justice to the practical demands of religion. Buber and others criticised the fictitious nature of Cohen's Judaism, which, they said, had been able to excite feelings of enthusiasm, but had failed to produce any practical impact.[14]

Leo Baeck arose to meet the challenge. First, he distanced himself from historicism: although he had noticed parallels in the history of the Jewish people over the centuries,

> he was not interested in constructing a line of development which Geiger had taken to be the basis of his reform movement.
> His (own) emphasis (was)on the unchanging directions of Jewish mind and will, out of which have come adequate answers to the needs of successive periods.[15]

Baeck wished that his students 'should develop a feeling for the permanent core of Judaism ... to be preserved in a productive dialogue with the currents of the contemporary world ... a living restatement of the classic tradition'.[16] In this way, the persistence of Jewish values would guarantee and strengthen Jewish physical perseverance; not development, but permanence *(Beharren),* was the factor that shaped Jewish destiny as its inner force. Just as Baeck combined the more traditional interpretation of Jewish sources, which he had practised at the Breslau Seminary, with the modern scholarship requirements without restriction taught at the Hochschule in Berlin, he sought to mediate in his theology between the lasting core of Judaism and its infinite variety of appearances.[17]

Leo Baeck's philosophical development owed, of course, a great deal to H. Cohen. Altmann even goes so far as to attribute 'the singular moral strength which enabled him to remain unperturbed and

12. Altmann, 'Theology', p. 194.
13. See Hans Liebeschütz, 'Jewish thought and its German background', in *Leo Baeck Institute Yearbook* 1 (London, 1956), p. 222-7.
14. See ibid., p. 225.
15. Hans Liebeschütz, 'Judaism and History of Religion in Leo Baeck's work', in *Leo Baeck Institute Yearbook* 2 (London, 1957), p. 14.
16. Ibid., p. 13.
17. See Liebeschütz, 'Between Past and Future', p. 7.

steadfast in the face of evil ... [to] the idealist faith which Cohen had planted in his soul'.[18] But Baeck went beyond Cohen by adding to the idealist concept of religion as one unending ethical task a passionate enthusiasm for the Jewish tradition.[19] God, to him, was more than an abstract notion. He reasserted the right of religion to speak to the heart and emphasised the reality of religious experience.[20] Baeck's primary concern was to recapture the living reality of God in individual Jewish lives, thereby defining theology as a 'reflection' *(Besinnung)* upon tradition.[21]

It seems that Leo Baeck was regarded as having been more a theologian rather than a philosopher,[22] although he incorporated successfully many philosophical notions of his period into his edifice of ideas. But how far these were presented in a 'system' – at a time when a system seemed to have been an indispensable feature of a philosophy proper[23] – remains to be discussed.[24] It would perhaps

---

18. Altmann, 'Theology', p. 198.

19. See Albert Friedlander, *Leo Baeck: Teacher of Theresienstadt* (London, 1973) (New York/Chicago/San Francisco 1968), p. 149.

20. The philosophical influences he received from Schleiermacher and Dilthey have been widely commented upon; from the first he took the notion of religion as 'Provinz im Gemüt' (a province within the soul, a sentiment), and from Dilthey's 'Psychologie des Verstehens' the idea that, whereas the natural sciences (*Naturwissenschaften*) provide causal explanation, the achievement of the humanities (*Geisteswissenschaften*) consists in comprehending meaning: 'Die Natur erklären wir, das Seelenleben verstehen wir.' The purpose of Dilthey's theory was to give to the humanities their own independent methodological foundation opposite the natural sciences. Comprehension was to be directed towards 'the real categories of life', an approach that allowed past ideas of former epochs to live again.

21. See Homolka, pp. 141ff.

22. Neither Julius Guttmann, in his *Philosophies of Judaism*, a history of Jewish philosophy from biblical times to Franz Rosenzweig (New York, 1964, 1973) nor Heinrich and Marie Simon in their *Geschichte der jüdischen Philosophie* (Munich 1984) mention Leo Baeck. See also Albert Friedlander, *Leo Baeck: Teacher*, p. 148: 'Baeck was a theologian, not a philosopher.'

23. This would explain why Rosenzweig (but not Buber) is represented in Guttmann's history of Jewish philosophy. Rosenzweig's attempt to conceptualise experience into a structure shows him following in the footsteps of German Idealists (Schelling in particular), in spite of his own declared opposition to traditional philosophy. See Guttmann, *Philosophies*, p. 423. In contrast, Buber made it clear that he had no system. His contributions were directed against the rationalistic trend and have their origin in Eastern European Hassidism, but also in German Romanticism. See Simon, *Geschichte*, pp. 224f. There is a tendency now in contemporary histories of Jewish thought to include, next to the 'rationalistic' thinkers (amongst whom are Cohen and Baeck) 'non-rationalist models', as they are called, and other 'drafts' which have not yet been categorised. See Eugene B. Borowitz, *Choices in Modern Jewish Thought* (New York, 1983).

24. Leo Baeck was opposed to systems, because he feared that religious notions might easiliy become 'fossilised' *(versteinert)*. Furthermore, he felt that a system was

not be wrong to say that Leo Baeck was also too modest to have wanted to produce a philosophy. He never wished to proclaim any knowledge about God; instead, he believed that the right approach for men towards the divine would more appropriately be achieved through deeds rather than by philosophical speculation.[25] But, while he chose not to follow Cohen's 'abstract' philosophy, a new criticism was brought forward: Baeck had transferred revelation, traditionally understood as a unique event in the past, into the continuity of Jewish experience, and he had thereby allegedly 'reduced' religious concepts to a humanist level.[26]

Apparently, Baeck's philosophy was seen as 'too theological' by some and his theology as 'too philosophical' by others – the dilemma of a thinker who tried to find a middle path.[27] Other reasons, too, might have been responsible for people's reluctance to adopt his thought: Leo Baeck's style of writing, although elegant and clear, had a most 'uncommon sense of structure': he expressed his thoughts lucidly, and with deep piety, but in a rather detached way. It was characteristic of him to balance firmly his 'paradoxa' of religious experience with a rational clarity of purpose.[28] Fritz Bamberger points out that Baeck did not want to teach children for the simple reason that they would expect simple and straightforward answers even to difficult questions. Baeck's conscience however could not accept any demand for simplification.[29]

Secondly, the scope of Baeck's knowledge was vast. He was generous in his use of sources, but unfortunately he did not think much of footnotes. He often aimed at giving a synopsis of the development and the interrelation of the important spiritual and religious phenomena by simply giving references based on a shared cultural background. Today, the comprehensive perspective is a rare phenomenon.[30] Baeck very much epitomised the scholar of his day and age: 'Was er

---

inappropriate for a 'seeker'. See Friedlander, *Leo Baeck: Teacher*, pp. 7, 144 and 149. In Baeck's opinion, the constant search for answers reflected the very nature of Judaism itself, the tension which lay at the root of its continuous vitality.

25. See Liebeschütz, 'Between Past and Future', pp. 11f.

26. See Altmann, 'Theology', p. 200.

27. 'The middle way is suspected by all the factions. And Baeck's teachings, quite simply, were not recognised for what they were.' Friedlander, *Leo Baeck: Teacher*, p. 208.

28. See Hans Bach, *The German Jew, a synthesis of Jewish and Western Civilization*, 1730–1930, (Oxford, 1984) (reprinted 1985), p. 170.

29. See Fritz Bamberger, 'Leo Baeck – der Mensch und die Idee', in *Worte des Gedenkens*, Reichmann (ed.), p. 77. For Baeck's method of teaching see also pp. 77–82.

30. See also Wolfgang Hamburger, 'The Hebrew Union College', in *Festschrift zum 80. Geburtstag von Leo Baeck* (London 1953), p. 105. The students at the Hebrew Union College, where Baeck taught in 1948, could often not follow his difficult

studierte, war unmittelbar und gegenwärtig in ihm'('Whatever he studied he made his own immediately and forever').[31]

Which course has Jewish theology taken since Baeck, and to what
extent have subsequent theological outlines made use of the rationalistic perspective?

At this stage it perhaps needs pointing out that attempts to formulate a Jewish theology have often been dismissed as an 'un-Jew-
ish' exercise, given that the core element of the Jewish religion was
seen to be the practical deed rather than speculation. While, in the
post-emancipation period, the traditional outlook towards practice
was challenged, the 'scholarly reconstruction' of what still mattered
to Judaism took place,[32] at first through the application of a historical perspective, to which religion too was subjected. The traditional
Breslau Seminary, although it carried the name 'Jewish *theological*
Seminary', had shown no intention of presenting the contents of
Judaism as a system of faith. Baeck, challenged by the Christian con-
notation of theology and the Greek ideal of perfection, completeness
and harmony, emphasised the Jewish never-ending task: to find
one's standpoint in life, continually, and to look toward something
that is beyond.[33]

Altogether, the 'reinvigoration' of Judaism was achieved by the
'concerted whole' of four outstanding thinkers of German Jewry:
Cohen, Baeck, Buber and Rosenzweig.[34] It was their common effort
which brought a new strength and resilience to Judaism in the twentieth century. The 'fence around the Torah' in the Talmudic period
had become a high wall during the Middle Ages until, through the
hopes and promises of a fraternal mankind, it was rebuilt in the nineteenth and twentieth century as a demarcation line only. While the
old fence had been held up by religious customs, the new fence, for
many, consisted just of religious ideas.[35] Recovering their vital power
became the aim of liberal Judaism. Baeck fully supported the new
programme, but he did not wish to abandon tradition. He spoke of
the 'elasticity of the fence'[36] which 'we must preserve ... to protect

---

style and frame of reference and were unable to respond to him. See Leonard
Baker, *Days of Sorrow and Pain: Leo Baeck and the Berlin Jews*, (New York/London,
1978), p. 327f.

31. Max Gruenewald, 'Leo Baeck – Zeuge und Richter', in *Worte des Gedenkens*,
Reichmann (ed.), p. 95.

32. See Leo Baeck's account of how theology emerged as a need of the new age, in
'Theologie und Geschichte' (1938), in *Aus drei Jahrtausenden* (Tübingen, 1958).

33. See Leo Baeck, 'Jewish Existence'. A Lehrhaus Lecture (30 May 1935), translated
by C. Cassel, *European Judaism* 1994/1, p. 13.

34. See Bach, *The German Jew*, p. 169.

35. See ibid., pp. 246f.

36. See Leo Baeck, *The Essence of Judaism* (New York, 1976), p. 270.

the existence and ... the task of Judaism'. Therefore, Baeck's position cannot be labelled as clearly liberal,[37] nor was it any longer straightforwardly orthodox. Orthodox thinkers criticised his 'failure to give due prominence to the halakhic tradition'[38] and that Halacha itself had been acknowledged more as an idea and as a concept than as an efficient life force.[39] Halacha, so it was alleged, had been brought by Baeck into a 'state of suspension', while Baeck himself was reproached for his 'indecision'[40] in these matters and for avoiding a clear position. And yet, Baeck's liberalism had contested neither the status nor the validity of the Halacha.

On the other hand, his portrayal of Judaism was seen to be highly commendable, because it 'shows a balance and penetration unequalled elsewhere'.[41] At a time when religious liberalism thought it had fulfilled its task, Leo Baeck reinterpreted Judaism and gave new meaning to the character of the Jewish people as a people and as a religious community, as well as to Jewish history.[42] W. Kaufman appreciates in Leo Baeck in particular his 'renewed awareness of the existentialist reality of the Jewish people' and points out that 'the pragmatic value ... lies in its hope in man as exemplified in the Jewish people's perennial capacity for rebirth'.[43] Regrettably perhaps, Leo Baeck's existentialist contribution has hardly been noticed. Instead, one turned to the works of Rosenzweig and Buber who had outlined a structure of a programme for a Jewish theology, but while their philosophical ideas expressing existentialist concerns were studied in depth, their theological outline seems to have been neglected for quite a while.

In this context it is interesting to point out, that Leo Baeck himself drew a parallel between his own thinking and Heidegger's notorious formula about 'das Seiende, dem es in seinem Sein um dieses selbst geht'[44] when he defined: 'Jewish thinking is just the thinking in which man is included, which concerns him in his concrete reality, in his appointed concrete hour in which he is just now'.[45] Jewish thinking means obedience to the commandment, and Leo Baeck points out that Heidegger – either consciously or otherwise – used a biblical

37. See Friedlander, *Leo Baeck: Teacher*, p. 197.
38. Altmann, 'Theology', p. 200.
39. See Jeschajahu Aviad-Wolfsberg: 'Zu Leo Baecks Gedächtnis', in *Worte des Gedenkens*, Reichmann (ed.), p. 147.
40. See ibid., pp. 149f.
41. Altmann, 'Theology', p. 200.
42. See Georg Salzberger, 'Leo Baeck und seine Bedeutung für die Geistesgeschichte des neuzeitlichen Judentums', in *Worte des Gedenkens*, Reichmann (ed.), p. 139.
43. William E. Kaufman, *Contemporary Jewish Philosophies* (New York, 1976), p. 263.
44. 'a being such that in its being its being is in question'. This translation is given by D. W. Hamlyn, *The Pelican History of Western Philosophy* (London, 1989 (1987)), p. 324.
45. Baeck, 'Jewish Existence', p. 14.

thought when he said: 'To be *[Dasein]* does not mean to be present *[Vorhandensein]*, but to be at hand *[Zuhandensein]*.'

This is how Jewish thinking should be looked upon: not as dreaming or contemplating, but as realising what the commandment orders, so that life is always at hand.[46]

While Buber and Rosenzweig were studied in Europe, Reform Judaism in America turned to Kaufmann Kohler rather than to Baeck. We want to consider briefly which direction liberal theology took there and what its main characteristics and concerns were.

Kaufmann Kohler was born into an orthodox home in Fürth (Bavaria) in 1843.[47] For his increasingly liberal views he felt particularly indebted to S. R. Hirsch who 'liberated [him] from the thraldom of blind authority worship and led [him] ... from not thinking into the realms of free reason and research ...'[48] The other major influence on him was Abraham Geiger.

After his studies at various German universities he later became the President of the Hebrew Union College in Cincinnati. His *Jewish Theology* (New York, 1918) had set itself two aims: one was to 'investigate historically ... the fundamental principle underlying a doctrine, to note the different conceptions formed at various stages, and trace its process of growth'. Secondly, 'a systematic theology of Judaism must [present Judaism] in relation to the most advanced scientific and philosophic ideas of the age, so as to offer a comprehensive view of life and the world.'[49] Kohler believed in both reason and religious intuition, but was criticised by Altmann for having described 'the true Judaism as "pure inwardness"',[50] and Gershom Scholem claimed that the rationalist Kohler had used a concept of revelation that could be shown to be 'mystical' rather than rational.[51]

The rationalistic line which Kohler, based on his German spiritual inheritance, had initiated in America was continued by Samuel S. Cohon, Reform rabbi and professor of theology at HUC. In his *Jewish Theology*[52] he granted reason the highest status possible with

---

46. See ibid., p. 15.
47. See Max J. Kohler, 'Biographical sketch of Dr. K. Kohler', in *Studies in Jewish Literature* issued in honour of Prof. K. Kohler on the occasion of his 70th birthday, Georg Reimer (ed.) (Berlin, 1913).
48. Ibid., p. 3.
49. Kaufmann Kohler, *Jewish Theology*: Systematically and historically considered (New York, 1918), pp. 4 and 6.
50. Altmann, 'Theology', p. 200.
51. Scholem quotes F. Kohler as looking upon revelation as 'the appearance of God in the depth of the mirror of the soul', in: Scholem, 'Reflections on Jewish Theology' (1974), in *On Jews and Judaism in Crisis* (New York, 1976), p. 272.
52. The subtitle is: *A historical and systematic interpretation of Judaism and its foundations* (Assen, 1971).

regard to religion: that of a 'corrective' to religious practice and as a guide, to clear the religious path of obstructions, of inconsistencies and self-contradictions.[53] He sees the scope of Jewish theology expressed in the three questions; what are our beliefs and practices? How did they arise and assume their present character? And what is their value for us today?[54]

The American reconstructionist rabbi Jacob Bernard Agus reminds us of H. Cohen in his 'yearning for the "purity" of logical thought'[55] and also of Leo Baeck, when he defines liberal faith as always 'becoming, never a possession'.[56] He underlines the perpetual movement from the particular to the universal and declares that the opportunity of spiritual growth arises out of the constant tension and alternation of viewpoint.[57] The 'nature and task of liberal Judaism' is summed up by two commitments, each complementing the other: one to our sacred tradition, the other toward the universal ideas of mankind. However, in this reconstructionist approach there is always a subjective element: one begins with 'the prompting of one's own heart and mind, not with a book or a set of books ... it challenges each person to discover the meaning of the Divine image in his own soul'.[58]

At this point we continue with Scholem who rejoices that not even a rationalist like Cohen could help but relocate the revelation at Sinai into the human heart[59] (not into the mind!). He also finds the progressive idea of one's own access to revelation, thereby combining divine authority with human freedom, quite extraordinarily audacious.[60] And yet, it is difficult to see how a subjective element in our approach to revelation can be avoided, and Scholem points to a further complication: if revelation is the word of God, which was originally thought to be sensibly perceptible, then an assertion that ascribes a sensible activity to God is nothing less than an anthropomorphism![61] In Scholem's view, however, a modification of the problem of subjectivity was achieved by placing 'tradition' next to 'revelation', with the result that 'the infinite meaning of revelation ...

---

53. See ibid., pp. 2–4.
54. See ibid., p. 13.
55. B. Agus, *Dialogue and Tradition, The Challenges of Contemporary Judeo-Christian Thought* (London/New York/Toronto, 1971), p. 556.
56. Ibid., p. 554.
57. See ibid., pp. 559f.
58. Ibid., p. 557.
59. See Scholem, *On Jews,* p. 272.
60. See ibid., p. 270. But how can the listener, who is at the same time an interpreter, make sense of the message conveyed at all, if he is not already familiar with the 'skopos'?
61. See ibid., p. 266.

[would] unfold only in continued relation to time'. It was through tradition that Judaism was able to realise its concept of revelation,
although the authoritative character of this continual revelation 'fell
victim to historical criticism', leaving behind the category of tradition, 'a doctrine conducive to vagueness and ambiguity' with regard
to the idea of 'inspiration'.[62]

The belief that the divine origin of the Jewish tradition was incom-
patible with an application of modern thought was also held by the
Reform rabbi Max Wiener.[63] At first, Wiener felt close to (neo-)Kan-
tianism and Cohen – perhaps while he worked as second rabbi under
Leo Baeck in Düsseldorf. Hans Liebeschütz describes the difference
and the similarity between the two rabbis: 'Both had a deep interest
in philosophical thought and both refused to search for the right
speculative and metaphysical formulation as expression of religious
truth.' But, while Baeck would avoid judgements out of respect for a
great thinker, Wiener, by contrast, 'felt the urge to reach clear-cut
concepts'. Wiener did not even hesitate to pass an unfavourable
judgement about Baeck's *Essence of Judaism*: the book could 'not have
been intended as a theological book as it had avoided specifically
theological problems, which today challenge us to test them ...'.[64] In
about 1928, Wiener was greatly concerned that a definition of the
essentials of Judaism as expressed in mere rational ideas would lead
to a general religion and exclude any genuine impact of the Jewish
past.[65] He voiced his fears in a most challenging contribution entitled
Jüdische Religion im Zeitalter der Emanzipation[66] (1933), a standard work
that apparently still awaits its proper appreciation and review.

One of the central questions for Wiener was: to what extent did
the reconstruction of Judaism, which had become necessary since the
challenges of the Enlightenment period, follow its own inner
impulses, and to what extent had Judaism given in to the temptations
that had demanded new constructs in order to conform to the so-
called *Zeitgeist*? Did these new constructs, in the broad light of day,
not turn out to be a fictitious cover-up of an actual capitulation?[67]

62. See ibid., pp. 271–4. For a good overview of the hermeneutical problem that
    Scholem addresses here, see also Michael Fishbane, 'Hermeneutics', in *Contempo-
    rary Jewish religious thought*, Arthur A.Cohen and Paul Mendes-Flohr (eds) (New
    York/London, 1988), pp. 353–61.
63. See Hans Liebeschütz: 'Max Wiener's reinterpretation of liberal Judaism', in *Leo
    Baeck Yearbook 5*, 1960, pp. 41f.
64. Ibid., p. 45, footnote 23.
65. See ibid., pp. 43f.
66. Berlin 1933. See the extract in Schalom Ben-Chorin and Verena Lenzen (eds),
    Jüdische Theologie im 20. Jahrhundert (Munich/Zurich, 1988), pp. 103–32.
67. See ibid., pp. 131f.: 'Es erfordert grosse Aufmerksamkeit, darüber zu entscheiden,
    in welchem Umfange der religiöse Wiederaufbau ... inneren Antrieben auch

Both Wiener's and Scholem's merit was to have pointed out some challenging problems that continue to present themselves to a questioning mind and that a liberal theology of today should consider. Both Wiener and Scholem challenged the idea of reason as a 'replacement' for religion, which perhaps some of the pioneers of liberal Judaism had come close to, when following in the footsteps of German Idealist philosophy.

While Wiener was against any metaphysical formulation of the essence of Judaism, Scholem's aim was to restore, against its old rival rationalism, the glory of mysticism, although his 'Reflections on Jewish Theology' administers such a critical sweeping blow all around, that he does not even spare the mystics themselves. And, as regards the above-mentioned problem of revelation, he states mockingly that 'not even the existentialist theologians have been successful in obscuring or obliterating from memory this destructive state of affairs, although one must admit that they – above all, Martin Buber and Abraham Joshua Heschel – employed their considerable eloquence for the purpose of evading the issue'.[68]

In a discussion on the position and possibilities of Jewish theology today the following questions should be asked according to Scholem:[69] what are the authoritative sources of the theology in question and how are its fundamental religious categories legitimised? Which central values can be established from such sources? What is the position of Judaism in today's world and what impact do the events of the Holocaust, and the creation of the state of Israel, have upon us Jews?

Scholem diagnoses our age as one of 'secularisation of all aspects of the human' and draws attention to the 'dwindling of visible religious authority'.[70] The 'most prominent characteristics ... of the conception of God's actions in the world, namely severity and compassion, have been transferred', according to Scholem's own unique sense of irony, 'from the hands of God into those of the materialists and psychoanalysts'.[71] Scholem also criticises the uninhibited optimism apparent in the belief that the technological rev-

---

gefolgt, und wie weit er den Versuchungen erlegen ist, in Anpassung an sogenannte Zeitgemässheit Konstruktionen aufzurichten, die bei Licht besehen sich als fiktive Deckungen einer tatsächlichen Kapitulation erweisen.'

68. Scholem, *On Jews,* p. 274.
69. See ibid., p. 261.
70. Ibid., p. 291.
71. Ibid., pp. 290f. See also Eugene B. Borowitz, for whom 'the autonomy which once was fulfilled in conscience and social responsibility now is directed to getting in touch with oneself, one's body, one's sensations ... and one's inner satisfactions'. He describes our society as infected with 'callousness and moral rot', where selfishness has done damage to the old concept of personal autonomy characteristic of early liberalism. See Borowitz, *Choices,* p. 261.

olution would solve problems of value, and emphasises that technology excludes the religious sphere by definition. However, there is still a streak of optimism in the dark picture he paints: he sees in the state of Israel, even if widely secularised, a guarantee for the continuity of the Jewish religion.[72]

In these reflections on Jewish theology, written about twenty years ago, Scholem addressed many of the topoi that appear in Buber's 'table of contents', the outline of a programme for a new Jewish theology.[73] While Scholem's first question about the authority of religious sources reflects in part Buber's second main topos entitled 'elements', the problem of the relationship between state and religion (Buber's Part I) is dealt with by Scholem on the basis of a diagnosis of current present-day characteristics. Finally, Buber's last point (III.4) about the role Judaism could play in solving the spiritual problems of the age has perhaps been given a hopeful expression by Scholem: 'if technology, sociology and psychology ... were porous, so that something else could become transparent in them, then at least a situation would be created in which religious attitude could develop into a fruitful dialogue with those areas'.[74]

In conclusion one should consider the one remaining point of Buber's outline, namely that of education and methods of teaching. It is at this point that one returns to Leo Baeck and the heritage he has left us.

The influence of Leo Baeck's thought has been felt through the work of his pupils, both in America, where he taught at the Hebrew Union College, and in England,[75] where, in the year of his death, in 1956, the Leo Baeck College was founded for the training of rabbis and teachers. The college regards itself as the direct heir to the *Hochschule für die Wissenschaft des Judentums* in Berlin. Leo Baeck was never before so disheartened as when he learned that it was closed down by the Nazis in 1942.[76] Shortly afterwards he expressed his hope that the work of the Hochschule should be continued in England.[77] He felt that there should be a special obligation and responsibility to transmit the heritage of German Jewry to future generations.[78] To fulfil this expectation has also been the endeavour of the Leo Baeck Institute, with its research centres in Jerusalem,

---

72. See Scholem, *On Jews*, p. 297.
73. See Homolka, pp. 99f.
74. See Scholem, On Jews, p. 291.
75. See Friedlander, *Leo Baeck: Teacher*, p. 50. See also Friedlander, *Riders towards the Dawn*, pp. 150ff. and pp. 121f.
76. See Baker, *Days of Sorrow and Pain*, p. 264.
77. See ibid., p. 260.
78. See ibid., p. 65.

New York and London.[79] Both the Institute and the College are
aware of their indebtedness to their spiritual founder, even though
some may believe that it is difficult to match the outstanding achievement of the German Jewish legacy. We will also have to admit that
the wide scope and richness of Leo Baeck's spiritual world based on
German *Geistesgeschichte* could not be replanted in its entirety outside
Germany. And furthermore, 'when we consider the content and the
aim of his [Leo Baeck's] thought, and writing in defining the spiritual
function of the Jewish inheritance, we cannot avoid the conclusion
that there is nothing on his level to replace his contribution.'[80] This
leaves us with a tremendous feeling of loss. However, we must reflect
upon our task which Leo Baeck has outlined for us: 'Verständnis und
Ehrfurcht sollen das Wesen des liberalen Judentums ausmachen.
Jüdisches Lernen und das Wissen um den Bund zwischen Israel und
seinem Gott sind die beiden Aufgaben, die dem Judentum unserer
Tage gestellt sind' ('Understanding and reverence must belong to
the essence of liberal Judaism. Jewish learning and the knowledge
about the Covenant between Israel and its God are the two tasks
which have been placed before the Judaism of our time').[81]

As early as 1938, Leo Baeck formulated the tasks for a Jewish theology: it would have to embrace a well-founded knowledge of the
whole history of Judaism and its own particularity. Secondly, it
would have to trace the idea of the tension between the infinite and
the finite, out of which emerges the task: to reflect upon the past and
to give meaning to the present (reflection means here: *Be-sinnung auf
Vergangenes und Sinn-gebung*).[82]

Leo Baeck wanted to stir the community to respect learning, so
that the reflection upon past values would give meaning to our practices of today.

In order to fulfil the task, we will have to consider the spiritual
heritage of Baeck's own time also, including the grand rationalistic
schemes that German Jewish philosophy has bequeathed to us.

Scholem's and Wiener's critical outlines of the possibilities of a
Jewish theology might still function as starting points for further fruitful discussions. Both have shown that a philosophical, critical
approach is indispensable to modern theology, even though they
were both sceptical as to what reason could achieve for religious
thought. Scholem does not believe in a secular morality built on rea-

79. See Hans Seidenberg, 'Eine Lücke in der deutschen Geschichtsschreibung', in *Leo
    Baeck: Lehrer und Helfer in schwerer Zeit*, Arnoldshainer Texte 20, Werner Licharz
    (ed.) (Frankfurt am Main, 1983), pp. 188–193.
80. Liebeschütz, 'Between Past and Future', p. 26.
81. Leo Baeck, quoted by Ernst L. Ehrlich, in Licharz (ed.), *Leo Baeck*, p. 96.
82. See Baeck, 'Theologie und Geschichte', in *Aus drei Jahrtausenden*, p. 39.

son alone: 'Morality as a constructive force is impossible without religion, without some Power beyond Pure Reason.'[83] And yet, Scholem calls himself an admirer of reason, because he regards reason as an important tool that serves both construction and destruction.[84]

Max Wiener, too, had great philosophical talents. Clarity and exactitude of language were matched by an acute awareness of problematic issues. Despite his depreciation of certain philosophical trends, he succeeded Julius Guttmann to the chair of philosophy and soon became a very successful teacher of Jewish philosophy in his own right.[85] While, initially, he saw the position of philosophical thought in Judaism 'as merely marginal', the anti-philosopher Wiener returned to philosophy during the last years of his life. A posthumous manuscript testifies to his urgent

> plea for an education which would kindle interest in philosophical reflections as the final aim in teaching both the arts and scientific subjects. Only thus can an impulse for the formation of a comprehensive view of the world be given, which is the necessary presupposition of any serious interest in religion.[86]

Is philosophy still interwoven with theology today?

Albert Friedlander points out that 'our theologians are afraid of classic philosophy', and we agree with him that existentialism is responsible for having 'brought a particular type of anti-intellectualism into modern theology'.[87]

A Jewish theology for today needs philosophical underpinning, particularly in a world that experiences a disorienting loss of cultural consensus and a lack of conceptual coherence.[88]

Leo Baeck's way was the middle way between philosophy and theology, and he was attacked by both sides. Let us hope with A. H. Friedlander, in accordance with Geiger's dictum, that 'the middle way may well be the path which will endure'.[89]

---

83. 'With Gershom Scholem. An interview', in Scholem, *On Jews,* p. 32.
84. See ibid., p. 31.
85. See Liebeschütz, 'Max Wiener's reinterpretation', pp. 44ff.
86. Ibid., p. 56f.
87. Friedlander, *Leo Baeck: Teacher,* p. 268.
88. For a discussion about the present relationship between Jewish philosophy and theology see also Esther Seidel, 'Jewish philosophy and Jewish thought', in Irene Kajon (ed.), *La storia della filosofia ebraica,* Biblioteca dell'Archivio di Filosofia 9 (Padua, 1993), pp. 509–24.
89. Friedlander, *Leo Baeck: Teacher,* pp. 268f.

Not only would this middle way make us realise Leo Baeck's influence upon Jewish life in our own time and bring us closer to our own self-knowledge,[90] but, by combining the duties of the heart with the demands of reason, we shall perhaps be able to fulfil the hope that Leo Baeck once expressed: the hope arising from 'the great opportunity of Judaism in our day to be again a universal religion, if only we would rise to the opportunity'.[91]

90. Friedlander, *Leo Baeck: Leben und Lehre* (Stuttgart, 1973) (Munich, 1990) (new version of the formerly quoted English edition of *Leo Baeck: Teacher of Theresienstadt*), p. 66.
91. Leo Baeck quoted in Norman Bentwich 'Tribute', in *Worte des Gedenkens*, Reichmann (ed.), p. 206.

BIBLIOGRAPHY

Ackermann, Aron, *Judentum und Christentum* (Leipzig, 1903)
Aland, Kurt, *Hilfsbuch zum Lutherstudium*, 3rd edn (Witten, 1970)
Allgemeine Zeitung des Judenthums: ein unparteiisches Organ für alles jüdische Interesse, founded by Rabbi Dr Ludwig Phillipson; Editor: Dr Gustav Karpeles (from 1909 Ludwig Geiger) (Berlin, 1870 onwards)
Althaus, Paul, *Die Theologie Martin Luthers*, 2nd edn (Gütersloh, 1963)
_____, *Um die Wahrheit des Evangeliums* (Stuttgart, 1962)
Altmann, Alexander, 'Franz Rosenzweig and Eugen Rosenstock-Huessy: An Introduction to their Letters on Judaism and Christianity', in *Essays in Jewish Intellectual History*, Alexander Altmann (ed.) (Hanover, New Hampshire/London, 1981), pp. 246–65
Altmann, Alexander, 'Hermann Cohens Begriff der Korrelation', in *In zwei Welten: Festschrift für Siegfried Moses*, Hans Tramer (ed.) (Tel Aviv, 1962), pp. 377–99
Altmann, Alexander, 'Leo Baeck and the Jewish Mystical Tradition', in *Essays in Jewish Intellectual History*, Alexander Altmann (ed.) (Hanover, New Hampshire/London, 1981), pp. 293–311
Altmann, Alexander, 'Theology in Twentieth-Century German Jewry', in *Leo Baeck Institute Yearbook* 1 (1956), pp. 193–216
Altmann, Alexander, 'Zur Auseinandersetzung mit der "dialektischen Theologie"', in *Monatsschrift für Geschichte und Wissenschaft des Judentums* 79 N.S. 43 (1935), pp. 193–216
Andresen, Carl, ed., *Handbuch der Dogmen- und Theologiegeschichte*, vol. 1: *Die Lehrentwicklung im Rahmen der Katholizität* (Göttingen, 1989)
_____, ed., *Handbuch der Dogmen- und Theologiegeschichte*, vol. 2: *Die Lehrentwicklung im Rahmen der Konfessionalität* (Göttingen, 1989)
Antoni, Carlo, *Vom Historismus zur Soziologie* (Stuttgart, s.a.)
Apfelbacher, Karl-Ernst, *Frömmigkeit und Wissenschaft: Ernst Troeltsch und sein theologisches Programm* (Munich, 1978)
Asheim, Ivar, ed., *Kirche, Mystik, Heiligung und das Natürliche bei Luther: Vorträge des Dritten Internationalen Kongresses für Lutherforschung*, (Göttingen, 1967)
Baeck, Leo, *Aus drei Jahrtausenden* (Tübingen, 1958)

———, *Dieses Volk: Jüdische Existenz*, vol. 1, 2nd edn (Frankfurt am Main, 1955)

———, *Dieses Volk: Jüdische Existenz*, vol. 2 (Frankfurt am Main, 1957)

———, *Epochen der jüdischen Geschichte* (Stuttgart, 1974)

———, *The Essence of Judaism*, (Frankfort, 1930) (London, 1936)

———, *Geist und Blut* (Berlin, 1931)

———, *God and Man in Judaism* (London, 1958)

———, *Judaism and Christianity* (New York, 1958)

———, *Paulus, die Pharisäer und das Neue Testament* (Frankfurt am Main, 1961)

———, *Judentum, Christentum und Islam: Rede gehalten von Ehren-Grosspräsident Dr. Leo Baeck anlässlich der Studientagung der Districts-Gross-Loge Kontinental-Europa XIX in Bruxelles* (22 April 1956)

———, *Spinozas erste Einwirkungen auf Deutschland: Inaugural-Dissertation* (Berlin, 1895)

———, *Wege im Judentum* (Berlin, 1933)

———, *Das Wesen des Judentums,* 1st edn (Berlin, 1905)

———, *Das Wesen des Judentums*, 2nd edn (Frankfurt am Main, 1922) and (Wiesbaden, s.a.)

Baeck, Leo, 'Bismarck posthumus', in *Allgemeine Zeitung des Judenthums*, 14 April 1899, p. 169–71

Baeck, Leo, 'The Faith of Paul', in *Journal of Jewish Studies*, 3 (1952), pp. 93–110

Baeck, Leo, 'Haggadah and Christian Doctrine', in *Hebrew Union College Annual* 23,1 (1950/51), pp. 549–60 (paged also: 1–12)

Baeck, Leo, 'Harnack's Vorlesungen über das Wesen des Christentums', in *Monatsschrift für Geschichte und Wissenschaft des Judentums* 45 (1901), pp. 97–120

Baeck, Leo, 'Hat das überlieferte Judentum Dogmen?', in *Wissenschaft des Judentums im deutschen Sprachbereich*, Kurt Wilhelm (ed.), 2 vols (Tübingen, 1967), pp. 737–52

Baeck, Leo, 'Judaism in the Church', in *Hebrew Union College Annual* 2 (1925), pp. 125–44

Baeck, Leo, 'Das Judentum', in Carl Christian Clemen, *Die Religionen der Erde, ihr Wesen und ihre Geschichte* (Munich, 1927), pp. 283–318

Baeck, Leo, 'The Psychological Root of the Law', (Wingate Lecture at the Hebrew University in 1951), Hebrew University Garland, ed. by Norman Bentwich (London, 1952), pp. 11–17

Baeck, Leo, 'Romantische Religion', in *Festschrift zum 50jährigen Bestehen der Hochschule für die Wissenschaft des Judentums* (Berlin, 1922), pp. 3–48

Baeck, Leo, 'Some Questions to the Christian Church from the Jewish Point of View', in *The Church and the Jewish People*, Göte Hedenquist (ed.) (London, 1954), pp. 102–16

Baeck, Leo, 'Theologie und Geschichte', in *Bericht der Lehranstalt für die Wissenschaft des Judentums* 49 (1932), pp. 42–54

Baeck, Leo, 'Der Wandel der jüdischen Blickrichtung', in *Littera Judaica: Festschrift Edwin Guggenheim*, Paul Jacob and Ernst Ludwig Ehrlich (eds) (Frankfurt am Main, 1964), pp. 107–21

Baeck, Leo, 'World Religion and National Religion', in *Mordecai M. Kaplan Jubilee Volume on the Occasion of his Seventieth Birthday* (New York, 1953), pp. 1–7

Baker, Leonard, *Days of Sorrow and Pain: Leo Baeck and the Berlin Jews* (New York/London, 1978)

_____, *Hirt der Verfolgten* (Stuttgart, 1982)

Baron, Salo W., *Modern Nationalism and Religion* (New York/Philadelphia, 1960)

Barth, Karl, *Protestant Thought: From Rousseau to Ritschl* (New York, 1959)

Behler, Ernst, 'Kritische Gedanken zum Begriff der europäischen Romantik', in *Die europäische Romantik*, Ernst Behler, Clemens Heselhaus, Wolfram Krömer et al. (eds) (Frankfurt am Main, 1972)

Ben-Chorin, Schalom, 'Das Jesusbild im modernen Judentum', in *Zeitschrift für Religions- und Geistesgeschichte* 5 (1953), pp. 231–57

Bennigsen, Rudolf von, *Der liberale Protestantismus* (Berlin, 1888)

Benz, Richard, *Die deutsche Romantik: Geschichte einer geistigen Bewegung* (Leipzig, 1937)

Berkhof, Hendrikus, *200 Jahre Theologie: ein Reisebericht* (Neukirchen, 1985)

Berlin, Charles, *Index to Festschriften in Jewish Studies* (Cambridge, Mass./New York, 1971)

Blaser, Klauspeter, *Geschichte–Kirchengeschichte–Dogmengeschichte in Adolf von Harnacks Denken: Ein Beitrag zur Problematik der historisch-theologischen Disziplinen* (Mainz, 1964)

Birkner, Hans-Joachim, Liebig, Heinz and Scholder, Klaus, *Das konfessionelle Problem in der evangelischen Theologie des 19. Jahrhunderts* (Tübingen, 1966)

Boehlich, Walter, ed., *Der Berliner Antisemitismusstreit* (Frankfurt am Main, 1965)

Börsch, Ekkehard, *Geber–Gabe–Aufgabe: Luthers Prophetie in den Entscheidungsjahren seiner Reformation 1520–1525* (Munich, 1958)

Bonhoeffer, Dietrich, *Nachfolge*, 10th edn (Munich, 1971)

_____, *The Cost of Discipleship* (London 1949)

Bornkamm, Heinrich, *Luther im Spiegel der deutschen Geistesgeschichte* (Heidelberg, 1955)

_____, *Luthers geistige Welt* (Gütersloh, 1960)

Borowitz, Eugene B., *A New Jewish Theology in the Making* (Philadelphia, 1968)

Borowitz, Eugene B., 'Reason', in *Contemporary Jewish Religious Thought*, Arthur Cohen and Paul Mendes-Flohr (eds) (New York, 1987), pp. 749–54

Bosl, Karl, 'Die Reformation: Versuch einer Bestimmung ihres historischen Ortes und ihrer Funktion in Gesellschaft und Kultur Europas', in *Zeitschrift für bayerische Landesgeschichte* 31,1 (1968), pp. 104–23

Bousset, Wilhelm, 'Das Wesen des Christentums (Review)', in *Theologische Rundschau* 4 (1901), pp. 89–103

Bronsen, David, ed., *Jews and Germans from 1860 to 1933: The Problematic Symbiosis* (Heidelberg, 1979)

Brosseder, Johannes, *Luthers Stellung zu den Juden im Spiegel seiner Interpreten* (Munich, 1972)

Brunner, Robert, ed., *Gesetz und Gnade im Alten Testament und im jüdischen Denken* (Zurich, 1969)

Bürkle, Horst, 'Das europäische Christentum und die nichtchristlichen Kulturen', in *Zeitschrift für Missionswissenschaft* 1 (1985)

Bulhof, Ilse N., *Wilhelm Dilthey: A Hermeneutic Approach to the Study of History and Culture* (Den Haag/Boston/London, 1980)

Centralverein-Zeitung: Blätter für Deutschtum und Judentum, Organ des Centralvereins deutscher Staatsbürger jüdischen Glaubens (Berlin, 1922 onwards)

Clayton, John P., ed., *Ernst Troeltsch and the Future of Theology* (Cambridge, 1976)

Cohen, Hermann, *Der Begriff der Religion im System der Philosophie* (Gießen, 1915)
_____, *Deutschtum und Judentum* (Gießen, 1916)
_____, *Zur jüdischen Zeitgeschichte,* Jüdische Schriften 2 (Berlin, 1924)
_____, *Die religiösen Bewegungen der Gegenwart* (Leipzig, 1914)
_____, *Die Religion der Vernunft aus den Quellen des Judentums* (Leipzig, 1919)
Colpe, Hermann, 'Der Wesensbegriff Ernst Troeltschs und seine heutige Anwendbarkeit auf Christentum, Religion und Religionswissenschaft', in *Troeltsch-Studien,* vol. 3: Protestantismus und Neuzeit, Horst Renz and Friedrich Wilhelm Graf (eds) pp. 231–39
Courth, Franz, *Das Wesen des Christentums in der Liberalen Theologie* (Frankfurt am Main/Bern/Las Vegas, 1977)
Deissmann, A., ed., *Beiträge zur Weiterentwicklung der christlichen Religion* (Munich, 1905)
Delius, Hans-Ulrich, ed., *Martin-Luther-Studienausgabe* (Ost-Berlin, 1982)
Dietrich, Wendell S., *Cohen and Troeltsch* (Atlanta, Georgia, 1986)
Dilthey, Wilhelm, *Der Aufbau der geschichtlichen Welt in den Geisteswissenschaften* (Frankfurt am Main, 1981)
_____, *Ethica* (Berlin, 1915)
_____, *Grundriß der allgemeinen Geschichte der Philosophie* (Frankfurt am Main, 1949)
_____, *Leben Schleiermachers* (Berlin/Leipzig, 1922)
_____, *Das Wesen der Philosophie* (Stuttgart, 1984)
Dilthey, Wilhelm, 'Die Typen der Weltanschauung und ihre Ausbildung in den metaphysischen Systemen', in *Weltanschauung* (Berlin, 1911)
(Dilthey, Wilhelm), *Briefwechsel zwischen Wilhelm Dilthey und dem Grafen Paul Yorck von Wartenburg 1877–1897* (Berlin, 1923)
Döbertin, Winfried, *Adolf von Harnack: Theologe, Pädagoge, Wissenschaftspolitiker* (Frankfurt am Main/Bern/Las Vegas, 1985)
Doerry, Martin, *Übergangsmenschen: Die Mentalität der Wilhelminer und die Krise des Kaiserreichs,* 2 vols (Weinheim/Munich, 1986)
Drescher, Hans-Georg, *Ernst Troeltsch - Leben und Werk,* (Göttingen 1991)
Ebeling, Gerhard, *Luther,* 4th edn (Tübingen, 1981)
_____, *Lutherstudien,* 3 vols (Tübingen, 1971–85)
_____, *Umgang mit Luther* (Tübingen, 1983)
Ebeling, Gerhard, 'Das rechte Unterscheiden: Luthers Anleitung zu theologischer Urteilskraft', in *Zeitschrift für Theologie und Kirche* 85,2 (1988), pp. 219–58
Ebeling, Gerhard, 'usus politicus legis - usus politicus evangelii', in *Zeitschrift für Theologie und Kirche* 79 (1982), pp. 323–48
Edwards, Paul, ed., *The Encyclopedia of Philosophy* (New York/London, 1967)
Eisler, Rudolf, *Kant-Lexikon: Nachschlagewerk zu Kants sämtlichen Schriften, Briefen und handschriftlichem Nachlaß;* 8. unveränderter Nachdr. d. Ausg. (Berlin 1930) (Hildesheim/New York, 1979)
Eisler, Rudolf, *Philosophenlexikon* (Berlin, 1912)
Elbogen, Ismar, 'Ein Jahrhundert Wissenschaft des Judentums', in *Festschrift zum 50jährigen Bestehen der Hochschule für die Wissenschaft des Judentums in Berlin* (Berlin, 1922), pp. 103–144
Elbogen, Ismar, 'Neuorientierung unserer Wissenschaft', in *Monatsschrift für Geschichte und Wissenschaft des Judentums* 62 N.S. 26 (1918)
Encyclopaedia Judaica: Das Judentum in Geschichte und Gegenwart (Berlin, 1929)

Encyclopaedia Judaica (Jerusalem, 1971)

Ermarth, Michael, *Wilhelm Dilthey: The Critique of Historical Reason* (Chicago/London, 1978)

Eschelbacher, Joseph, 'Das Judentum im Urteil der modernen protestantischen Theologie', in *Schriften*, Gesellschaft zur Förderung der Wissenschaft des Judentums (ed.) (Leipzig, 1907), pp. 1–22

Eschelbacher, Joseph, 'Das Judentum und des Wesen des Christentums: Vergleichende Studien', in *Schriften*, 2nd edn, edited by Gesellschaft zur Förderung der Wissenschaft des Judentums (Berlin, 1908)

Fackenheim, Emil L., *Encounters between Judaism and Modern Philosophy: A Preface to Future Jewish Thought* (Philadelphia, 1973)

Feuerbach, Ludwig, *Das Wesen des Christentums* (Stuttgart, 1980)

Fiebig, Paul, 'Jüdische Gebete und das Vaterunser', in *Die Christliche Welt* 5 (1891), cols 313–21, 368–75

Fiebig, Paul, 'Rezension von J. Eschelbacher "Das Judentum und das Wesen des Christentums"', in *Theologische Literaturzeitung* 30 (1905), cols 418–21

Forstmann, Jack, *A Romantic Triangle: Schleiermacher and Early German Romanticism* (Missoula, Montana, 1977)

Friedlander, Albert H., *Leo Baeck: Leben und Lehre* (Stuttgart, 1973)

_____, *Leo Baeck: Teacher of Theresienstadt* (New York et al., 1968)

Friedlander, Albert H., 'Baeck and Rosenzweig', in *European Judaism* 20,2 (1986), pp. 9–15

Gabriel, Hans-Jürgen, *Christlichkeit und Gesellschaft: eine kritische Darstellung der Kulturphilosophie von Ernst Troeltsch* (Berlin (DDR), 1975)

Garthe, Barbara, 'Über Leben und Werk des Grafen Hermann Keyserling' (unpubl. diss. University of Erlangen-Nuremberg, 1976)

Geiger, Abraham, *Das Judentum und seine Geschichte* (Breslau, 1871)

Geiger, Ludwig, *Abraham Geiger's Nachgelassene Schriften*, 4 vols (Berlin, 1875–76)

Geiger, Ludwig, ed., *Abraham Geiger: Leben und Lebenswerk* (Berlin, 1910)

Geis, Robert R. (et al.), *Versuche des Verstehens* (Munich, 1966)

Gensichen, Hans-Werner, 'Das Christentum im Dialog der Kulturen: Kontextualität und Universalität', in *Zeitschrift für Missionswissenschaft* 1 (1985)

Goldschmidt, Israel, *Das Wesen des Judentums nach Bibel, Talmud, Tradition und religiöser Praxis* (Frankfurt, 1907)

Graf, Friedrich-Wilhelm, 'Konservatives Kulturluthertum', in *Zeitschrift für Theologie und Kirche* 85 (1988), pp. 31–76

Graupe, Heinz M., *Die Entstehung des modernen Judentums: Geistesgeschichte der deutschen Juden*, Hamburger Beiträge zur Geschichte der Juden 1 (Hamburg, 1969)

Greschat, Martin, ed., *Theologen des Protestantismus im 19. und 20. Jahrhundert*, 2 vols (Stuttgart et al., 1978)

Groeben, Margarete von der, *Konstruktive Psychologie und Erlebnis* (Stuttgart, 1934)

Grosse-Brockhoff, Annelen, *Das Konzept des Klassischen bei Friedrich und August Wilhelm Schlegel* (Cologne/Vienna, 1981)

Guttmann, Alexander, *The Struggle over Reform and Rabbinic Literature* (New York, 1977)

Guttmann, Julius, 'Die Normierung des Glaubensinhalts im Judentum', in *Wissenschaft des Judentums im deutschen Sprachbereich*, 2 vols, Kurt Wilhelm (ed.) (Tübingen, 1967), pp. 753–70

Guttmann, Julius, 'Religion und Wissenschaft im mittelalterlichen und modernen Denken', in *Festschrift zum 50jährigen Bestehen der Hochschule für die Wissenschaft des Judentums in Berlin* (Berlin, 1922), pp. 147–216

Guttmann, Michael, *Das Judentum und seine Umwelt* (Berlin, 1927)

Hägglund, Bengt, *Geschichte und Theologie,*(Ost-Berlin, 1983)

Harnack, Adolf von, *Erforschtes und Erlebtes: Reden und Aufsätze*, 4 vols (Gießen, 1923)

——, *Lehrbuch der Dogmengeschichte*, 3 vols, 4th edn (Tübingen, 1909–10)

——, *Reden und Aufsätze*, 2 vols, 2nd edn (Gießen, 1906)

——, *Das Wesen des Christentums*, with a preface by R. Bultmann (Stuttgart, 1950)

——, *Das Wesen des Christentums*, 2nd edn (Gütersloh, 1985)

——, *What is Christianity?,*(Philadelphia, 1986)

Hartmann, Eduard von, 'Das Wesen des Christentums in neuester Beleuchtung', in *Die Gegenwart 59* (1901), pp. 4–8, 210–12, 230–2

Henke, Peter, 'Erwählung und Entwicklung: Zur Auseinandersetzung zwischen Adolf von Harnack und Karl Barth', in *Neue Zeitschrift für Systematische Theologie und Religionsphilosophie* 18 (1976), pp. 194–208

Herms, Eilert, 'Die Bedeutung des Gesetzes für die lutherische Sozialethik', in *Von Wittenberg nach Memphis: Festschrift für Reinhard Schwarz*, Walter Homolka and Otto Ziegelmeier (eds) (Göttingen, 1989), pp. 62–89

Hirsch, Emanuel, *Geschichte der neuern evangelischen Theologie im Zusammenhang mit den allgemeinen Bewegungen des europäischen Denkens*, vol. 5 (Gütersloh, 1975),

Hirsch, Emanuel, *Hilfsbuch zum Studium der Dogmatik* (Berlin, 1964)

Hodges, H.A., *Wilhelm Dilthey: An Introduction* (London, 1949)

Hoffmann, Heinrich, 'Die Frage nach dem Wesen des Christentums in der Auklärungstheologie', in *Harnack-Ehrung: Beiträge zur Kirchengeschichte* (Leipzig, 1921), pp. 353–65

Hoffmann, Heinrich, 'Zum Aufkommen des Begriffs "Wesen des Christemtums"', in *Zeitschrift für Kirchengeschichte* 45 N.S. 8 (1927), pp. 452–9

Hoffmann-Axthelm, Diether, 'Loisys "L'Évangile et l'Église"', in *Zeitschrift für Theologie und Kirche* 65 (1968), pp. 291–328

Holborn, Hajo, 'Der deutsche Idealismus in sozialgeschichtlicher Bedeutung', in *Historische Zeitschrift* 174 (1952), pp. 359–84

Hollmann, Georg, 'On Baeck's article on Harnack's "Wesen des Christentums" in the *Monatschrift für Wissenschaft und Geschichte des Judentums*', in *Theologische Rundschau* 7 (1904), pp. 197–212

Holtzmann, Heinrich, 'Besprechung der Kontroverse zwischen F. Perles und W. Bousset', in *Theologische Literaturzeitung* 29 (1904), pp. 43–6

Homolka, Walter K., *Ein dem Untergang naher Aramäer war mein Vater . . . : das 'kleine geschichtliche Credo' und seine Wirkungsgeschichte im Midrasch der Pessach-Haggada* (Egelsbach/Cologne/New York, 1993)

——, *Jüdische Identität in der modernen Welt - Leo Baeck und der deutsche Protestantismus* (Gütersloh, 1994)

Homolka, Walter K., 'Continuity and Change. Liberal Jewish Theology in a Christian Society', in *Von Wittenberg nach Memphis*, Walter Homolka and Otto Ziegelmeier (eds) (Göttingen, 1989)

Homolka, Walter K., 'Die frühen Haskala-Bestrebungen in Polen', *Neue Jüdische Nachrichten*, vol. 5, no. 27 (Munich, 1981)

Homolka, Walter K. and Friedlander, Albert H., *The Gate to Perfection* (Oxford, 1994)

Isaak, Bernhard, 'Der Religionsliberalismus im deutschen Judentum' (unpubl. doctoral dissertation, University of Leipzig, 1933)

Jacob, Walter, *Christianity Through Jewish Eyes: The Quest for Common Ground* (Cincinatti, Ohio, 1974)

Jacobs, Louis, *Jewish Thought Today* (New York, 1970)

Jantzen, Grace, 'The Identity of Christianity: Theologians and the Essence of Christianity from Schleiermacher to Barth', in *King's Theological Review* 9,2 (1986), pp. 65–6

Jaspers, Karl, *Die geistige Situation der Zeit*, 4th printing of the 5th edn (Berlin, 1955)

Jelski, Israel, *Das Wesen des Judentums* (Berlin, 1902)

Joel, Manuel, *Religionsphilosophische Zeitfragen in zusammenhängenden Aufsätzen besprochen* (Breslau, 1876)

Joest, Wilfried, *Fundamentaltheologie* (Stuttgart et al., 1974)

Jonas, Hans, *Gnosis und spätantiker Geist* (Göttingen, 1964)

Jüdisches Lehrhaus Zürich: Leo Baeck Heft, Jahresbericht 8 (1959)

Kaltenborn, Carl-Jürgen, *Adolf von Harnack als Lehrer Bonhoeffers*, Theologische Arbeiten 31 (Berlin (DDR), 1973)

Kampe, Norbert, 'Akademisierung der Juden und Beginn eines studentischen Antisemitismus', in *Jüdisches Leben*, Berliner Topographien 4, Wolfgang Dreßen (ed.) (Berlin, 1985), pp. 10–23

Kampmann, Wanda, *Deutsche und Juden* (Heidelberg, 1963)

Kaplan, Mordecai M., *The Purpose and Meaning of Jewish Existence* (Philadelphia, 1964)

Karpeles, Gustav, 'Literarische Jahresrevue', in *Jahrbuch für jüdische Geschichte und Literatur* 6 (1903), pp. 15–47 and 9 (1908), pp. 25–72

Keller-Wentorf, Christel, *Schleiermachers Denken* (Berlin/New York, 1984)

Keyserling, Hermann Graf, *Reisetagebuch eines Philosophen* (Munich, 1913; 2nd edn 1919)

Kinder, Ernst and Haendler, Klaus, eds, *Gesetz und Evangelium*, 2nd edn (Darmstadt, 1986)

Koch, Klaus, *Ratlos vor der Apokalyptik* (Gütersloh, 1970)

Köhnke, Klaus Christian, *Entstehung und Aufstieg des Neukantianismus* (Frankfurt am Main, 1986)

Kohler, Kaufmann, *Grundriß einer systematischen Theologie des Judentums auf geschichtlicher Grundlage*, reprint (Hildesheim/New York, 1979)

Kohler, Kaufmann, *Jewish theology: Systematically and historically considered* (New York, 1918)

Kraus, Hans-Joachim, *Geschichte der historisch-kritischen Erforschung des Alten Testaments*, 3rd edn (Neukirchen-Vluyn, 1982)

Krause, G. and Müller, G., eds, *Theologische Realenzyklopädie*, (Berlin/New York, 1980 onwards)

Krauss, Samuel, 'Luther und die Juden', in *Wissenschaft des Judentums im deutschen Sprachbereich*, Kurt Wilhelm (ed.) (Tübingen, 1967), pp. 309–14

Krausser, Peter, *Kritik der endlichen Vernunft* (Frankfurt am Main, 1968)

Kroeger, Matthias, *Rechtfertigung und Gesetz* (Göttingen, 1968)

_____, *Theologische Klärung unseres Friedensverhaltens: Eine Zweireichelehre für den Frieden* (Stuttgart et al., 1984)

Krumwiede, Hans-Walter, *Evangelische Kirche und Theologie in der Weimarer Republik*, Grundtexte zur Kirchen- und Theologiegeschichte 2 (Neukirchen-Vluyn, 1990)

_____, *Geschichte des Christentums: III Neuzeit* (Stuttgart et al., 1977)

Kupisch, Karl, *Quellen des deutschen Protestantismus (1871–1945)* (Göttingen, 1960)

———, *Von Luther zu Bismarck: Heinrich von Treitschke* (Berlin/Bielefeld, 1949)

———, *Zwischen Idealismus und Massendemokratie: Eine Geschichte der evangelischen Kirche in Deutschland von 1815–1945* (Berlin, 1955)

Kupisch, Karl et al., *Judenfeindschaft im 19. Jahrhundert* (Berlin, 1977)

Lange, Dietz, ed., *Friedrich Schleiermacher* (Göttingen, 1985)

Lazarus, Moritz, *Die Ethik des Judentums*, 2 vols (Frankfurt am Main, 1904/1911)

Leese, Kurt, *Der Protestantismus im Wandel der neueren Zeit* (Stuttgart, 1941)

Leuze, Reinhard, *Theologie und Religionsgeschichte* (Munich, 1980)

Leuze, Reinhard, 'Das Christentum: die "absolute Religion"', in *Zeitschrift für Missionswissenschaft und Religionswissenschaft* 68,4 (1984), pp. 280–95

Lewkowitz, Albert, 'Religion und Philosophie im jüdischen Denken der Gegenwart', in *Monatsschrift für Geschichte und Wissenschaft des Judentums* 79 N.S. 43 (1935), pp. 1–11

Lexikon des Judentums (Munich, 1971)

Licharz, Werner, ed., *Leo Baeck: Lehrer und Helfer in schwerer Zeit*, Arnoldshainer Texte 20 (Frankfurt am Main, 1983)

Liebeschütz, Hans, *Das Judentum im deutschen Geschichtsbild von Hegel bis Max Weber* (Tübingen, 1967)

Liebeschütz, Hans, 'Between Past and Future: Leo Baeck's Historical Position', in *Leo Baeck Institute Yearbook* 11 (1966), pp. 3–27

Liebeschütz, Hans, 'Jewish Thought and its German Background', in *Leo Baeck Institute Yearbook*, 1 (1956), pp. 217–36

Liebeschütz, Hans, *Von Georg Simmel zu Franz Rosenzweig*, Schriftenreihe wissenschaftlicher Abhandlungen des Leo Baeck Instituts 23 (Tübingen, 1970)

Liebeschütz, Hans, 'Wissenschaft des Judentums und Historismus bei Abraham Geiger', in *Essays presented to Leo Baeck on the occassion of his eightieth birthday (Festschrift)* (London, 1954), pp. 75–93

Lindeskog, Gösta, *Die Jesusfrage im neuzeitlichen Judentum: Ein Beitrag zur Geschichte der Leben-Jesu-Forschung,* reprint (Darmstadt, 1973)

Lindeskog, Gösta, 'Jesus als religionsgeschichtliches und religiöses Problem in der modernen jüdischen Theologie', in *Judaica* 6 (1950), pp. 190–229 and 241–68

Lohse, Bernhard, *Martin Luther*, 2nd edn (Munich, 1982)

Loisy, Alfred F., *L'Évangile et l'Église* (1902)

Lübbe, Hermann, *Religion nach der Aufklärung,* (Graz/Vienna/Cologne, 1986)

Luther, Martin, *Sämmtliche Werke*, 1st edn (Erlangen, 1850)

D. Martin Luthers Werke: Kritische Gesamtausgabe (Weimar, 1883 onwards)

Macquarrie, John, *Twentieth Century Religious Thought* (London, 1963)

Mann, Ulrich, *Das Christentum als absolute Religion* (Darmstadt, 1970)

Marquardt, Friedrich W., 'Unabgegoltenes in der Kritik Leo Baecks an Adolf von Harnack', in *Leo Baeck: Lehrer und Helfer in schwerer Zeit*, Arnoldshainer Texte 20, Werner Licharz (ed.) (Frankfurt am Main, 1983), pp. 169–87

Marsch, Wolf-Dieter, *Institution im Übergang: Evangelische Kirche zwischen Tradition und Reform* (Göttingen, 1970)

Marsch, Wolf-Dieter and Thieme, Karl, eds, *Christen und Juden,* (Mainz/Göttingen, 1961)

Mayer, Reinhold, *Christentum und Judentum in der Schau Leo Baecks,* Studia Delitzschiana 6 (Stuttgart, 1961)

Mayer, Reinhold, 'Leo Baeck', in *Theologische Realenzyklopädie,* G. Krause and G. Müller (eds) (Berlin/New York, 1980), pp. 112–15

Mebust, John L., *Wilhelm Dilthey's Philosophy of History and its Influence on Wilhelm Herrmann and Ernst Troeltsch* (Princeton, Jersey, 1973)

Meinhold, Peter, 'Adolf von Harnack', in Peter Meinhold, *Geschichte der kirchlichen Historiographie,* Orbis Academicus III/5, 2 vols (Freiburg/Munich, 1967)

Merk, Otto, 'Judentum und Christentum bei Leo Baeck', in *Traditio, Krisis, Renovatio aus theologischer Sicht (Festschrift Winfried Zeller),* Bernd Jaspert and Rudolf Mohr (eds) (Marburg, 1976), pp. 513–28

Meyer, W., *Evangelische Kirche und deutscher Staat* (1935)

Mildenberger, Friedrich, *Geschichte der deutschen evangelischen Theologie im 19. und 20. Jahrhundert,* Theologische Wissenschaft 10 (Stuttgart et al., 1981)

Misch, Clara, ed., *Der junge Dilthey* (Leipzig, 1933)

Miskotte, Kornelis H., *Het Wezen der Joodsche Religie* (Amsterdam, 1932)

Modern Humanities Research Association, ed., *MHRA Style Book,* 4th edn (London, 1991)

Mommsen, Theodor, *Auch ein Wort über unsere Juden* (Berlin, 1880)

Morgan, Robert and Pye, Michael, eds, *Ernst Troeltsch: Writings on Theology and Religion* (London, 1977)

Mosse, Werner E., ed., *Juden im Wilhelminischen Deutschland: 1890–1914,* Schriftenreihe wissenschaftlicher Abhandlungen des Leo Baeck Instituts 33 (Tübingen, 1976)

Mulert, Hermann, 'Wann kam der Ausdruck "Das Wesen des Christentums" auf?', in *Zeitschrift für Kirchengeschichte* 45 N.S. 8 (1927), p. 117

Müller, Hans Martin, ed., *Kulturprotestantismus - Beiträge zu einer Gestalt des modernen Christentums* (Gütersloh, 1992)

Müller, Johann B., ed., *Die Deutschen und Luther* (Stuttgart, 1983)

Müntinga, Hermann, 'Das Bild von Judentum im deutschen Protestantismus', in *Judenfeindschaft im 19. Jahrhundert,* Karl Kupisch et. al. (eds) (Berlin, 1977), pp. 21–49

Neufeld, Karl H. (SJ.), *Adolf von Harnack: Theologie als Suche nach der Kirche,* Konfessionskundliche und kontroverstheologische Studien 41 (Paderborn, 1977)

_____ (SJ.), *Adolf von Harnacks Konflikt mit der Kirche* (Innsbruck et al., 1979)

Neufeld, Karl H. (SJ.), 'Christentum im Widerstreit', in *Stimmen der Zeit* 198 (1980), pp. 542-52

Newmann, Louis I., *Jewish Influence On Christian Reform Movements* (New York, 1925)

Niebergall, Friedrich, 'Rezension von L. Baeck "Das Wesen des Judentums",
2. Auflage', in *Christliche Welt* 37 (1923), col. 27

Niewöhner, Friedrich W., 'Judentum, Wesen des Judentums', in *Historisches Wörterbuch der Philosophie,* vol.4, Joachim Ritter and Karlfried Gründer (eds) (Darmstadt, 1976)

Niewöhner, Friedrich W., 'Isaac Breuer und Kant: Ein Beitrag zum Thema "Kant und das Judentum"', in *Neue Zeitschrift für Systematische Theologie und Religionsphilosphie* 17,1 (1975), pp. 142–50 and 19,2 (1977), pp. 172–85

Nowak, Kurt, *Evangelische Kirche und Weimarer Republik* (Göttingen, 1981)

_____, *Schleiermacher und die Emanzipation des Judentums am Ende des 18. Jahrhunderts in Preußen* (Berlin, 1984)

_____, *Schleiermacher und die Frühromantik* (Weimar, 1986)

Ollig, Hans-Ludwig, ed., *Materialien zur Neukantianismus-Diskussion* (Darmstadt, 1987)

Ollig, Hans-Ludwig, ed., *Neukantianismus* (Stuttgart, 1982)

Osten-Sacken, Peter von der, 'Rückzug ins Wesen und aus der Geschichte: Antijudaismus bei Harnack und Bultmann', in *Wissenschaft und Praxis in Kirche und Gesellschaft* 67 (1978), pp. 106–22

Palmer, Richard E., *Hermeneutics: Interpretation Theory in Schleiermacher, Dilthey, Heidegger and Gadamer* (Evanston, 1969)

Panck, W., *Harnack und Troeltsch* (New York, 1968)

Pannenberg, Wolfhart, *Systematische Theologie*, vol. 1 (Göttingen, 1988)

Perles, Felix, *Was lehrt uns Harnack?* (Frankfurt am Main, 1902)

Perlitt, Lothar, *Vatke und Wellhausen: Geschichtsphilosophische Voraussetzungen und historiographische Motive für die Darstellung der Religion und Geschichte Israels durch Wilhelm Vatke und Julius Wellhausen,* Beihefte zur Zeitschrift für alttestamentliche Wissenschaft 94 (Berlin, 1965)

Pesch, Otto H. and Peters, Albrecht, *Einführung in die Lehre von Gnade und Rechtfertigung,* 2nd edn (Darmstadt, 1989)

Petuchowski, Jacob J., 'Judentum und Christentum in jüdischer Sicht', in *Christlicher Glaube in moderner Gesellschaft* 26 (1980) pp. 136–51

Petuchowski, Jacob J., '"Rabbinische" und "dogmatische" Struktur in theologischer Aussage', in *Jüdische Existenz und die Erneuerung der christlichen Theologie,* Martin Stöhr (ed.) (Munich), pp. 154–62

Plantinga, Theodore, *Historical Understanding in the Thought of Wilhelm Dilthey* (Toronto, 1980)

Plaut, W. Gunther, *The Growth of Reform Judaism* (New York, 1965)

——, *The Rise of Reform Judaism,* 2nd edn (New York, 1969)

Raab, Heribert, ed., *Kirche und Staat* (Munich, 1966)

Rasch, Wolfdietrich, 'Zum Verhältnis der Aufklärung zur Romantik', in *Romantik,* Ernst Ribbat (ed.) (Königstein/Taunus, 1979), pp. 7–21

Ratschow, Carl H., 'Wesen des Christentums', in *RGG,* 3rd edn, vol. 1 (Tübingen, 1957), pp. 1722–9

Rauwenhoff, D.L.W.E., *Religionsphilosophie,* 2nd edn (Braunschweig, 1894)

Reardon, Bernard M.G., *Religion in the Age of Romanticism: Studies in Early Nineteenth Century Thought* (Cambridge et al., 1985)

Reichmann, Eva G., ed., *Worte des Gedenkens für Leo Baeck* (Heidelberg, 1959)

Reinharz, Jehuda, *Fatherland and Promised Land: The Dilemma of the German Jew 1893–1914* (Ann Arbor, 1975)

Rendtorff, Trutz, 'Christentum', in *Geschichtliche Grundbegriffe: Historisches Lexikon zur politisch-sozialen Sprache in Deutschland,* Otto Brunner, Werner Conze and Reinhard Koselleck (eds) (Stuttgart, 1972), pp. 772–814

Rendtorff, Trutz, 'Das Verhältnis von liberaler Theologie und Judentum um die Jahrhundertwende', in *Das deutsche Judentum und der Liberalismus: German Jewry and Liberalism,* edited by Friedrich-Naumann-Stiftung (Sankt Augustin, 1986), pp. 96–112

Rengstorf, Karl-Heinrich, 'Leo Baeck als Theologe und im theologischen Gespräch', in *Worte des Gedenkens für Leo Baeck,* Eva G. Reichmann (ed.) (Heidelberg, 1959), pp. 125–32

Renz, Horst and Graf, Friedrich W., *Troeltsch-Studien,* vols 1, 3, 4 (Gütersloh, 1982/1984/1987)

Richarz, Monika, ed., *Jüdisches Leben in Deutschland (1918–1945),* Publication of the Leo Baeck Institute, 3 vols (Stuttgart, 1976/78/82)

Ringer, Fritz K., *Die Gelehrten: Der Niedergang der deutschen Mandarine*

1890–1933, translated from U.S. English by K. Laermann (Stuttgart, 1983) (Cambridge, 1969).

Ritter, Joachim and Gründer, Karlfried, eds, *Historisches Wörterbuch der Philosophie* (Darmstadt, 1976)

Rogge, Joachim and Zeddies, Helmut, eds, *Kirchengemeinschaft und politische Ethik: Ergebnis eines theologischen Gespräches zum Verhältnis von Zwei-Reiche-Lehre und Lehre von der Königsherrschaft Christi* (Berlin, 1980)

Rolffs, Ernst, 'Adolf von Harnack und die Theologie der Krisis', in *Die Christliche Welt* 52,2 (1938), cols 61–5

Rosenblüth, Pinchas E., 'Die geistigen und religiösen Strömungen in der deutschen Judenheit', in *Juden im Wilhelminischen Deutschland: 1890–1914*, Werner E. Mosse (ed.) (Tübingen, 1976), pp. 549–98

Rosenstock-Huessy, Eugen, ed., *Judaism despite Christianity* (University of Alabama, 1961)

Rosenzweig, Franz, *Kleinere Schriften* (Berlin, 1937)

Rosenzweig, Franz, 'Geist und Epochen der jüdischen Geschichte', in *Wissenschaft des Judentums im deutschen Sprachbereich*, Kurt Wilhelm (ed.) (Tübingen, 1967), pp. 269–80

Rotenstreich, Nathan, *Jewish Philosophy in Modern Times: From Mendelssohn to Rosenzweig* (New York et al., 1968)

Ruddies, Hartmut and Graf, Friedrich W., eds, *Bibliographie Ernst Troeltsch* (Tübingen, 1982)

Rürup, Reinhard, *Emanzipation und Antisemitismus: Studien zur Judenfrage der bürgerlichen Gesellschaft*, Kritische Studien zur Geschichtswissenschaft 15 (Göttingen, 1975)

Rürup, Reinhard, 'Emanzipation und Krise: Zur Geschichte der "Judenfrage" in Deutschland vor 1890', in *Juden im Wilhelminischen Deutschland: 1890–1914: Ein Sammelband*, Schriftenreihe wissenschaftlicher Abhandlungen des Leo Baeck Instituts 33, Werner E. Mosse and Arnold Paucker (eds) (Tübingen, 1976), pp. 1–56

Rupp, George, *Culture-Protestantism: German Liberal Theology at the Turn of the Twentieth Century* (Missoula, Montana, 1977)

Sandmel, Samuel, *Leo Baeck on Christianity*, Leo Baeck Memorial Lecture 19 (New York, 1975)

Schäfer, Rolf, *Ritschl* (Tübingen, 1982)

Schäfer, Rolf, 'Welchen Sinn hat es, nach dem Wesen des Christentums zu suchen?', in *Zeitschrift für Theologie und Kirche* 65 (1968), pp. 329–47

Schanze, Helmut, *Romantik und Aufklärung*, 2nd edn (Nuremberg, 1976)

Schlegel, Friedrich, *Kritische Schriften*, 3rd edn (Munich, 1971)

Schleiermacher, Friedrich D.E., *Über die Religion* (Hamburg, 1958)

Schlenke, Dorothee, *Normativität und Geschichte* (Munich, 1986) (unpublished)

Schlippe, G. von, *Absolutheit des Christentums bei Ernst Troeltsch auf dem Hintergrund der Denkfehler des 19. Jahrhunderts* (Neustadt an der Aisch, 1966)

Schmauch, Werner and Wolf, Ernst, eds, *Königsherrschaft Christi: Der Christ im Staat*, Theologische Existenz heute N.S. 64 (Munich, 1958)

Schmidt, Werner H., *"Rechtfertigung des Gottlosen" in der Botschaft der Propheten Festschrift für Hans Walter Wolff* (Neukirchen, 1981)

Schmitz, Hermann-Josef, *Frühkatholizismus bei Adolf von Harnack, Rudolph Sohm und Ernst Käsemann* (Düsseldorf, 1977)

Schnädelbach, Herbert, *Philosophie in Deutschland 1831–1933* (Frankfurt am Main, 1983)

Schoeps, Julius H., *Neues Lexikon des Judentums* (Gütersloh/Munich, 1992)

Scholem, Gershom, *Major Trends in Jewish Mysticism* (New York, 1946)

Schreiner, Martin, *Die jüngsten Urteile über das Judentum: Kritisch untersucht* (Berlin, 1902)

Schrey, Heinz-Horst, ed., *Reich Gottes und Welt: Die Lehre Luthers von den zwei Reichen,* Wege der Forschung 108 (Darmstadt, 1969)

Schultz, Franz, *Klassik und Romantik der Deutschen,* 2 vols (Stuttgart, 1934/1940)

Schwartzman, Sylvan D., *Reform Judaism Then and Now* (New York, 1971)

Schwarz, Reinhard, *Luther* (Göttingen, 1986)

Schwarzschild, Steven S., 'Modern Jewish Philosophy', in *Contemporary Jewish Religious Thought,* Arthur Cohen and Paul Mendes-Flohr (eds) (New York, 1987), pp. 629–34

Schwarzschild, Steven S., *The Theologico-Political Basis of Liberal Christian-Jewish Relations in Modernity',* in *Das deutsche Judentum und der Liberalismus: German Jewry and Liberalism,* edited by Friedrich-Naumann-Stiftung (Sankt Augustin, 1986), pp. 70–95

Schweitzer, Albert, *Geschichte der Leben-Jesu-Forschung,* 9th edn (Tübingen, 1984)

Schwöbel, Christoph, *Martin Rade – Das Verhältnis von Geschichte, Religion und Moral als Grundproblem seiner Theologie* (Gütersloh, 1980).

Selge, Kurt-Victor, ed., *Internationaler Schleiermacher-Kongreß Berlin 1984,* 2 vols (Berlin/New York, 1985)

Seligmann, Caesar, *Geschichte der jüdischen Reformbewegung von Mendelssohn bis zur Gegenwart* (Frankfurt am Main, 1922)

Simon, Ernst, *Brücken: Gesammelte Aufsätze* (Heidelberg, 1965)

Smart, Ninian, *The Phenomenon of Religion* (London, 1973)

Smart, Ninian, Clayton, John, Katz, Steven and Sherry, Patrick, *Nineteenth Century Religious Thought in the West,* 3 vols (Cambridge, 1985)

Sohm, Rudolph, *Das Verhältnis von Staat und Kirche* (Tübingen, 1873)

Spiegel, Yorick, *Theologie der bürgerlichen Gesellschaft* (Munich, 1968)

Stephan, Horst and Schmidt, Martin, *Geschichte der evangelischen Theologie in Deutschland seit dem Idealismus* (Berlin/New York, 1973)

Stöhr, Martin, ed., *Jüdische Existenz und die Erneuerung der christlichen Theologie* (Munich, 1981)

Stoodt, Dieter, *Wort und Recht* (Munich, 1962)

Strauß, Bruno, ed., *Hermann Cohens Jüdische Schriften,* 3 vols (Berlin, 1924)

Strich, Fritz, *Deutsche Klassik und Romantik oder Vollendung und Unendlichkeit,* 1st edn (Munich, 1922); 2nd edn (München, 1965)

Stupperich, Robert, *Die Reformation in Deutschland* (Gütersloh, 1980)

Sykes, Stephen W., *The Identity of Christianity: Theologians and the Essence of Christianity from Schleiermacher to Barth* (London, 1984)

Sykes, Stephen W., 'Ernst Troeltsch and Christianity's Essence', in *Ernst Troeltsch and the Future Theology,* John Powell Clayton (ed.) (Cambridge, 1976), pp. 139–71

Sykes, Stephen W., 'Note to "What does Essence of Christianity mean?"', in *Ernst Troeltsch: Writings on Theology and Religion,* Robert Morgan and Michael Pye (eds) (London, 1977), pp. 180–81

Tal, Uriel, *Christians and Jews in Germany: Religion, Politics and Ideology in the Second Reich, 1870–1914* (Ithaca/London, 1975)

Tal, Uriel, 'Liberal Protestantism and the Jews in the Second Reich 1870–1914', in *Jewish Social Studies* 26 (1964), pp. 23–41

Tal, Uriel, 'Theologische Debatte um das "Wesen des Judentums"', in *Juden im Wilhelminischen Deutschland 1890–1914,* Werner E. Mosse (ed.) (Tübingen, 1976), pp. 599–632

Timm, Hermann, *Die heilige Revolution: Schleiermacher, Novalis, Friedrich Schlegel* (Frankfurt am Main, 1978)

Toury, Jacob, *Die politischen Orientierungen der Juden in Deutschland: Von Jena bis Weimar*, Schriftenreihe wissenschaftlicher Abhandlungen des Leo Baeck Instituts 15 (Tübingen, 1966)

Troeltsch, Ernst, *Die Bedeutung des Protestantismus für die Weiterentwicklung der modernen Welt* (Munich/Berlin, 1906)

——, *Die Kirche im Leben der Gegenwart* (Munich/Berlin, 1911)

——, *Gesammelte Schriften* (Tübingen, 1913)

Tyrrell, George, *Christianity at the Cross Road* (London, 1909)

Ucko, Sinai, 'Geistesgeschichtliche Grundlagen der Wissenschaft des Judentums', in *Wissenschaft des Judentums im deutschen Sprachbereich*, Kurt Wilhelm (ed.) (Tübingen, 1967), pp. 315–52

Urbach, R., 'Judentum und Christentum (Zwei Bücher über das Wesen des Judentums)', in *Monatsschrift für Geschichte und Wissenschaft des Judentums* 50 N.S. 13 (1906), pp. 257–80

Veit, Otto, *Christlich jüdische Koexistenz*, 2nd edn (Frankfurt am Main, 1971)

Verband der deutschen Juden, edited by, *Die Lehren des Judentums nach den Quellen*, 5 vols (Berlin, 1920–9)

Volkow, Shulamit, 'Das jüdische Projekt der Moderne', in *Historische Zeitschrift*, vol. 253/3 (Munich, 1991)

Wagenhammer, Hans, *Das Wesen des Christentums: Eine begriffsgeschichtliche Untersuchung* (Mainz, 1973)

Wehler, Hans-Ulrich, *Das Deutsche Kaiserreich 1871–1918*, Deutsche Geschichte 9, 4th edn (Göttingen, 1980(1973))

Wellhausen, Julius, *Israelitische und Jüdische Geschichte*, 3rd edn (Berlin, 1897)

Weltsch, Robert, 'Die schleichende Krise der jüdischen Identität', in *Juden im Wilhelminischen Deutschland 1890–1914*, Werner E. Mosse (ed.) (Tübingen, 1976), pp. 689–704

Wenz, Gunther, *Subjekt und Sein* (Munich, 1979)

Wiener, Max, *Jüdische Religion im Zeitalter der Emanzipation* (Berlin, 1933)

Wiener, Max, ed., *Abraham Geiger and Liberal Judaism* (Philadelphia, 1962)

Wiener, Theodore, 'The Writings of Leo Baeck', in *Studies in Bibliography and Booklore*, vol. 1, No. 3 (Cincinatti, Ohio, 1954)

Wilhelm, Kurt, 'Zur Einführung in die Wissenschaft des Judentums', in *Wissenschaft des Judentums im deutschen Sprachbereich*, Kurt Wilhelm (ed.) (Tübingen, 1967), pp. 1–58

Willey, Thomas E., *Back to Kant: The Revival of Kantianism in German Social and Historical Thought 1860–1914* (Detroit, Michigan, 1978)

Wobbermin, Georg, *Luther, Kant, Schleiermacher* (1939)

Wobbermin, Georg, 'Psychologie und Erkenntniskritik der religiösen Erfahrung', in *Weltanschauung* (1911)

Wohlstein, Josef, 'Das Wesen des Judentums', in *Allgemeine Zeitung des Judentums*, 21 July 1905

Wolf, Abraham, 'Dr Bäck's "Judaism"', in *The Jewish Quarterly Review* (1907), pp. 425–7

Wolf, Abraham, 'Professor Harnack's 'What is Christianity?'', in *The Jewish Quarterly Review* 16 (1904), pp. 668–89

Wolf, Arnold J., 'Leo Baeck's Critique of Christianity', in *Judaism*, 12 (1963), pp. 190–4

Wyman, Walter E., *The Concept of Glaubenslehre: Ernst Troeltsch and the Theological Heritage of Schleiermacher* (Chico, Calif., 1983)

Yasukata, Toshimasa, *Ernst Troeltsch: Systematic Theologian of Radical Historicality* (Atlanta, Georgia, 1986)

Yule, George, ed., *Luther: Theologian for Catholics and Protestants* (Edinburgh, 1985)

Zahn-Harnack, Agnes von, *Adolf von Harnack*, 2nd esp. edn (Berlin, 1951)

Ziegler, Jakob, 'Neue Bahnen für die jüdische Wissenschaft', in *Allgemeine Zeitung des Judentums* 15 May 1903, pp. 235–7

INDEX